American Foreign Policy

Fighting Nuclear, Chemical, & Biological Terrorism

OTHER BOOKS BY E. TED GLADUE

NONFICTION

China's Perception of Global Politics

Gamble for Survival: Nuclear, Chemical, & Biological Conflict

with, Leo P. Brophy

China's Diplomatic Behavior in the United Nations.

Ph.D. Dissertation

FICTION

Survival: The Adventures of Sean Semineaux

A novel

Semineaux: Miami/New York

A novel

Semineaux: New Zealand/Antarctica

A novel

Semineaux: Ch'in Shih Huang-ti & The Birth of China

A novel

Escaping Sandy (to be released Summer 2014)

A novel

POETRY

Green Light: A Collection of Poems

Poetry in Green: Poetry & Stories From Around the World

American Foreign Policy

Fighting Nuclear, Chemical, & Biological Terrorism

E. Ted Gladue, Ph.D.

Irish Lighthouse Press of Harbor Lights Press

Philadelphia, Pennsylvania
Dublin, Ireland
2014

Harbor Lights Press

Philadelphia 2014

PUBLISHED BY IRISH LIGHT HOUSE PRESS

USA

Library of Congress Cataloguing-in-Publication Data

ISBN-13: 978-1499149982
ISBN-10: 1499149980
Manufactured in the United States of America
Cover design by Steve Andrews

4

FIRST EDITION

Dedication of this book

to

Elie Wiesel

Nobel Peace Laureate

"IRAN MUST NOT BE ALLOWED
TO REMAIN NUCLEAR"

" If there is one lesson I hope the world has learned from the past, it is that regimes rooted in brutality must never be trusted. And the words and actions of the leaders of Iran Leave no doubt as to their intentions.

Should the civilized nations of the world trust a regime whose supreme leader said that Israel is 'doomed to annihilation,' and referred to my fellow Jewish Zionists as 'rabid dogs.'

Should we who believe in human rights, trust a regime which in the 21st century stones women and hangs homosexuals?

Should we who believe in freedom trust a regime which murdered its own citizens in the streets of Tehran, when the people protested a stolen election in 2009.

Should we who believe in the United States trust a regime whose parliament last month erupted in "Death to America" *chants as they commemorated the 34th anniversary of the storming of our Embassy in Tehran?*

Should we who believe in life trust a regime whom our own State Department lists as one of the world's foremost sponsors of terrorism?

I once wrote that history has taught us to trust the threats of our enemies more than the promises of our friends. Our enemies are making serious threats.

It is time to take them seriously. It is time for our friends to keep their promises."

Table Of Contents

11

Chapter One

American Foreign Policy

Prologue to chapter: American Spying

I began writing this chapter in early 2012 but two issues of vital importance to American Foreign Policy needed immediate attention: the fallout in Spring and Summer of 2013 from the leaks of American intelligence contractor Edward Snowden convinced me to write this short preface, for these revelations may change American Foreign Policy as did the events of 9/11, but in more subtle ways. Secondly, the growing dependency of drone strikes is not only a tactical mistake, but one that will bring strategic problems in future scenarios only envisioned by science fiction writers. As important is how the US Drone War may be at great odds with the character and values of most Americans.

Those old enough to have lived through the turmoil caused by Daniel Ellsberg's leaking of the Pentagon Papers remember it as a moment of truth: how the U.S. government lied about the Vietnam war while thousands of U.S. men and women were being killed and wounded in a war that had nothing to do with America's national or vital interests. By 2013 we again experience a whistle blower's exposure of a U.S. government working beneath the radar of public knowledge in a colossal program of spying on the very allies who have supported the U.S. in not only its "war on terrorism" but in the misconceived and unnecessary wars in Iraq and a decade too-long Afghanistan war. The shock of 9/11 brought Europeans to our side; the N.S.A. (National Security Agency) program used to spy on our allies has decimated the accrued good will gained from both the end of the Cold War as well as 9/11. This spy program called "Prism" might be labeled "Prism-gate;" while noting that Nixon only spied on Democrats at Watergate.

It might be called "Prism-gate," for it is incomprehensible that the President of the United States would go so far as to argue during a speech on June 19 that this spy program was about counter-terrorism and that it served the interest of all our allies. As Steve Erlanger reported from Paris, the spying on the European Union offices in both Brussels and Washington struck many " as unlikely places to find terrorists." Many Washington officials and ex-officials argue that spying is something all allies do, that it is the name of the game so to speak. But as Erlanger points out the U.S. has a " huge qualitative advantage over its partners" and quotes the author James Bamford in his book about N.S.A.: Our allies "don't have anywhere the capacity to do to us what we do to them." "The difference is, you're comparing eavesdropping with a nuclear weapon to eavesdropping with a cannon."

President Obama, like Nixon and Johnson in other eras, kept digging himself into a deeper hole when he spoke during a trip to Tanzania and rationalized U.S. behavior by comparing it with every other intelligence service. " Here's one thing they are going to be doing: they're going to be trying to understand the world better and what's going on in world capitals around the world, from sources that aren't available through The New York Times or NBC news...and if that weren't the case then there'd be no use for an intelligence service...that's how intelligence services operate."

Wow. Was my first honest reaction to the above rationalization by President Obama. Secondly, he is dead wrong. Two valuable lessons from working in intelligence, four years with U.S. military intelligence and six years working for the Acting Director of Political & Security Affairs in the Secretariat of the United Nations, with the later specialty getting into foreign Think Tank research facilities, most of which were difficult to breach, for they were often kept separate from the main government buildings, with no addresses and bank vault like security.

The most important thing I learned was that rarely, and I mean a "rarely" that is so close to never as to be most often indistinguishable; there is no "secret" information that would allow anyone to have an edge over others in trying to get at the truth or correct decision in international politics. It is nowhere comparable with insider trading on Wall Street. In politics, basic research or advanced research or whatever facts are uncovered are not as important as the analysis of what is known to anyone in the world who takes the time to study. And the best analysis of international and state behavior is most accurate when examined against knowledge of cultural, historical, economic, psychological, political, anthropological and current events of the time. Getting into some of the worlds most sophisticated think tank files on China during the Cold War revealed information similar to my files back in my personal home library.

This is why President Obama was dead wrong: a correct analysis of a world problem is a result of good basic thinking about what is already known. It is not what you know, but how you interpret the facts that are being presented by one or many sides. That is, when we are presented with facts, not lies as we witnessed with Vietnam and Iraq as I will discuss below, or study the lies told to European peoples before the most insane war of world history, WW I. Or, just make a life of studying the history of lies that started wars.

Just study the period after WW II with the dangerous standoff between Soviet and American forces in Germany. What was to be done? There were no secrets that would give American policy makers answers; just good clear thinking and debates about what to do with what we knew. The answer that came out of all the debates was the concept of "Containment, " attributed to one thinker, George Kennan, despite the bastardization of Kennan's original concept turning it into the creation of NATO, centering the response to Soviet aggression with a military response rather than a more subtle and defusing political order intended by Kennan.

Edward Snowden's revelations has opened up the public to aspects of government surveillance that in the past America often criticized previous Communist and autocratic spy agencies: they spied on their own people and we eagerly read novels written by those who survived lives with no privacy.   We called it a police state mentality, an Orwellian nightmare. We took pride in the fact our government is bound by Constitutional rules. We believed that the intrusiveness of the East German Statsi and the Soviet KGB would never be experienced in America.   Now we know differently.

You can hear the rumble from our founding fathers in their graves, for in America there now exists a legal authority above the Supreme Court, it is a secret court called the "Foreign Intelligence Surveillance Court" made up of appointed judges who make decisions about the depth of government spying in national security investigations.   The key here in the court ruling is the interpretation of one word...RELEVANT.   And from this, the NSA, under guise of the Patriot Act, has collected the phone records of the majority of Americans: records, internet, and phone conversations of ours plus all our European allies and their institutions such as the EU headquarters in Belgium and parliaments throughout the 28 nation European Union. Even U.S. criminal suspects have more protection against irrelevant evidence.

Jennifer DeVries and Siobhan Gorman reported in the Wall Street Journal that Mark Eckenwiler, former Justice Department's main authority on federal criminal surveillance law pointed out that " if a federal attorney ' served a grand-jury subpoena for such a broad class of records in a criminal investigation, he or she would be laughed out of court.'"   In this same article the journalists quote one of the authors of the Patriot Act, Wisconsin Republican Jim Sensenbrenner who argued that the government should only request such records that are relevant to a particular investigation: "to argue otherwise renders the provision meaningless...it's like scooping up the entire ocean to guarantee you catch a fish."

But the U.S. Director of National Intelligence, James Clapper, has defended the entire national and international collecting of huge databases of information by the United States. Clapper is quoted: " More narrow collection would limit our ability to screen for and identify terrorism-related communications." That is why his face on this page: he is the new face of America.

Clapper, and what he represents, has turned a wavering soul over to a deep admiration for Edward Snowden. A great nation's foreign policy before the era of nuclear weapons could be based on its ability to project force if need be with any friend or adversary. Not so anymore, the use of that force can also mean suicide; when everybody has muscles, no one can stand alone as king. America's foreign policy must be based on trust, if not, we have few allies we can trust. The above examples of Washington's thinking, exposed by Snowden, have created nearly as much confusion about where to go now as existed in 1946.

I know something about secrets, with experience holding the highest security clearance as a military cryptographer who often coded, decoded, and recoded messages from generals or intelligence operatives overseas to Andrews Air Force base where they were taken directly to the President of The United States after being decoded. Which meant that I was one of only two people who read a message going to the President. We cryptographers signed government documents making us aware that if we ever talked about America's code systems, even when we were old civilian men, we could be imprisoned at the military prison in

Leavenworth, Kansas. So I understand and appreciate the courage of Edward Snowden. And most importantly, he only gave away information on our spying, not the procedures, codes, and software presently used with American cryptographic systems. U.S. cryptographic systems were not compromised.

My support for Snowden is actually more basic than the above foreign policy concerns, for it goes to the very heart of what makes America different from any other government or nation in the world: the Forth Amendment in the U.S. Constitution's Bill of Rights, which states:

The right of the people to be secure in their persons, houses, papers, and effects, against unreasonable searches and seizures, Shall not be violated, and no warrants shall issue, but upon probable cause, supported by an oath or affirmation, and particularly describing the place to be searched, and the persons or things to be seized.

The Bill of Rights are what is at the heart of American culture, and in order to understand any nation's foreign policy you best understand its culture, for foreign policy is an extension of that culture. This is why Snowden's actions were so important, for we must ask the question; are we, as American's still protected by these rights hammered out by our founding fathers, all of whom were students of British Common Law that emphasized that not even the King could enter a peasants home without just cause; unlike laws on the continent during those centuries.

How can Americans trust our government to conduct a foreign policy that secures the safety of our nation if we cannot even trust our government at home. The September 6, 2013 revelations of the extent to which our trust has been disrespected by our government was reported by the New York Times by Nicole Periroth, Jeff Larson, and Scott Shane; a report that U.S. intelligence agencies requested the New York Times not publish. These reporters did write it up and revealed to the American republic for the first time what Eric Snowden had revealed.

By the time of the early September 2013 G-20 summit meeting in St Petersburg, Russia, President Obama had to do some backtracking from his original defense of the Snowden revelations, having to face two of the most important allies of American foreign policy in Latin America, Brazil's Dilma Rousseff and Mexico's Enrique Pena Nieto; both of whose personal emails were spied upon, as well as Ms Rousseff's communications with members of Brazil's parliament (so much for the values of democracy that professors like to teach about), and tapping into the communications of Mr Nieto during his recently successful presidential campaign. The spontaneous anger coming from south of the border is understandable for they know not only what a close ally they are, but also America's third largest trading partner.

When I went to the beginning of this chapter after having written three quarters of it, to write what I labeled a prologue, I did so more out of a gut instinct that U.S. spying on our allies was going to be big; it has become our most serious geopolitical blunder with our European allies since WW II. Sophisticated " wiretapping" of the cell phone of Europe's most prominent leader and currently closest European ally, German Chancellor Angela Merkel, implants such a deep mistrust of the United States that it will take a very long time to heal. It goes deep, like shame does to many Asians. As an American who has spent much time living and working in Europe, and intend more in the future, I am ashamed of the extent to which we have violated the sanctimony of their expected privacy. It will affect European perceptions of America for a long time, stemming from the same part of the brain or culture itself that abhors child abuse, or wife beating; serious norms have been violated, and they are not so easily patched-up.

As Roger Cohen has written in " **The Spy Who Didn't Love Me**" the Germans even have a word for it: " Handyuberwachung:" spying of cell phone calls. Cohen writes of this changed perception of America in Europe:

The perception here is a United States where security trumps liberty, intelligence agencies run amok (vacuuming up data of friend and foe alike), and the once admired 'checks' and 'balances' built into American governance and studied by European schoolchildren have become, at best, secret review of secret activities where opposing arguments get no hearing.

Cohen's brilliant explanation above, written in Berlin, was followed with: " This disquiet of Snowden that turned him into a whistle-blower now encounters overwhelming sympathy."

And just when we thought we have heard the worst part of this story the bottom falls out bringing us to lower levels of shame in German eyes. As Smale, Eddy, and Sanger reported from Berlin on October 28, 2013, the Germans are now aware that Chancellor Angela Merkel has been a "target" of American spying since 2002; and the spying operation to listen to calls on her personal cell phone was conducted out of the United States Embassy in the heart of Berlin near the historically significant Brandenburg Gate. Sanger and his team raised the question as to why did the U. S. government spy on one who had been " a rare stalwart supporter in Europe of the Bush administration's plans to invade Iraq."

The article adds to what Cohen had written about the changing European perceptions of America, by reporting the rationalization of U.S. motives as expressed by a member of Congress, the Republican Mike Rodgers, who believed Europeans misunderstood the "scope and intent" of America's spying. Rodgers claimed that our spying was intended to "protect them...from the threat of terrorist attacks." Think for a moment; of people in Europe reading these words that represent not just Rodgers, but many other Americans; and then imagine what you would think if Obama's personal cell phone calls had been tapped into since 2002 by a German spy network.

The severe damage done to the conduct of American foreign policy for the remainder of Obama's term, and perhaps beyond, is front and center here in German/American relations, the most crucial for America's interests in Europe. Ms Merkel is said to be very angry and feels betrayed, and said that "spying between friends is simply unacceptable" at this breach of trust, and a personal embarrassment to her.

On the other side of the world the Chinese, having learned that these sophisticated vacuum sweeper data collection spying systems were operating out of the American Embassy in Beijing and consulates in Chengdu and Shanghai, were most likely wondering if the cell phones of Mr. Zi and other top Chinese leaders had also been compromised. The Chinese Foreign Ministry on Oct 31 gave the U.S. a lesson in international law in a statement released to the press:

"We demand that foreign entities and personnel in China strictly abide by the Vienna Convention on Diplomatic Relations, the Vienna Convention on Consular Relations and other international treaties, and they must not, in any form, engage in activities that are incompatible with their position and status and that are harmful to China's national security and interest."

This is not a New York City politician complaining about foreign diplomats not paying their parking tickets; we are talking about basic foundations of international law and diplomacy that go back to the 17th century, at a time when the first American settlers were attempting to force the Indian tribes into accepting the white mans concepts of justice and law.

Germany: Realeconomics

Bismarck, the 19th Century German Chancellor gave us " realpolitik " played out into the creation of the German nation. Germany's shock from the revelation their Chancellor's cell phone has been tapped by American spies since 2002 has not just changed the political dynamics of German/American foreign policies; but is beginning to change the very nature of the power relationship between the two countries. Bismarck's Realpolitik, or hard power, was backed by what he called " blood and iron;" armies, guns, and cannons. Germany's new realeconomics, a soft power, is backed by economic policy and financial decisions. Realpolitik brought Germany to dominance in Europe after the defeat of France in 1870; the spying revelations of 2013 surreptiously brought the reality of German power to the surface, that its economic supremacy in Europe gives it by default, the position of Europe's number one power, as sure as was the case in 1870. All the European countries must place Germany, not the United States, at the center of their future decisions, for they too have been badly damaged by the spying on their own leaders for the past decade and the reality that America's inability to get its own financial house in order leaves them with no other choice.

As David Sanger has written from Berlin the U.S. "appears paralyzed in many ways," while the German Chancellor's formation of a new government will most likely include the left leaning Social Democrats from across the aisle, and displaying "power in ways unknown since 1945." The most amazing development as reported by Sanger from a Cyber-security conference in Germany was that German corporations and business people were setting up new internet systems to not only block American spies but to create European-wide electronic systems reflecting the new power realities in Europe, and the fallout of American influence (as evidenced by the early 2014 occupation of the Crimea by Russian troops).

This means that the breach of trust has extended beyond politics into the board rooms of European corporations who are now aware of how American firms with which they have been doing business for decades have actually been part of the U.S. spy network by allowing American spies to view and copy data of phone and internet communication of European businesses and individual executives. The reality that some of these dealings may have been forced upon American businesses by court orders makes little difference. And further disclosers may reveal much of the business spying to be of a contractual nature between the CIA and American corporations, making the revelations ever worse.   In the recently published "**America's most celebrated Publishing House, Farrar Straus & Giroux**" by Boris Kachka, is the story of the CIA contracting (paying good money) with the company president Roger Straus to put a special " hot line" secret phone in his office to be used by CIA agents in spying upon European leftist writers and dissidents during the Cold War, for at the time the publishing house had deep influence in European circles thought important by the CIA. But this was the Cold War period of the 1970s; how do you square that in 2013? As this is written it seems incomprehensible and counter-productive to American national interests, as it may to you, but Sanger leaves the reader with the reality of the mindset of the American intelligence community by quoting an American intelligence official (and Mr. Sanger must know quite a few big shots), rationalizing the seriousness of America's spying: " The reluctance is that you never know what you may need, in a month, or a year, or 10 years."

As written above, this spying revelation's impact of American foreign policy has profoundly changed the political playing field, and we see parallels in the economic field. It came at a time when a new trade agreement appeared to be binding Europe and American continents into one trade block. It is too soon to predict the future, but one can wonder what outcome a gambler would put their money upon.

There are two questions of importance to ask in conclusion: Where were Clapper's National Security Agency investigators before the Boston Marathon bombing? Why were security forces in Boston not at least notified that Russian intelligence had sent warnings. It is difficult to comprehend that the Russian tip-off on the Tsarnaev brothers to U.S. intelligence was not pursued sufficiently. Just look again at the tapes of the two brothers walking behind all those people watching near the finish line carrying bombs on their shoulders. Even a New York City cop would have profiled those two; in this case a racial profile would have been helpful (two guys who look like they could be from the Caucasus'), though this type of profiling is un-American.

Speaking of un-American takes me to the second issue, the increasing use of drones as a weapon against terrorists in far off lands, remote from even their own major cities and cultural centers. Think for a moment. Do these drone bombing make American citizens any safer? – as claimed by President Obama. Is this new method of warfare one that does not reflect the values for which thousands of Americans have fought for in so many wars of the past?

End of prologue

American Foreign Policy

America's founding fathers suggestions on the birth of our nation's foreign policy are often either misunderstood or misappropriated for narrow ideological goals. Their warnings of "entangling alliances" did not mean we should be isolationists. These men were all heavily aware of the complexities in human nature and the world derived not just by experience but careful readings of the histories of empires and the philosophical debates on the state of politics from Aristotle, Plato, Socrates onto Augustine, the Romans, the Enlightenment, to the writings of

Locke, Hobbs, and Rousseau. Unlike today's shoot-from-the-hip, self-confidant ideologues dominating TV and social media, they understood that a crisis may leave little wiggle-room between good and evil, cause and effect, and ideology should never dominate an analysis in search of the correct path.

Take the decision to invade Iraq in 2003. The American public were told lies about the reasons for the invasion, but Chaney, Rumsfield, Wolfowitz, Richard (you go first) Pearle, Elliot Abrams, and John Bolton to name a few of those expected to be knowledgeable of the pitfalls of a regime change in Iraq. Ideology drove them, or perhaps arrogance, or a greed for oil. As this is written in 2013 we know what regime change has meant for the lives of most people living through the terrible consequences, they no longer have a dictator but the horrors they face everyday may be worse to most. What people want of any government are health, welfare, and education. In Iraq, people die just shopping in the market place, praying in their places of worship, or even while attending funerals of loved ones who died in this war without end.

Like Robert McNamara (Corporate brilliance) and Mc George Bundy (Yale University brilliance) before them in regard to Vietnam, the Bush administration failed to accept or understand the accumulating wisdom against their actions in their rush to war. This is what the creators of our Constitution warned against. The hubris of those who should know better, whose job it is to make sure our men and women in uniform are not called upon to risk their lives for causes not critical to America's vital interest, as with the three longest wars in American history; Vietnam, Iraq, and Afghanistan.

The military "surge" decisions to dramatically increase U.S. troops in both Iraq and Afghanistan were a waste of young American lives upon the altar of wrong-headed thinking on the part of those who are paid to know better. General Petraeus, West Point graduate, Ph.D. in International Politics from Princeton, pushed his counterinsurgency doctrine, COIN, enthusiastically supported politically by some Washingtonians who had not only never served in uniform, but have actually dodged attempts to put them into uniform.

Sitting here in 2013 and thinking about the 21st century; what could we say may be helpful in understanding how American Foreign Policy should be conducted? There are many lessons, many voices, many books on foreign policy, which ideas will best guide us? An Internet search will reveal hundreds of authors beginning with our second president John Adams and ending with contemporary journalist Fareed Zakaria. Adams whose skill in attempting to navigate between a dangerous Franco/British war, and Zakaria whose judgment will always be tarnished with his support of the Invasion of Iraq. In between A and Z, where can we find the wisdom needed as this century unfolds with an emerging China, economic crises, terrorism, nuclear, chemical, and biological challenges, and Putin's Russia using military mobilization to push his agenda 100 years after the start of WW I, to say nothing of severe ecological problems facing every corner of the world.

Lets take a break and think. If you wanted the best American novel, or the best American poet, or the best American historian; to whom would you turn? You might choose J.D. Salinger's " Catcher In The Rye" as the best novel; Walt Whitman's " Leaves of Grass" for poetry, and the historical writing of David McCullough. This is just one person's take and as you see it is subjective. But when it comes to foreign policy, it best to be objective, for it does not just involve a personal judgment on art, but judgments on how best America can prosper and survive the uncertainties of this 21st century.

But first it must recognize that when a problem is put before us, there is something more fundamental than ideology that we bring in our attempting to understand the dynamics of the problem, as well as the approach itself. We all employ different strategies in solving problems in our personal life; just as statesmen do on the international level. Sometimes we mix up our strategies but mostly we rely on only one that serves as our primary guideline, and often prevents us from even considering evidence that may undermine what we consider the facts, or the truth.

The facts and the truth? Think the 2008 economic shock and how you as an individual thought about it in terms of how to bring our economy back where it was in 2007. The number one problem, good jobs. Some argued that the problem was the enormous debt and unless we cut spending and got the debt down recovery would take a long time before the private sector would begin hiring again. Industry, corporations, and businesses were afraid to hire until they were certain the economy was back on track.

So we have witnessed austerity measures being enforced here and in Europe that should have given those who control the " Means of Production" more "certainty" about the future with the governments and financial leaders tightening the screws on the budgets. But still too few jobs, but the big banks, financial institutions, and corporations have been amassing record level profits. With these same financial interests giving money to the majority of Senators and Congressional representatives for re-election campaigns, hiring former government and military leaders with unequal knowledge as Washington lobbyists to influence those who write our laws, most Americans do not realize they have little representation.

Why does a government exist beyond keeping order and defending the homeland? Under normal times we could say to make sure all Americans enjoy the protections of our Bill Of Rights, the United States government's most fundamental obligation to all its citizens. There may be a more fundamental position if we start with the fact that none of us had any choice of our being born. A believe that everyone born has a basic human right to a place in which they can bathe and clean, cook food, and sleep with a roof over their head. I love being an American with my freedom to say what I want, to write what I want, to assemble with whomever I wish, and believe in any God, or not believe. The American revolution of 1776 and the French revolution of

1789 opened up new eras in human conceptions of the responsibilities of governments that brought us to the 21st Century. We need new concepts of government responsibilities in our new global age when poverty, hunger, human degradation can no longer be hidden away from human consciousness. We no longer need Stanley and Livingston to tell us what is happening in Africa; we can all see it every day if we can to tune in. China could not hide the bodies of over 5,000 dead children after the earthquake of 2008 as a result of faulty construction; Bangledesh could not hide the bodies of the hundreds garment workers who died from fires and building collapses due to government corruption.

There will always be murders, violence, wars, and misery in this world, but there can be less of it, and this is the main reason governments exist; not to create an environment where a few can dominate the economy at the expense of all others, for an "economy" is about jobs for most people and what happens when the private sector does not create them or the pay is so low it is difficult to pay one's room and board.

Back to American foreign policy and the thought of what strategy best serves the nation, or, ways to think about policy options, taking into consideration that individuals use different methods of problem solving that are no much unlike those used by statesmen.

STRATEGIC THINKING

Which strategy do you identify with?

First: There are those who believe that every problem has a solution as long as we open it up to discussion and let all be heard, the community can solve it. These are **idealist** who does not see just a problem, but a solution just around the corner based on a belief that no problem is beyond our ability to solve.

Second: Some approach every problem accepting that we may not be able to solve it immediately, nor perhaps in the near future, and their motto is " that Rome was not built in a day." Like an addict trying to overcome addiction; taking one step at a time solves problems. Find something we can all agree to before moving forward. This is the mind of the **pragmatist.** It is nice to think that if we put our collective minds to the problem we can solve it. What can we accomplish today, or in this meeting, that we can all agree to. One step at a time.

Third: Everyone knows that if you hope to make money in the market you go to the most successful stock analyst, if your child needs a brain tumor operation you find the best neurosurgeon in the field, if you wish to buy expensive art you better have an expert to advise you. I have a friend who buys and sells old watches. What do they all have in common? They are **analysts.** Those who know the art of deductive theory first explained by Aristotle eons ago. Go from the general to the specific. Eliminate, eliminate, eliminate, until you narrow down your decision to the one remaining truth, or the most beautiful diamond, the greatest work of art, or a watch not worn since the 1920s that has never been duplicated. Upon what information do you chose a bottle of wine for dinner?

Forth: In many families there is always the one who is either "out there," or is the one considered a "little" eccentric, to say the least, and likes to learn what is new or different. The dreamer is at times loved, and at times loathed. At family gathering they may or may not show up; and often, if they do, they may be dressed differently, or bring a date that makes everyone nervous. Sometimes they become sellers of washing machines and dream of riding a star through space, as did Albert Einstein. It is sometimes uncomfortable to have them at meetings, for their suggestions often upset the harmony created by like-minded people with like-minded solutions to the problem at hand. These type we call a **synthesis;** and they like to throw objections at what everyone agrees is "the " solution: "No," they say, that is wrong. They are rarely found in organizations that stress groupthink, harmony, and an unwillingness to think outside the box. It is not until the complete failure of a policy or a business strategy that the synthesis and their input is appreciated and sought.

Fifth: Then there is the one who sits above it all, but takes in all the opposing and contradictory points of view and sees merits in all their positions, but does not commit to any one view, having wisdom that only experience teaches: knowing how quickly life and the world changes. Their objective is to examine all the facts, all the opinions, the unknowns and the unthinkable. Their aim is to get to the truth of the matter, if possible. They want to understand not only what the others think are the problems, but also what is the reality of the situations under investigation and discussion, the context. We call them a **realist.** To them, it is good to find common agreement, to take intelligent steps toward a resolution; to narrow down the critical elements of the problem, to come up with innovative ways to solve the problem, but the most important thing is gather together all the facts. Show me what are considered the facts the realist claims, and then we can get at what is more important, what is truth and what is not truth.

It was this later type of analysis, the realist, who was missing before Vietnam, before Afghanistan, before Iraq. American foreign policy has gone off the edge long before these wars with an idealist like President Woodrow Wilson who, after the most murderous war in human history, WW I, with his dream of the "League of Nations." To Wilson, WW I was the "war to end wars." A great idea but he lacked the pragmatism and realism to bring his dream to the reality of the world stage, for he had a personality defect that impacted him as a politician; he would not back down or compromise if he believed he was right. Wilson's grand design for peace never got out of the American Congress. If America had joined the League of Nations could WW II have been avoided? Would U.S. leadership in the League of Nations have affected German military and naval buildups and occupations in the Ruhr and elsewhere, blunting German aggression? Consider the current nuclear ambitions of Iran and North Korea. Would there be any hope today of curbing these threats without the U.S. in the United Nations? Rewriting history remains with the fiction writer, but with the stakes so high in our nuclear era we must allow ourselves to play God with a cubed puzzle.

WHO IS A REALIST?

The realist's knows his potential, and knows his limitations, both based on the facts and the reality of how those facts may shift within the changing of context. Strange, how it took a realist like FDR to bring Wilson's dream to reality during a top secret code named "Riciera" meeting with Winston Churchill on a vessel off the coast of Newfoundland in 1941, for though FDR was a realist his pragmatism brought him to appreciate the importance of Wilson's ideas on an international organization that could help maintain peace.

Which takes me back to the question explored earlier about choosing the best novelist, or poet or historian; for, if we wish to understand the intellectual intricacies of "realism," whom would we choose? We could go back to the first realist, Nicole Machiavelli and his writings about the "Prince;" but for our nuclear age it is crucial that we choose the very best realist thinker, for to err would have been like putting Dick Chaney, Richard Pearle, and John Bolton in command of American foreign policy during the Cuban Missile Crisis: none of us would have been here right now.

I am tempted with the amazing mental dexterity of statesman and scholar George Kennan, the thinker behind the idea of "Containment" that somehow got us through the Cold War without dire consequences. But I choose the philosopher, intellectual, political theorist, and teacher of realism, Hans J. Morgenthau whose writings influenced every post-WWII thinker, from Kennan to Henry Kissinger. His classic text " Politics Among Nations" had a profound impact on thinkers, statesmen, and diplomats for decades after WW II, but is not used as a text in political science departments today for many professors are not capable of teaching from a text so deep in historical, philosophical and psychological understanding.

As a young university professor in Western Pennsylvania decades ago I was assigned to teach my first International Politics course and my students and myself were assigned Morgenthau's text, "Politics Among Nations." My class was made up of very bright senior year political science honor students and we struggled, for I had not yet reached a sufficient intellectual depth to bring his text to life. I hoped they could not tell, but I knew it. I soon switched to another text after they openly complained to me how overwhelmed they were trying to utilize what they had just learned during the past four years. They were relieved and I saved face. But I continued to study Morgenthau at night, and a few years later I sat in rapture before a TV as Morgenthau took his realist principles before an international audience debating the two main architects of the Vietnam War, Robert MacNamara and McGeorge Bundy. MacNamara, considered the genius who ran Ford Motor Company and Bundy who some considered the brightest political scientist Yale ever produced believed that it was in America's interest to stop Communism in Vietnam. They attacked Morgenthau on an intellectual and personal level; but Morgenthau, not only held his ground but also told them to debate with him directly without having all the aids running to their sides with advice on pieces of paper. Morgenthau as a realist knew Vietnam was a major American mistake and history has proven him right no less than those of us who opposed the Iraq invasion planned by Chaney and Bush.

A few years after that TV debate I found myself sitting in a small yearlong Ph.D. seminar on International Political Theory at City University of New York Graduate Center where Morgenthau last taught. During that year I had been studying Clinical

Psychiatry at Mt. Sinai hospital in a special program combining political scientists along with M.D.s and I pressed him to address the deeper questions of unconscious variables in the motivations of nations which often went against what he had written in his classic text. I was often surprised that Morgenthau stepped in to defend me against the onslaughts of my fellow students who dismissed my arguments. These were precious intellectual debates that I was later able to discuss with Morgenthau as I came to know him on a personal level during many occasions at the New York residence of John G. Stoessinger who was Morgenthau's best friend and my boss at the United Nations and with whom I taught courses in International Politics at Hunter College

Henry Kissinger himself learned much from Morgenthau's realism, which he displays in his writings and many of his major foreign policy positions, but who also let his ego interfere from what Morgenthau's ideas taught him. Vice President Chaney, the most dangerous civil servant in American history, showed no intellectual evidence that he even tried to absorb Morgenthau's lessons

Within the first hundred pages of his classic text Morgenthau discusses the core of his political theory that I will outline and then take the liberty of applying it to our 21st Century world, influenced not just by his writings but direct involvement with this great man in a full year's study of political theory

Morgenthau outlined six principles of "political realism" that are rather dense intellectual arguments that most likely confuse today's students used to simplistic text message arguments. Let me briefly lay them out for you to think about, and will suggest some simple attempts at applying them.

Principle # 1: He argued that if there are any laws that govern the way in which nations deal with each other, they " have their roots in human nature." The news of the day or news of the world displays what many wish to ignore: that we seem to be animals first, and humans second. Or perhaps beasts first, for how else can one accept the news of atrocities around the world in any 24 hour period. In fact, animals are less cruel to each other than humans; for they just kill for food and defense. So if we look at the brutal news coming out of Syria, Nigeria, Iraq, Afghanistan, Congo, Honduras, Boston, Newtown Conn., and many other places...we must ask? What are the roots of human nature? At bottom line: to think as a statesman we have to separate truth from opinion, when analyzing politics or society in general.

Principle # 2: He claimed that the most fundamental litmus test of "political realism" is the concept of one's "Interest Defined In Terms Of Power." And the statesman does not concern himself with ideology or motivations (an aspect of Morgenthau's theory that I have not agreed with and have written about). But politics must be set apart from other spheres of action such as economics, for here interest is defined in terms of wealth. China and Japan currently playing this out with their display of armed coastal naval ships in the South China Seas and off-shore islands, or the history of the United States sending military forces into Central America. Or it could be a more subtle display of power such as China's reluctance to curb North Korea's nuclear ambitions, or Putin's annexation of Crimea in 2014, or the United States refusing to support a democratically elected populist government in Honduras in 2009.

Power can be subtle without even having to be on display for it is about having control over others behavior. As with ancient Chinese wisdom the most successful battle is the one won without having to use weapons. From birth to death most people live within invisible straight jackets imposed upon them by their culture, parents, spouses, schools, bosses who control their behavior most often without any display of power. A small nation tucked between two powerful neighbors understands this quite well. Anyone having the misfortune of living with a control freak often exists on raw uncomfortable edges.

23

This was on display during some dangerous years of the Cold War when US/USSR nuclear weapons were pointed at each other, sometimes with hair-trigger periods of dangerous suspense, which could have destroyed our civilization. My experience during these years, at the United Nations or working on U.S. military bases more fully opened my eyes to these fearful realities. Thus, in the theory chapter at the end of my book on Chinese perceptions, I restate this principle to reflect the reality of the times: That nations begin to define their interest, not in terms of power, but in terms of survival; which at the same time corresponds to Morgenthau's emphasis that a "rational" foreign policy is a "good foreign policy, for it minimizes risks while at the same time complies with the moral precept of "prudence,"

Principle # 3: The previous principle is an objective truth and it is universally valid. It exists everywhere. It is true in the animal kingdom as well as among people in any given society. In the Mayan hills of Central America roosters display their territorial interest over the hens. The dominant alpha male in so many animal species, as well as human matriarchal societies, clans, tribes, and Empires in history. An environment of live and let live is rare on this earth. Yet interests do change and this is reflected in a nation's foreign policy; they are not set in concrete. A nation itself is a product of history, and is "therefore bound to disappear in the course of history."

Principle # 4: Political realism recognizes the inherent tension between morality and politics. The political actor must first and foremost consider the nation's vital interests when dealing at the geopolitical level, the morality of that decision not always clear cut and obvious, in the complex real world of conflicting moral opinions in their abstract universal formulations. The highest moral of the state is "Survival;" therefore when weighing the consequences of alternative political actions, the supreme virtue in politics, is "Prudence."

Principle # 5: The moral aspirations of a particular nation are not synonymous with the moral laws that govern the universe. The European powers learned this a long time ago, during the wars of religion; the thirty Years War from 1618-1648 that were so brutal and violent that it gave birth to the today's concepts of International Law, as written down by Hugo Grotius. The bloodshed resulting from today's religious wars from Afghanistan to the Middle East witness similar motivations to 17th century Europe.

Principle # 6. Realist politics is an autonomous sphere of activity that should not be reduced to other spheres of activity. This may be the most interesting of Morganthau's principles for the realist must be as precise as the neurosurgeon with his knife. He is alone, with no one to guide his actions in the sphere of an operation on the brain. How does the Israeli head of state decide when his intelligence information tells him that Iran may soon have a nuclear weapon that could wipe Israel off the map? Or the South Korean head of state with American military commanders who receive intelligence that North Korea is about to fire a nuclear-armed missile at South Korea? Or that Iran was sending Assad of Syria missiles capable of reaching Israel with chemical weapons? These are questions that have no pat answers; somewhat similar to those posed to John F. Kennedy at the Cuban Missile Crisis of 1962. The realist must show that the nation's interest may differ from the moralistic and legalistic viewpoints expressed by others, and this difference is real and profound.

Geopolitics

At this point I want to add another concept into the mix; one that has dominated the politics throughout the world for thousands of years: Geopolitics. Everything begins with geography, and this includes demography, economics, and politics all linked together. If you mixed up the world by moving Arabs to the US, or Europeans to China, and moved all of China to Europe, there would ultimately be no difference in the pursuit of the national interest in any part of the world. The new population would eventually take the same positions with regard to the same interests being pursued by the current population. Geography not only produces people with different physical characteristics, but different ways of thinking, that thinking grounded in economic and survival pursuits, encoded into their culture, which in itself is a manifestation produced by the geography. I have studied many peoples to learn something new; the philosophy and history of Germans, Chinese, Arabs, Inuit, Maoris, Mayan's and others. The deserts of the Arabs and the white winter ice of the Inuit produce a psychology of self-reliance and freedom as surely as the crowded landscapes of Chinese have produced a psychology of group think and conservatism, or the Germans whose demands for order lie at the heart of their psychology.

For American foreign policy to be successful it must be grounded on realism and geopolitics. The recent miscalculations of the Obama foreign policy in the Middle East are good example of realism and geopolitics not being applied to decision-making.

For example, the belief that the Arab Spring was going to bring democracy to the Middle East was as dreamy as those anticipating the emergence of a democratic Russia at the end of the Cold War or a democratic Iraq after killing Saddam. Wish should not drive foreign policy. Culture drives politics as we have seen with ancient distrust and hatreds from Tunisia through Egypt, Libya, Syria, and Iraq; preventing the seeds of democracy from ever taking hold, for democracy like love needs to be nourished to survive. The first country to liberate in the Arab Spring, Tunsia, remained deadlocked in sectarian conflict, but in late 2013 there appeared to be some hope for acceptance of consensus politics, but all in all, the Middle East became even more unstable because of US policy lacking in correct decisions with regards to Syria and more seriously with Iran. The later a primary example of the mistake of ignoring realism and geopolitics in developing policy; just consider, Israel and Saudi Arabia, America's most reliable allies in the Middle East as well as being bitter enemies, now allied in their opposition to the Geneva agreements reached between the US and Iran; Wahhabists and Zionists in alliance. The chapter on Iran deals with a deeper analysis of Iran's motives, but Israel's Netanyahu whose opinion of Iran's new leader "as a wolf in sheep's clothing," may not be flattering, but may be accurate reflects its conclusion in a statement. A realist would conclude that the vital political decisions in Iran remain in the hands of the religious leader, a theocratic authority who had also released enough of the reins on the previous leader to permit him to not only deny the Holocaust but to threaten Israel's very existence. Has the Theocratic religious ruler become more tolerant, thereby allowing a smiling professor looking type to make his own decisions? The Saudi/Israel positions are driven by geopolitics, for Saudis perceive Shiite Iran as the greatest threat to the Arab Sunni world and Israel sees Iran as an existential threat to its existence.

Syria by the end of 2013 began to look like Spain in 1936; only with all the warring religious parties from the 17th century thirty-years war mixed it. Obama dropped the ball and the time for offense passed, for the geopolitical nature of it had long eclipsed the earlier ideas of regime change as in Tunisia and Egypt, or democracy, and now even the reality Assad may remain in power. Syria is not of vital interest to the US, but Obama should have early on found ways to strengthen the early rebel forces to the point of toppling Assad, without American troops in Syria under any circumstances. The dynamics have changed drastically with Iranian soldiers and weapons pouring into the battle, Russians supply weapons and intelligence, and competing rebel forces with goals so hostile to each other it makes for a less effective revolutionary army.

The perception of Obama's lack of leadership and decision after the chemical weapons attacks on innocent men, women, and children, has not been reversed with the agreement for Assad to give up all his chemical weapons, for too much damage has already occurred. In an interview with reporter Matthew Kaminski a respected member of the Saudi royal family, Prince Alwaleed bin Talal, summed up the differing US/Saudi views of Assad:

> "The US policy is to have the devil you know,
>
> Saudi Arabia is to have any devil in Syria,
>
> other than the devil you know."

Today American foreign policy is confronted with many problems, not the least of which a rising China and Terrorism. At the end of WW II we were faced with paralysis over how to deal with our wartime ally, The Soviet Union and Communism; the later two problems for American Foreign Policy being the subject of the first writing of this very book. The 1980s was the most dangerous decade in world history. Leo and I took to writing this book with the same passion as those who work to end women's choices, or give women the decision over abortion, or fight for or against capital punishment. We believed that our combined backgrounds allowed us insights into these deadly choices of war and peace during the Cold War; Leo Brophy had been the Chief Historian for the U.S. Army's Chemical and Biological Services and author of many books such as " **The Chemical Warfare Service: Organizing for War,**" as well as books on the " **U.S. Army in WW II**" and acting as chief editor of classic studies on chemical and biological weapons. He was a most distinguished professor of history, a scholar, researcher, with a fiery spirit driven by his sense of justice, nurtured by his families experience as Pennsylvania coal miners in Carbon County, home to the Molly Maguire's, union men hung for demanding work and justice. Leo would not shy away from an intellectual battle; like a Harry Truman or a Dean Acheson. And our objective was anything but academic; we wanted to speak to the general population, and hopefully the decision-makers. I had learned from my experiences in military intelligence, at the United Nation working with peacekeeping, as well as my contacts with not just Chinese and Russians, but interesting people from around the world. In short, we believed we had a responsibility to contributing in any way we could, for the times were more dangerous than most people realized.

Now, this study looks at China and Terrorism (with an interesting interruption with the Russian invasion of Crimea this past week), but there are so many lessons to be learned from understanding how we dealt with Cold War problems whose challenges were so much more daunting. We have many levels of close ties with China than we ever had with the USSR: Kissinger's "Détente" suggestions that economic and cultural ties would help to bridge friendly relations between the two Superpowers is just a faint historical memory considering the millions of such ties between China and America. But China does possess a modern military equipped with enough nuclear weapons to inflict end of world damage on America, is developing a shore to ship missile system sophisticated enough to threaten U.S. Naval surface fleets currently keeping Pacific Ocean shipping lanes open to ships of all nations, and plays into U.S. concerns about a potential check to its number one power position in the world no less than Germany's challenge to Britain at the end of the 19th century and beginning of the 20th, Japan in the Pacific for America in the 20th century, or the emergence of the USSR as a power to watch after WW II for America.

It is easy to write about a "Flat World" where all this technology and trade makes it necessary to keep the peace as Tom

Freidman has written, but at the core of international politics is the fact of geopolitics, and it is an animal compared to Freidman's civilized "Flat World". its like we walk around in suits and dresses acting professional while beneath all our skins lie emotions, anxieties, fears, that can dominate us like a demon, and ruin it all. Like the DNA of each country's geography, geopolitics could ignite primitive passions that make no sense in our modern commercial times. Just look at the escalating tensions over small outcrops of islands in the China seas that began with fisherman bumping other's boats and public claims rarely acted upon. My 1982 case study on this issue published in the "Law Of The Sea" chapter in my "China's Perceptions Of Global Politics" book dealt with concerns about potentially huge deposits of oil in the seabed around some of these outcroppings called islands. I remember the optimism of a pal of mine who used to work on the offshore drills conducting explorations on the seabeds in the late 1970s and early 80s But today, a very dangerous situation has developed, renewed Nationalism. Oil is easier to bargain than national pride, for the later brings out the ghosts of other times and eras, fired-up with emotional passions that are always unpredictable. I never dreamed when I wrote the earlier case study that I would come to see the day when these disputes could possibly ignite a major Pacific war. Think about it: the modern cities of Asia destroyed (or flattened, pun intended) in a war over control of large rocks in the China seas. I do not see this happening; but who thought a nut case with a pistol in Serbia could start WW I. Geopolitical claims backed by nationalistic passions are not easily resolved. Let's now look at something closer to home.

We should be still learning from the past but we don't. Take Cuba. If it weren't 90 miles from Key West would the U.S. have risked so much in 1962? What we recently learned about the Cuban Missile Crisis makes me wonder this very day, what future historians would write about us, knowing now about the Russian submarine commander who prevented WW III by not following an order, his only order, to release nuclear missiles. The evidence is so new we have yet to digest its meanings. Would missiles in Cuba be any worse than the nuclear war that would have ignited had that Russian Admiral not have overruled other submarine Captains under his command who were already turning the keys in preparation for launching? Think about that. All our American families would have been wiped out, our civilization. Just think Hurricane Sandy: lot of people in its aftermath living like it were the Middle Ages in the states most damaged. Cuba, the island, would still be 90 miles from the most southern tip of the Florida peninsular. Our world we know now would not be here.

This chapter could be only about Cuba and all the problems and lessons of the complexities of foreign policy making are there in a nutshell, covered with dozens of layers more like an onion. Just like we are who we are; our personalities mostly remain the same throughout our lifetimes, and even with many makeovers, we will revert back to whom we are when exposed to unexpected failure or danger. Cuba will be Cuba in spite of changes. Paris will always be Paris; before and after Louie the 14th, the guillotine and the French revolution, Hitler and America tourists. San Francisco will always be San Francisco. Havana will again be a playground for the rich, just a matter of time, as it was before Castro. It is hard to wrap my mind around the above fact that America gambled on its very existence in 1962, a fact we played with since, until the above story of the Russian commander opens it up to science fiction.

Who is this Cuba? I was driving around Havana in my red and white Ford convertible in the winter/spring and early summer of 1958 when the Cuban army of over 35,000 men was holding off Castro's group of bandits in the mountains, numbering little more than a few hundred men. I had just drove from Texas where I had been discharged from the military and was very curious due to the privileged military intelligence reports I had read about American investment interests in Cuba. None of those reports gave the rebels a chance of success. I had seen first hand what Mao's little band of rebels had accomplished in China, and knew more about

31

guerilla warfare from that experience to make me very skeptical of what I had read in recently de-coded military documents, as well as the newspapers of the day. I had put my car on a ferry then running out of Key West, Florida to Havana.

The first two days I drove around town enjoying my recent freedom from military life until I encountered the first of many things that gave life to my suspicions. Havana was a city filled with rumors; but then rumors ended on my third day when Castro's voice filled the streets from thousands of makeshift speakers around the entire city. Castro was up in the Sieria Maestra mountains; he now had his propaganda machine in the form of Radio ReBelde, or Rebel Radio. I remember the moment as clearly as I remember the tense night in 1962 when we all froze in horror as Kennedy informed us of our nuclear war alert. I was sitting at an outside restaurant table with three wealthy Cubans who had just come from gambling at a casino, a Mafia New York guy who owned the restaurant, and a pal of mine from military intelligence then stationed in Havana. We said nothing to each other, but we could read each other's minds that day. It was just a blurb in human history; but one of those moments that would be at the core of a science fiction story, but an event dismissed by millions of journalists and intelligence agencies around the world. What we all knew at the time was that the Cuban Army was a professional army in that they considered being a soldier a job, not a warrior, and had no intention of dying in uniform. We also knew that Batista's military forces had severe logistical problem because of U.S. sanctions due to the horrendous human rights abuses of the regime. Batista could not even get parts for his airplanes. As Castro's voice blasted, I thought about what propaganda had done for Mao's rebels in China.

Batista had sent an army of 12,000 into the mountains to capture Castro and his right hand man Che Guevara but were defeated by a few hundred rebels. An entire battalion was defeated, 240 captured, and the rebels lost only three men. About the time I was forced to put my car on a ferry to Key West Castro's rebel forces of around 300 men were nearly destroyed in a battle at Las Mercedes that had been a trap set up to destroy the revolution. It nearly succeeded, for Castro asked for a cease-fire. It was a trap similar to the one laid out by the Kuomintang in South China whose objective was to destroy all of Mao's rebels in one decisive battle. Castro was encircled, as was Mao; and like Mao he escaped the encirclement after stalling in negotiations for seven days. By August 8 Castro and his band of rebels were back up in the mountains, and I had landed in Philadelphia where I was going back to college, to learn how to classify what I had experienced in four years of military, from professors who read and wrote books about it.

So the first question a realist asks is: who is Iran, who is North Korea, who is Syria, who is China, who is Russia. For beyond what they appear to be, what they produce, what they say about themselves, what their behavior is at a given time, who they are, is whom we will be dealing with, if a crisis occurs. Like a husband and wife often not knowing what lies at the core of their partner, sometimes spending a lifetime without truly knowing the other. Here in 2014, who is Iran? Is Iran the ancient culture I write about in another chapter, giving hope to those who believe Iran's threats to wipe Israel off the map should not be used to determine vital foreign policy decisions leading to bombing its nuclear facilities; or is the recent intelligence information about the horrible, cowardly, killing of many young American students over Lockerbie, Scotland in 1988 may not have been carried out by Libya's Colonel al-Gaddafi, but by Iranian agents who found Gaddafi quite willing to take the blame for the bombing of the airliner. Which Iran do we see in this hour of decision for our ally Israel, with regards to whether to bomb or not to bomb Iran.

With Iran currently doing its best to cover up its nuclear developments, does this latest information on such a successful long-term cover-up on the Lockerbie killings have any bearing on how to deal with the current crisis?

As I learned long ago in military intelligence, assume nothing. Based on what we are being told, Iran does not yet have the bomb. But, perhaps they do. After all the known intelligence there are those in both Israel and the U.S. who would take that leap of faith in a so called "preventative strike." As we now know, there were several in that 1962 war room that pushed Kennedy to take "preventive measures." We also know now about the Soviet submarine Captains who had already begun to turn the keys. It's not too abstract to think about just what one nuclear bomb would do to the State of Israel. In our nuclear age a bad foreign policy decision of going to war does not necessarily mean the wrong war at the wrong times. It could mean the end of two nations, as we now know them. How do we wrap our minds around these choices?

Lets do a case study of one day of American Foreign Policy

If we just take one day, say, August 30, 2012, and look at American Foreign Policy to see how decisions illuminate how ignorant our young nation is to global history and the realities of international and geopolitical forces in the world.

This Day 8/30/2012: U.S. troops teaching Afghans to fight. Come on; they have defeated Empires for centuries. Worse yet, allowing military commanders, regardless of advanced academic degrees, to devise a policy where our guys became embedded with Afghan soldiers whom they are training to fight the Taliban. Many of the recruits are the Taliban. I cannot image loosing a son this late in this war that should have ended in 2004. What would President Obama tell the parents? Your son died for a culture that stones women to death for not marrying an old man her parents had wanted her to marry, or men who throw acid on the faces of young women who want to learn to read and write, or to protect men who burn down schools and kill the teachers that educate women. Here is an American flag. Your son or daughter died for their country, the USA. My answer to this cannot be printed.

This Day 8/30/2012: Welcome to American Foreign Policy 101. Now, suppose your son or daughter in uniform dies in Honduras tomorrow, August 31, 2012. Yes, we have military boots on the ground. Our leaders were so afraid that the Central American countries were about to de-criminalize drugs in order to cut down on the violence and murders in their countries, they bribed them with amounts of money that I could not find in any of the budgets so avidly discussed in this election season; Honduras, Costa Rica and other Central American countries have agreed to allow the U.S. military to use lethal force again drug smugglers, perceived or real; like the killing of two pregnant women in the back woods of an Honduras river. A blip in time in the vastness of space; but, perhaps, one of the babies in the bellies of those two women might have one day become a leader of enormous persuasion for peace and prosperity. U.S. troops have fought in Central America to protect the interests of the United Fruit Company (now Dole Fruit Company), to stop the spread of Communism, and now to stop the flow of drugs into America. Is it not time for American policy in Central America to deal with the realities of the 21st Century and lead, as a great nation should, not with the heavy hand of boots on the ground.

Letter from Ernest Hemmingway to newly elected President J.F. Kennedy:

Hemmingway who not only wrote about war in his novels, but served in war, got wounded in war, and covered war as a journalist, was moved to write this to the new President: " … It is a good thing to have a brave man as our President in times as tough as these for our country and for the world."

History shows that those who experienced war are more likely to attempt resolution of a conflict than draw the sword. Many who experience extreme violence of any sort come away with a wisdom that guides them in times of crisis, a compass that is not measurable by any standards. Be it Truman who tried to hold back General McArthur from expanding the Korean war into China; or Eisenhower who kept men like General Lemay from using nuclear weapons against China, or J.F. Kennedy who most likely may have not sent more advisors into Vietnam had he lived.

This is a debate whose time has come, for with the proliferation of nuclear, chemical, and biological weapons not just within the short reach of nation states but deranged individuals and terrorist groups, is it not best to have those at the helm who understand the nature of the beast. Think for a moment: Johnson's Vietnam buildup and Bush/Chaney's invasion of Iraq and the prolonged war in Afghanistan. How much bloodshed followed these decisions of these two Presidents, and neither ever fought in war. Some think military experience does not have any relevance in determining whether one would make the wise decision on questions of war and peace. We heard these discussions with the nomination of Senator Chuck Hagel for Secretary of Defense, such as a January 20, 2013 editorial in the NYT by no other than the paper's chief editor at the time.

Chuck Hagel received awards for valor and two purple hearts serving this country in Vietnam, which the editor, Bill Keller, states " was unquestionably honorable...but the notion that experience of war imparts a special wisdom is one of our enduring fallacies...and should be regarded with skepticism," and the qualities that make a good defense minister is unlikely " to have been perfected in the jungles of Vietnam," and Keller concludes by stating that Hegel's " military service could be a handicap."

This is an argument that does not stand up in the annals of history, be it ancient Greece, Rome, or the literature of the world. It does not even stand up to basic male behavior; for it has been my experience that the really tough guys are the gentlemen, who fight only when it is imperative. It is the weak that often fight, for they crave the respect given to the warrior who controls his passions. Looking at the pretty scar-free face of Bill Keller I suspect he has never been in a street fight, nor less fought in combat. Being the son of the Chairman and chief executive of the Chevron Corporation, George Keller, he was able to avoid serving in Vietnam when graduating from Pomona College in 1970 when other young men from working class families were not so fortunate

Getting personal, yeah; but what is more personal than loosing a son or daughter sent into combat in Iraq by the likes of men like the draft-dodging Vice-President Chaney, Richard (chicken) Pearle, Elliot Abrams, and George the reservist Bush. New York Times Keller was shouting invasion from the rooftops in 2003 with his article: " The I-can't Believe-I'm-A-Hawk Club" arguing that Colin Powell "Should Go," because his strategy of **diplomacy** had failed. Is was bad enough, that Keller, the journalist, was not even savvy enough to walk across town to the UN to uncover that Powell had been duped and set up by Bush and Chaney; but Keller went on to praise assistant defense Secretary Paul Wolfowitz as being a " Sunshine Warrior."

Words don't kill; but sending our young men and women to fight the wrong wars does. Bill Keller has only the power of the word with the NYT, but his words may empower other men like him who sit in Washington with the power to send more honorable young American men and women into the fires of death for causes not vital to American interest or security. This is what concerns me as American foreign policy is refocusing on the world, with Asia, Central America, and Africa in our crosshairs. Kerry and Hegel may not have all the answers; but at least they have the scars that may allow them more prudence in dealing with matters of life and death than others who have lived a sheltered life because of the sacrifices of others.

Shift in American Foreign Policy

In April 2012 U.S. policy makers admitted a shift in American foreign policy with an announcement of the creation of a new intelligence apparatus responsible for gathering information on China, terrorism, and nuclear proliferation, thereby downgrading expenses and intelligence gathering information on Iraq and Afghanistan. Wow.... Is that intelligent, or not? Yea, maybe if this was 2002, on the eve of American taxpaying citizens allowing Bush/Chaney to slice open the pregnant belly of America's treasures of financial surplus, genetic pool of brave young men and women, onto the altars of Iraq and Afghanistan markets for the likes of Halliburton, big US oil, and others backed-up by a decade of lawmakers more interested in food stamp cheats, government paid abortions for minority teenagers, students learning scientific truths about how life is more about accident than ordained by God and changing textbooks to reflect their own mistakenly intelligent positions based on minds blinded by dumb-downed religious principles. It would be funny if so many families across America were not now suffering the pain of loosing a loved one in these far off countries that has little to do with America's vital interests, or the multitudes that displayed the stars and stripes on their cars, homes, and brains after 9/11, or those unemployed sitting tonight starring at a wall and wondering what happened to the home they owned, or the job they had, or sadly enough, the families they once loved and supported. 2002 was the time to focus on China, terrorism, and nuclear proliferation. Would the likes of Congressman Paul Ryan, Senator Mitch McConnell, and Eric Cantor recognize these realities?

What Happened America? Were we as blind and desperate as those Germans who bought into Hitler in the 1930s? It felt so good to attack those terrorist nests in Afghanistan that bred those that caused our brothers and sisters to jump out the windows of the Twin Towers, kill so many lovely innocent people and so many gallant responders. Kill those terrorists swinging on bars and undergoing commando training. Yes, but... but... now a decade old, and hey, those same guys are not yet back in power, but may be. I will even go so far as to write once we pull out Karzai is gone and the Taliban will take over. That we could get rid of a dictator in Iraq with our firepower and allow a democracy to flourish. Wave the flags, put those proud stickers on our cars that we have loved ones who have put their bodies and lives out there, for an Iraq that is further from Democracy in 2014 than it was in 2003, for the majority in Iraq wish nothing less than compliance to their blueprint for society, sharing power with no-one.

Now we are in 2014 being asked to trust our government with protecting us from terrorists, threats from weapons of mass destruction, and a China whose behavior we need to be taken as a possible threat to our hard won hegemony inherited from the long and dangerous Cold War, don't blink or I will shoot, the 24 hour cloud of Armageddon threats. It's like we have heard before. When a patriarch is judged not by his willingness to commit to a truth, but to an ideological position based more on a misperception of reality based more on a wish than what is.

The problem for most Americans is that we not only have our perceptions of foreign policy manipulated, but even the way we see ourselves served by the only institutions than can protect us and our Constitutional rights from being eroded into meaningless..

By 2014, the most serious problems facing America Foreign Policy is what to do with Iran, and what the future holds for Africa after Mali/Algeria.

Iran

The solution for Iran, and the entire Middle East is a lasting peace, and that is achievable. There must be created a **Middle East Nuclear Free Zone**, one that sees not just Iran relinquishing its desire to have nuclear capabilities, but for Israel to surrender its nuclear arsenal like others have done, such as the Ukraine after the fall of the Soviet Union. As you shall read in the text, I suggested the creation of a Middle East nuclear free zone over thirty years ago, then a dream; but now, it is imperative. It does not seem likely that Iran will give up its nuclear ambitions, and no Israeli government can ever give up its right to protect itself against the historic threats to its very existence that began with conventional warfare in 1948 and now Iran's threat of total annihilation. Nuclear weapons are the elephant in the room. If Israel and Iran were parties to a nuclear free zone, the Palestinian problem would be adjudicated within the context of this historic settlement, changing the dynamics in the region from Lebanon to Saudi Arabia.

The key to this goal lies in diplomacy, something that has gotten pushed aside since 9/11 supplanted by military and intelligence types who have been the point-men for America's interests, in war and peace. The military and intelligence types represent hard power, and what have they left us with after a dozen years. An Iraq we have yet to admit was no less a pull-out than Vietnam, despite arguments to the contrary that the " The Surge" was a success in that it allowed us to leave, as a NYT editor claims, allowed the U.S. " withdrawal without shame." I do not think historians will come the same conclusions. As cited above, Iraq was a failure. Look what we found and what we left. Let common sense answer that.

Afghanistan is another matter. As argued before, the initial objective of knocking the Taliban from power was a decision no one regretted; but where are we by 2013? In a phase so difficult for our guys in uniform who have to worry about getting shot in the back by those Afghans they are training to fight after we leave. And whom are they going to fight? The Taliban. This, after a dozen years at war.

Its time to realize that military and intelligence types should not be the ones conducting foreign policy, even those holding Ph.D.s in International Politics like General Petraeus. This is not an opinion, but an experience. Having taught graduate level International Politics to Air Force, Navy, Marine, Army, and Intelligence officers in bases overseas I have a unique perspective. True, in my classes the spread from left to right thinking was similar to any university in which I taught. But when it came to the fine art of diplomatic thinking, a line was drawn in the sand so to speak; or more precise, the military mind and others. I taught not just international political theory and international law, but courses dealing with past concerns, the USSR, and our present concern, the PRC. In my teachings and in seminar discussions and research papers I took my students to the brink of intellectual discourse, pushing them to think outside "the box." I would chide them to "think like a Philly boy;" to hell with convention. For this was a university classroom, not a military academy or military course on how to. In my experience most of my students, military or intelligence types (the number of civilian intelligence officers at bases like Ramstein in Germany and Chicksands in England would be more substantial), were not very willing to cross that boundary of negotiating with the enemy. Those few who did, would tell me they were planning on getting out of the military. It is time to leave foreign policy to the foreign service types.

Roger Cohen of the NYT wrote in **"Diplomacy Is Dead"** that what we need now is the type of "effective diplomacy" that solved so many crucial political problems in the later 20th century such as Nixon's breakthrough with China, the end of the Cold War, and the Dayton peace accord in Bosnia, that requires " patience, persistence, empathy, discretion, boldness, and willingness to talk to the enemy." This is the "realpolitik" that George Kennan and

Hans Morgenthau wrote about. And as Cohen writes, " not for the squeamish."

Yes, Iran's nuclear threats are not beyond diplomacy, and I would argue the only way to prevent Iran from having nuclear weapons. Bombing Iran will not stop it from this goal. Again, this is not my opinion, but my experience.

I studied and experienced the craft and art of diplomacy for nearly a decade, in an area of the greatest concentration of diplomats in the world, the United Nations. I worked for the Director of Political & Security Affairs as well as writing a Ph.D. dissertation: **"China's Diplomatic Behavior In The United Nations "** bringing me into daily contact with diplomats from around the world. My experience was intense; my investigation of Chinese diplomacy brought me under the scrutiny of not only the Russians, most of whom were KGB agents working under UN cover, but the FBI and CIA. Perhaps more important for our current world, I was not just satisfied with understanding China's positions and diplomacy the issues of the day, but other countries experiences with Chinese diplomacy. I was so intent on finding out how Third World and other less powerful countries were dealing with China that one university professor in my doctoral program complained that I was " researching more like a journalist than a scholar, and he should be slowed down."

It is that experience of listening to representatives of these countries revealing just how much patience, perspective, and realpolitik was involved in negotiations with countries who viewed them as minor pawns in the international chess game called diplomacy. I learned more about the Chinese from them than the Chinese themselves, or the thousands of hours of testimony, both spoken in meetings and printed in documents. The United Nations provided this, for most nations cannot afford elaborate embassies around the world and New York was it. The political elites from their countries, those closest to the decision makers, were here in New York, not in embassies around the world. This was were the action was for them, and I listened and learned, not realizing then that this would give me strong convictions that the call for a **nuclear free zone for the Middle East** does not have to be the pipe dream of peaceniks, or as Cohen writes, ignored because of " wimpy associations."

The day following Cohen's piece his colleague, Thomas Friedman wrote a column, **" Break All the Rules"** suggesting that in order to gain "leverage in diplomacy" we should bypass governments and rulers using social media to reach their citizens, thereby putting pressure on their leaders to deal with our diplomats in more constructive ways than presently exercised. He argues:

"We live in an age of social networks in which every leader outside of North Korea today is now forced to engage in a two-way conversation with their citizens. There's no more just top-down. People everywhere are finding their voices and their leaders are terrified. We need to turn this to our advantage to gain leverage in diplomacy."

I would not comment on the above if it were written by a college undergraduate in political science, but this is from a writer with thee Pulitzer Prices in 1983, 1988, and 2002 who was elected as a member of the Pulitzer Board in 2005. Granted, columnists no longer have the ears of Washington power brokers like a Scotty Reston once did, but this guy does have a wider audience than the populations of many countries he writes about in his column, and he is dead wrong. There is no way America is going to solve its two most important problems of the near future, Iran or African terrorism, by appealing to the people of Iran in Farsi to understand their problems are a result of their government. They already know that, they don't need to be told.

Friedman's ideas were fairly harmless when he was writing about technological advances and globalization, but when he crossed over into politics he is open game. His Pulitzer Prize in

2002 was for " illuminating the worldwide impact of the terrorist threat," so here we are in 2014 and the suggestions in the column under discussion would bring forth terrorism on a level we can not image at this time, which I will return below.

Friedman the journalist supported the 2003 invasion of Iraq and argued that the establishment of a democratic state in the Middle East would force other countries in the region to liberalize and modernize, and he attacked the French for their advocating the prudence of not attacking without concrete evidence. Friedman was a total hawk. By 2014 there is no doubt that the invasion of Iraq has resulted in more terrorism than could have been imagined in 2003.

Now Friedman is advocating that a solution to the problem of governments not dealing with us as we wish they would, to go directly to their citizens. Just think of the citizens of two countries we "liberated," Iraq and Afghanistan. They are facing not only more terrorism now than before, but also more violent forms. Stirring up peoples long held down does not produce the democracy Friedman predicted in 2003, nor will the people put pressure on their governments or leaders to deal with our diplomats; all it would do is unleash hatreds that have their roots in recent and ancient history.

The advancement of American diplomacy by utilizing the technology of social media in reaching populations long suppressed is about as far off from the reality of how the world works as his 2005 book **" The World is Flat: A Brief History of The Twenty-first Century."**

As I watched Barack Obama's second inauguration I thought about how we needed radical new ideas and tactics to solve the quintessential threat that is Iran. And as Cohen writes, " Breakthrough diplomacy is not conducted with friends. It is conducted with the likes of the Taliban, the ayatollahs and Hamas." I think about all those diplomats I learned from at the U.N. and think about how many of their nations in the Middle East and Africa today that could be of enormous help in bringing about peace in the area through a nuclear free zone. This is in the interests of so many nations, not just the U.S., Israel and others fearful of an Iran/Israel nuclear war. Suspicions and fears of China in the late 1960s and early '70s were just as intense as Iran today; and one must remember, China did have the bomb. Today's neocons would have considered Nixon's so called " ping-pong diplomacy" wimpy; but what it produced was an entire restructuring of geopolitics and was truly the beginning of the end to the Cold War with the Soviet Union. It was not President Reagan's military build-up that brought an end to the Cold War, but Russia's "Vietnam" mistake of invading Afghanistan and the consequences of ignoring thousands of years of history as we have done in staying too long. It depleted Soviet resources no less than our two wars have done to the treasure chest left by President Clinton, with even more dire consequences for the Soviet economy. It was then that the Reagan diplomacy succeeded. I always wrote and taught that Russians never back away from threats; but will always engage in realpolitik diplomacy.

It is an opportunity for President Obama to do for peace in our time what other presidents have done in 1972, 1989, and 1995, and as Cohen suggested allow him to earn "that Nobel Peace Prize." A nuclear free zone in the Middle East may do just that.

Fast forward to summer 2013

The sanctions have had a devastating effect on Iran's economy; causing the Real to lose half it value, raising the price of food and any imported product bringing terrific pain and hardship to the population. But, the government is still rushing to develop that nuclear weapon as they time and again have played with Western governments with nothing to show for negotiations. More and more Iran's negotiating style have begun to resemble Korea's.

To understand the dilemma, an American would have to climb into the minds and perceptions of Israel leaders, for if this is not handled correctly Israel will pay the fatal price. As Netanyahu has said, we will not let anyone determine the fate of Israel except Israel.

Africa & America's next military commitments

The problems for American foreign policy in Africa has first been exposed by the crisis in Mali involving terrorism, a problem that brings together two of my early intellectual interests, African tribal life and Chinese history. As an undergraduate student I often took geography courses for two reasons; one, I had traveled extensively during four years of military service before college, the secondly because of a great teacher in that department. His name was Mr. Hawthrone and with him we studied the geography of Africa. He was ahead of his time, and rather than study Africa as if it were economic geography as others did in most universities at the time, he took us through a fascinating study of tribal life in Africa, teaching us that tribal diversity and cultures were as distinct from each other as were Finns from Spaniards or English from Greeks. We studied maps of Africa without any political divisions, only geographical features of mountains, jungles, rivers, savannas, and the like and the tribes that inhabited these lands. We learned how the land on which the tribe lived determined their economy, their language, their family life and structure, the way they resolved conflicts, authority and its decision making, in other words the land determined the entire culture and the way the people thought of themselves and the way their viewed the world around them. It was not until we understood these fundamental truths about Africa that we then superimposed the political boundaries upon the map of Africa. Boundaries that the tribes had no say in determining. Boundaries determined by the very colonial masters who ripped apart families and sold them as slaves around the world. This is the Africa we have inherited in the 21st century.

We have witnessed in America how abused or problem children grow up to be mass murders' with automatic weapons in their hands. Yet, the general public, for decades now, have little sympathy with the horrendous murderers and conflicts that come to the surface in Africa, Rwanda and the Congo just to site a few from the recent past. Few Americans understand that the root of this violence is not just tribal, but a result of western imperialism and its impact on the minds of Africans, consciously or unconsciously damaged by efforts to brainwash them into accepting a slave/master relationship. The westerns tried to psychologically mold the mind of Africans.

Years ago an Algerian psychiatrist, who had treated Africans fighting for independence from the French in Algeria wrote a book , **"The Wretched of the Earth"** based upon his case studies of thousands of Africans who came for treatment. The doctor and author, Franz Fanon, discovered something deeper in the psychic of these patients than the current conflict. It was a mental cancer developed when a human being is subjected to someone else's control, like an occupation of one's mind, by an individual or a foreign occupier. Generations pass it from generation to generation like a bad gene or defective DNA, in these cases it was the result of European imperialism on the minds of black Algerians; a disease of the spirit, whose only relief is to go out and kill those who have shackled you to their wills. Kill a white man. Fanon came to the conclusion that violence, to many, was not only justified, but also necessary for the mental health of the individuals, and eventually would lead to political liberation.

Many somewhat understand the motivation of a woman physically abused for years by a husband picking up a knife and driving it through his heart in a flash of anger; but, how about the young kid kicked, humiliated, and scorned in his own country by a foreigner, a white foreigner.

47

I have been to several African countries but my real learning began at the United Nations, for it brought me into contact with many interesting Africans, those who were from the ruling power in their countries, from every part of Africa. (and true, that most of these did not represent the masses). It was the 1970s and African liberation movements and decolonization, begun in 1960s, were continuing. I dealt with Angolans, Mozambicans, South Africans and other dreaming of kicking out the colonialists and imperialists from their countries.

The year 2013 will be the year that Africa became front and center in World Politics. But most westerners retain the same reaction to today's Africa that my students did back in the 1970s. A complete disconnect. Let us just look at the recent violence Mali and Algeria. It is the beginning of a problem the 21st Century will have to deal with.

When Latin and Central American countries were confronting their pasts and futures in the 1970s and 80s the two 800 pound gorillas in the room were Socialism and its radical cousin to its left, Communism; for many believed they were good weapons to use against not only foreign imperialist but their own elites who sold them out. In Africa today, there are two 800-pound gorillas roaming the land; tribalism and Islam. Tribalism; whose DNA is planted across the boundaries of many contemporary African states, and Islam; a new weapon to use against the interests of former colonizers and their own rulers who sometimes sell them out.

The crisis in Mali and its offshoot in Algeria have exposed the dangers in not just that region, but also all of Africa: tribalism and Islam. People abused or ignored by history do not go away, and will grab onto an idea or movement that enables them to take back what they believe belongs to them. Right here on the home front: American Indian tribes lost the lands of the great western plains, only to end up owning casinos taking wealth from the descendents of those who drove them into reservations or elimination.

The complexities of Africa for American foreign policy is subtly illustrated in its dealings with Nigeria, a nation thought to be a U.S. ally in Africa, think oil here. How does Secretary of State Kerry deal with Nigeria in 2014 when the Nigerian military are dealing with their Islamic insurgency, the Hoko Bono, with a program of genocide. Nigerian policy in the past had to deal with the traditional tribal conflicts as well as the conflict ignited by the south not sharing in the oil wealth of the nation. By now we know that there does not seem to be any diplomatic solutions available for any society to deal with Islamic Fundamentalist with their stealth weapons of suicide bombers and uncompromising mental brainwashed ideology whose objective is a theocracy of unbearable and unforgiving societal rules.

U.S./China & Africa

Here the realist has many questions. While the U.S. has been so busy with fighting terrorism since 9/11 the Chinese have been signing contracts with African nations for access to raw materials and has been Africa's largest trading partner with hundreds of billions of dollars a year; up exponentially from only $10 billion in 2000, on the eve of 9/11. The last time the U.S. was Africa's major trading partner was 2009. In 2010 the African Development Bank reported that Chinese firms signed 20 contracts in Africa for every one America signed. Some economic forecasters predict that China/African trade could reach $400 billion by 2016. Think: in 1980 it was a paltry $1 billion.

A little history here is interesting. China was out of the African business for quite some time; for during 1970s and 80s China was busy promoting its brand of revolution in an Africa at war with western imperialism, so when they would, for instance, build a railway in Tanzania it was to gain a foothold in a nation that had become independent in 1961, and hopefully spread its revolutionary gospel to other African states as I wrote about in the chapter **"China's Perceptions of Africa"** in my China's perception book. Whether it was Chinese, Soviet, or American aid or development projects they all came with political expectations. The Chinese message was "self-reliance," the U.S. message based on such economic development theories as Rostow's doctrine of " The Stages Of Economic Growth," arguing that growth was some mechanistic matter that had little to do with human problems, and aid is just a means of helping developing countries get from one level of growth to another; like growth stages of a child. And somewhere in this mix was politics; where African development would take place only when western democratic principles and free market forces were put in place. Unfortunately, the end of the Cold War left many African countries out in the cold when it came to developmental help from East or West.

Back in 2000 China's total investment in Africa was about ten billion in dollars, but by 2005 it had reached $39.7 billion, then $55 billion in 2006, 2011 it was $166.3 billion. In 2009 China replaced the U.S. as Africa's largest trading partner, with the U.S. at around $100 billion annually. In 2010 China signed 20 contracts for every one signed by an American company. One third of China's oil supplies come from Africa and close to 1000 Chinese corporations are doing business in Africa.

CHINESE INVESTMENT OFFERS IN AFRICA SINCE 2010

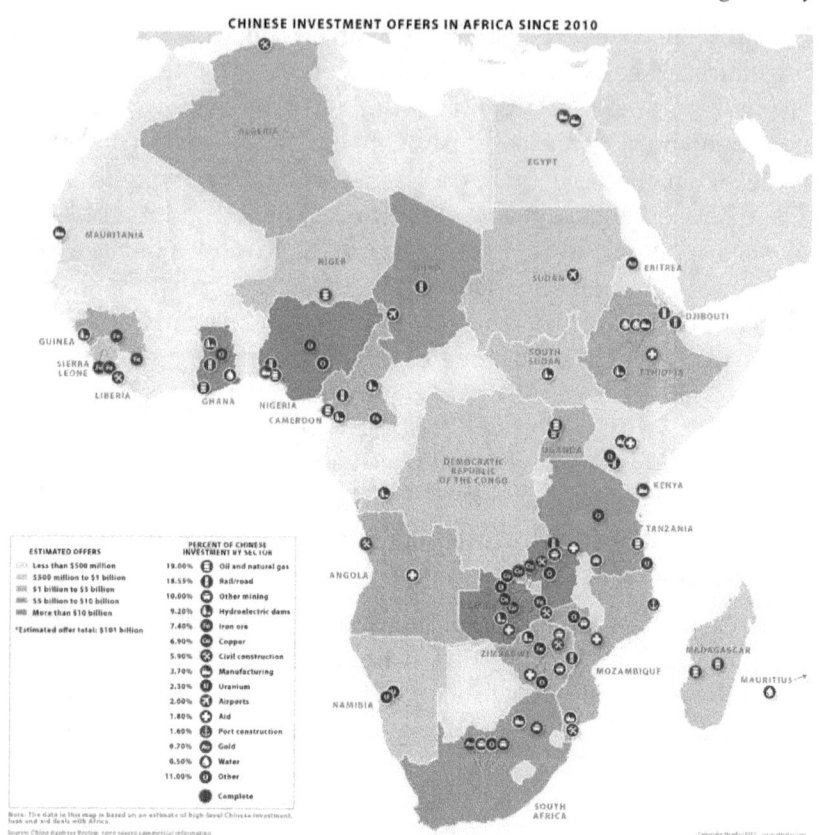

Enter discussion: Erik   Prince,   author   of   "Civilian Warriors…Blackwater."

As I wrote earlier, one of my current heroes is Edward Snowden, for representing that special part of American DNA, authentically home grown, an honest originality, and as tough as need be. We also have Erik Prince, authentic and original, and important in the conclusions to this chapter in many ways. The history of Blackwater is a serious contribution. It brought me back to a conservative and traditional graduate school in history at a fine Philadelphia university, when non-serious scholars washed out, for it was an intellectually challenging two year Master's program. We tried to get through the cobwebs of time in seeking raw and original evidence in attempting to study contentious historical periods; and a book such as Prince wrote would be like a diver finding that shell fish with the perfect pearl.

What had Americans known about PMCs (Paid Military Contractors) during two of the most controversial wars in American history? In 2003 I believe that the American people were tricked by Bush and Chaney when knowing more troops were necessary to fight these wars, declined to order up a Draft; instead, called up the State Guards, transforming them overnight into the National Guard. Prince's book brings another reality out of the shadows that again reveal Dick Chaney's bloody hand, the use of over 160,000 PMCs who were contracted to perform everything from cleaning kitchens, protect State Department personnel, and assist the CIA with assassination kill teams or running drone strikes into Pakistan.

As Prince pointed out in an interview with Rachel Martin that from the beginning of our nation: " As you know as Americans sit down to their thanksgiving meal… they should think about guys like Miles Standish or John Smith, the guys that helped build the original colonies – worked for a publicly traded company on the London Stock Exchange. You know, the Jamestown Colony was such a company." So the point he makes, has been the case with all of America's conflicts, but never at this level before. But he argues in this interview that with the defense and intelligent budgets not just large, but "bloated," and the private sector can not just help cut these funds in our trying economic times, but do the job better. In Prince's words: "I am perfectly happy to have that discussion or debate with somebody on the value and the merits of the private sector innovation and out-maneuvering any government bureaucracy – anytime, anywhere."

I wanted Eric Prince in this discussion, for it is a discussion that has ramifications beyond American defense and security agencies budgets, and ties into the our future with regards to Africa and China, with Prince remaining in the picture. Here again, an important discussion with another journalist, David Feith, about American policy in Africa, China's African policies, and Eric Prince's new role in China and Africa.

Journalist David Feith argues correctly that it is easier for China's state owned firms for they do not have to deal with such " trifles " as human rights, financial transparency, or environmental problems. " When a tyrant like Sudan's Omar al-Bashir can't get Western financing for a mega-dam across the Nile River, China arrives with an easy loan, some state owned firms to build the dam and some others to claim oil or mineral concessions elsewhere in the country."

When Brophy and I began our book began in 1983 the United States was supporting dictators, autocrats, thugs who murdered their own people; anyone who would join our anti-Communist side. You were with us or against us; the shadows of injustice within their countries air brushed and the thugs were given " foreign aid " allowing them to buy American weapons. In David Feith's interview with Erick Prince " **Out of Blackwater and Into China** " he caught my attention having just read Prince's " **Civilian Warriors: The Inside Story of ' Blackwater ' and the Unsung Heroes of the War on Terror."**

Prince, Feith writes, prefers to look on the bright side. That any good investment in Africa is, for Prince, " by and large the best for the people of Africa that have a job, that have electricity, that might have clean water, that might have those things that we in the west take horribly for granted." My kind of thinker, thank you Mr. Prince.

Prince argues: "Its Capitalism 101." When someone needs copper, or wood or an ag product and they invest capital somewhere to make that happen, and people get jobs from that, and that good gets introduced to the world stage and it gets traded and moved, the whole world benefits.

With the question of China's patronage of a president for life, such as Bashir, Eric Princes' CEO, Gregg Smith, a former U.S. Marine says: " There's thousands of tribal conflicts in Africa every decade that have nothing to do with anyone from the outside. It has everything to do with tribal conflicts that have been going on for centuries, and the fact that the economies cause folks not to have jobs…It's not about who backs Omar al-Bashir." Spoken like an Oxford African specialist.

Prince argues that China's newly developed empire in Africa does not come at the expense of America's interests, for the expansion of trade that is generated from this benefits both China and America, who remain each other's largest trading partner, and countries that trade together as less likely to shoot at each other.

And shooting at each other is something Eric Prince knows something about. As an ex-Navy SEAL, ex-CIA spy, ex-CEO of the private-security firm Blackwater, that he carved out of a North Carolina snake infested swamp and employed ex-military special forces guys to train others in the art of war, the war to protect clients from the bad guys, whose private company had eventual responsibility, or mission, in protecting U.S. government and State Department men and women in Iraq and Afghanistan for nearly a decade. Outcome: not one State Department personal or government official under their protection was killed during all this time. In his interview with Martin he described such a mission carried out hundreds of times a day in Iraq or Afghanistan; "when you are required to drive the congressionally mandated American vehicle…on the same predictable routes…it's very easy for the enemy to set up on you 'cause they know your' coming." He said his people were about to do that mission about 100,000 times, with not one killed or wounded. Except, 41 men of Blackwater killed in action supporting that mission.

Eric Prince's reward from the U.S. government: betrayed by the CIA, and "blowtorched by politics." In 2009, the CIA Director Leon Paetta leaked to Congress that Blackwater was a CIA asset. Prince writes in his book that the CIA had committed a gross act "of professional negligence," and totally regrets " in every way, shape, and form for ever saying 'yes'" to a CIA or State Department contract.

Eric Prince brings to my mind another great American compatriot who was done an injustice for his contributions, ex-FBI agent John O'Neil. What I found fascinating was that Prince was actually using his own money to recruit " and deploy a world-wide network of spies tracking al Qaeda operatives in 'hard target' locations where even the CIA couldn't reliably operate." Feith points out that this work remained secret until CIA's Penetta leaked it to Congress.

So now Eric Prince has taken his talents in another direction. He has a new firm in Hong Kong posed to acquiring business with China in Africa, now Africa's largest trading partner. In Prince's words: " This is not a patriotic endeavor of ours – we're here to build a great business and make some money doing it ... China has the appetite to take frontier risk, and that expeditionary risk of going to those less-certain, less-normal markets and figuring how to make it happen, with hundreds of billions of dollars in investments

So the U.S. became Africa's second largest trading partner in 2009, where are we in 2014? Unlike the Chinese who gave up their political aspirations in Africa a long time ago, we are beginning to play out our normal role again. Eric Schmitt in his article " **U.S. Takes Training Role in Africa as Threats Grown and Budgets Shrink** " points out that American officials describe the mission in Africa as "enabling;" one without American boots in combat situations but one supporting local and international forces in their war on terror. But, in 2013 there were 3,500 U.S. military from the First Infantry Division conduction over 100 missions ranging from " a two-man sniper team in Burundi to humanitarian exercises in South Africa." Army Green Berets from Fort Carson, Colorado helped train African troops in Niger to conduct patrols and to disrupt terrorist ambushes. American transport planes ferried 1,700 peacekeepers from Burundi and Rwanda to the strife-torn nation of Central African Republic.

How many Americans know we have Green Berets training troops in Niger, a country of borders with the most dangerous states of Mali, Nigeria, and Libya, and in two years spent $33 million dollars to develop Niger's counter terrorism capabilities. U.S. Army soldiers are helping to train an 850 man battalion of Nigerian rangers to deal with the increasingly violent and capable Boko Haram militants (the name itself, Boko Haram, in the northern language means "Western education is sinful" and often take aim at schools.

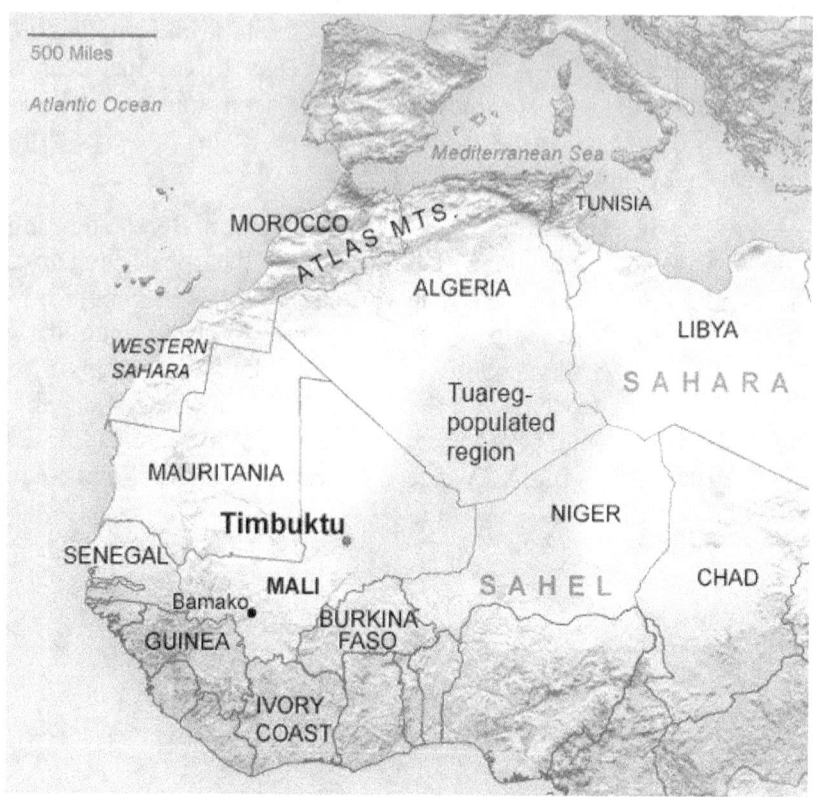

In February 2014 Boko Haram raided a boarding school in northeast Nigeria during the night and set it afire, killing 29 students most of whom were reduced to ashes. In June 22, 2013 students in the village of Mamudo were killed, and again in 2014 an entire village was razed and as the people tried to escape they were slaughtered, over 200 of them.

Boko Haram are more violent and complex than anything America has faced in both Iraq and Afghanistan, and it will get worse. Looking at America's involvement here bringing up historical memories of previous low level involvement in places like Vietnam in the early sixties and Central America in the 1980s. But worry not, for as Schmitt tells us American officials point out that they " will intervene directly," only, when "vital" interests are at stake. I think we have heard that before; and who decides when it is "vital," Congress, the President, or some Army Captain in Africa, whose "boots" are not on the ground.

It does not end. On March 23, 3014 Helene Cooper reported that **"More U.S. Troops to Aid Uganda Search for Kony,"** as President Obama has sent 150 Special Operations forces along with CV-22 Osprey aircraft to help the Ugandan government find Mr. Kony, a former Catholic altar boy wishing to overthrow the Uganda government and to rule the country with the Ten Commandments. His army, the L.R A., or Lords Resistance Army has brutally raped, killed, and kidnapped tens of thousands of men, women, and children in Central Africa. Even President George W. Bush sent advisors to Uganda and provided millions of dollars in aid and military equipment but these efforts not only failed but forced Kony to regroup in neighboring countries than led to an escalation of violence where it had not been, such as the Congolese jungles where entire villages were wiped out and the rest raped and kidnapped Vietnam, Afghanistan, Iraq, and slowly, but deliberatively, Africa. Will American sleep through history again, until it is too late?

The interesting thing about human history is that since the bomb we have created a threat that could end all creation, leaving no one around to blissfully go about life as we always have. Can America affect the world in any way that can prevent this? Is there any hope that the United Nations can be effective in preventing this? Perhaps some have answers to these questions I cannot answer, especially in light of the fact that the most dangerous enemy of the future is unlike all before. The Japanese warrior fought with a mind-set that allowed no compromise or surrender, why so many Americans died invading the islands. But after defeat, American and Japanese developed a future together. In

Vietnam, we did not lose a war, we lost a battle against a mind-set, that drove men to never give up till the Americans were driven out of Vietnam; even more psychologically driven than Americans during our revolutionary war with the British. Today, how many American cities do not have Vietnamese restaurants. The Soviet bloc Communist nations spent decades in the cross-hairs of nuclear weapons that would have left nothing of their lands or peoples than smoldering, charred, charcoal pieces of things and the ashes and dust of all the men, women, children, animals, birds, trees, grasses, crops, leaving a wasteland not much unlike the lifeless planets in the sky. After the Wall came down, many Communist wanted to be Capitalists. Today, the dreams of Vietnamese, Japanese, Americans, and many of those peoples enclosed within the USSR are similar and complementary.

Today's threat to modern cosmopolitan societies and forward progress working toward a better future, Islamic Fundamentalism, is a threat unlike anything in the history of the modern world; for their visions of a future will never be compatible with modern societies. In no foreseeable time will this enemy of the modern world ever sit down to have tea with us. And the problem is their perceptions of the world remain fixated in the 7th century while they have access to 21st century weapons, with dreams of acquiring those now beyond their reach, nuclear, chemical, and biological weapons.

It reminds me of UN peacekeeping operations in the 1970s when blue helmeted peacekeepers were called soldiers without guns. I used to argue at the UN at this period, that " you can not break up a street fight using pillows," for in the midst of potential or violent confrontations neutrality is never respected and often becomes part of the problem. Only a show of strength prevents violence in the face of bad guys. A fact we often learned too late in the genocides of our times.

CASE STUDY: how existential realities get buried, even with brilliant people.

America is the most powerful nation in the entire history of the world, whose military controls more destructive firepower than all the nations of world history combined. Therefore, it is imperative that America's Foreign Policy be conducted in a manner worthy of its responsibilities that come with such awesome power. Where to begin this conclusion, so we can have an international dialogue, is a tricky one for there are so many opinions and talking heads that cross every spectrum of the political imagination. But what is most concerting is when respected scholars, those who should know better, come to give advice and their conclusions and recommendations are flawed, based upon their own misperceptions of reality.

I have talked about " talking heads " and scholars; but let me take the ideas of one such scholar, Niall Ferguson. I have carefully read and respected his books such as " **The War of the World,** " " **The Ascent of Money,** " but for this conclusion I would like to foscus on his Wall Street Journal article (2/23/2014) " **America's Global Retreat,** " in which he argues that America's view of geopolitics is all wrong.   He is a professor at both Harvard University and a senior fellow at Stanford University's Hoover Institution with many many many distinguished honors and awards; but I want to use him to show that even a scholar of such renoun as he, can be wrong. In fact, he is deadly wrong.

In this WSJ piece he correctly argues that President Obama made several geopolitical mistakes; calling for the overthrown of a longtime U.S. ally in Egypt, Hosni Mubarak and later backing the government of Mohammed Morsi after the Muslim Brotherhood won the 2012 elections, then backing a coup against Morsi. On Libya, Obama was relunctant in backing the effort to oust Moammar Gadhafi in 2011, and later failed to protect U.S. diplomats in Benghazi who were killed in 2012. Ferguson was also right that Obama's hesitation to intervene "effectively" in Syria was a mistake, as well as Obama's weak response to Assad's use of chemical weapons, especially following his " cross the line " threats, that would result in the use of American air strikes..."if" Congress approved.

Then the professor goes on to claim that "Syria has been one of the great fiascos of post-world war II American foreign policy." I can accept this coming from one of the non-intellectual talking heads on American TV, but from such a scholar, it is disturbing. He goes on to explain what we all see, that the American inaction has caused not only thousands of deaths but has " escalated into a sectarian proxy war between Sunni and Shite Muslims, with jihadist groups such as the Islamic State of Iraq and Syria and the Nusra Front fighting against Assad, while the Shiite Hezbollah and the Iranian Quds Force fights for him." But what is "disturbing" is that he, the great historian, distorts history by putting the blame on this reality on Obama. Ferguson writes:

" It is now almost certain that more peple have died violent deaths in the greater Middle East during this presidency than during the last one." (meaning Bush)

Every graduate student of history learns to distinguish between cause and effect, here is a distinguished scholar who seems to be blind to this distinction. Ferguson's blindness goes so far as to accuse Obama supporters of portraying Bush as a "warmonger," when in truth he was not only a warmonger, but one who unleashed all the hatred of the region now resulting in the violence Ferguson writes about. Ferguson seems to have amnesia about the time before the Bush/Chaney decision to invade Iraq, the war fought to topple a Dictator, then to bring Democracy to the Middle East only to turn it into a nightmare for those living there as age-old hatreds suppressed within the minds and bloodstreams were freed to explode in their cities, towns, and villages; destroying not just lives but dreams of millions wishing a better life in a modern world which global media brought to feed these dreams. Perhaps, Ferguson the historian should have taken a few courses in anthropology, for he fully supported the Bush/Chaney invasion in 2003, his words:

"It's all very well for us to sit here in the west with our high incomes and cushy lives, and say its immoral to violate the sovereignty of another state. But if the effect of that is to bring people in that country economic and political freedom, to raise their standard of living, to increase their life expectancy, then don't rule it out."

Long after Ferguson's 2003 statement, the death of 4,489 American military personal with 32,021 wounded physically, thousands upon thousands with brain injuries and mental problems destroying many for life.

The Iraq civilians who remained in Iraq a decade after 2003 find life impossible to live as suicide bombers and religious zealots killed them where they shopped for food, prayed in their houses of worship, and followed them to kill them in their funeral processions or when they buried their loved ones . Bush did violate their sovereignty and this is what we left in our wake.

This Bush/Chaney/Ferguson belief that Iraq peoples consciousness had so absorbed the images of a modern life that could be theirs, that they would welcome the invaders as liberators, bringing them opportunites of a better life, forgot to put the animal into the equation. At the conclusion of my book on China and global politics is my very scholarly sounding chapter, " **A Psychodynamic Theory of Global Politics,**" that addresses this serious misperception of politics that leads to serious miscalculations. It simply recognizes that peoples perceptions change as their awareness of new and different ideas become known, even changing their consciousness. Somewhat like children changing as they experience others with different values and beliefs that are different or in conflict with the family.

But, as I wrote back in 1982, what must be understood about human nature, the human animal: " There always remains a consciousness of uniqueness among all peoples, a projection of collective spirit which cries out for recognition, or demands self-determination." Can foreigners really understand these shadows walking behind everyone, as if the foreigner is not one but two people? One like us, one only like them that we could never understand unless we lived with them. There is a collective spirit known only to those who possess it; just as mysteriously as one wakes up with a spouse after twenty years to find out they know nothing of the other, a uniqueness that remained repressed or supressed for twenty years. I suppose Bush/Chaney/Ferguson believed that Iraqi Sunni and Shiiti would become bed-partners in this new world of democratic government being brought to their shores behind bombs, tanks, artillery, and armored men breaking down the doors to their homes at night.

With regard to Syria, Ferguson writes: "Syria had been one of the great fiascos of post-World War II American Foreign Policy," for the U.S. missed the opportunity to intervene. The deaths, tortures, and exodus of millions was a result of this hestitation by Obama. Not only that, but escalation into sectarian wars between Sunni Shiite Muslims, jihadist "groups such as the Islamic State of Iraq and Syria, and the Nausa Front fighting against Assad, while the Shiite Hezbollah and the Iranian Quds Force fight for him. Here we are, in Feburary 2014 not yet out of Afghanistan and Ferguson wants the U.S. to be involved with this fight. Even Abraham Lincoln knew that the nations should only, if possible, fight one war at a time. As an historian, how does he miss the major cause of all this turmoil; the 2003 invasion of the Middle East.

Let me insert one of my journalism pieces into the equation.

WHY WE CANNOT BOMB SYRIA

We have lost the moral high-ground

Just imagine for a moment, if this were October 11, 2001, and President Assad was killing his people with chemical weapons and President Bush was considering a retaliatory strike. How much public opinion world-wide and at home would be behind such action?

After 9/11 America was on the high ground; not so today. A war in Afghanistan that eliminated the Taliban training grounds and then went on for ten more years in an attempt to "nation build" in the image of a western democracy, then a war in Iraq built upon lies about weapons of mass destruction, now a nation currently trapped within the violence of religious hatred not seen since the religious wars of Europe, 1618-1648 that led to the birth of modern international law dealing with the laws of war, written by Grotius.

We cannot bomb Syria because we have lost the high moral ground of a great nation after 9/11. Let me tell a story. There was a powerful ancient Chinese emperor who was not just in love, but obsessed with his favorite concubine whose beauty was legendary. But, she was always unhappy and never smiled. The emperor tried everything to make her happy or make her smile. Nothing worked. In those days the greatest threat to the kingdom came from the barbarian tribes to the north, beyond the walls. One day the spies in the north of the kingdom messaged the Emperor that the barbarians were about to attack. Before the internet, bells were rung from town to town, village to village warning of the invasion that was a threat to all. Kings and Lords from all of northern China immediately summoned all their armies and came charging north to stop the invasion.

When the thousands of horsemen and soldiers arrived in the capital for combat the emperor noticed something unique. His beloved concubine was smiling for the first time. She was truly excited by the passion and intensity of the moment. It just so happened that this time there would be no attack. The enemy had for whatever reason turned around and galloped back to the Mongolian deserts. Afterwards, the beloved woman reverted back to her miserable self.

The emperor, determined to make her happy decided to again ring the bells, and in their continued desire for self-preservation the kings and lords of the land responded with all their troops and horsemen. The emperor again was so pleased to see his lady happy and smiling at the display of enormous power and response. To the kings and lords this was about survival, as well documented centuries later when the Mongols would overcome all of China for several hundred years. So the emperor rang the bells again and again only to see his beautiful lady smile; but, there came a time when the men on horseback did attack, the bells were rung, and nobody came. The emperor, along with his beautiful lady, died in the sacking of his city.

On September 12, 2001 America had the support of not just the Congress and the American people, but the support of most of the world in seeking justice and revenge for the perpetrators of 9/11. Then we blew it. Not satisfied with driving Osama bin Laden out of his training camp in Afghanistan we made two fatal mistakes: one, attempting to transform a primitive nation essentially run by tribal leaders into a modern democracy and allowing 9/11 emotional capital to be dragged through the trash pit of lies and deceptions by the likes of Chaney, Rumsfeld, Wolfowitz, you go first Richard Pearle, John Bolton, Elliot Abrams and the rest of the bell ringers to dump Saddam Hussein; America lost its moral high ground. The very moral high ground a great nation must travel to grow.

So here we are in the summer of 2013 with a nasty situation where the president of Syria is using banned chemical and biological weapons on his own people and the president of the United States is appealing for support to retaliate against this beastly act. Woops. Not so fast. I do not believe America should bomb Syria at this time, despite my being applauded by Assad's killing those beautiful children and their mothers asleep in their beds.

First, we have lost the moral high ground we earned as a result of 9/11, and secondly, as a result of our miscalculations in Afghanistan and Iraq, the credibility of our decision-making is distrusted. And, what do we do after we blow up specific targets? What do we do next? Bomb more sites?

Like the ancient Chinese emperor, we have rung the bells too often and exhausted our calls to battle.

Back to text

On a more profound level Ferguson found a President Obama statement to the New Yorker magazine…"truly stumning:"   The president had said "I don't really even need George Kennan right now,"   speaking of the man whose insights brought about the "Containment " of the USSR, prompting Ferguson, who wrote that a George Kennan is " exactly what he (Obama) needs."   Then Ferguson goes on to suggest maybe it is not a Kennan that is needed, but a Kissinger, for it is Kissinger who understood what is needed in today's Middle East, "equilibrium" and "balance of power."   Fegruson wishes to teach us about the balance of power by referring us to Kissinger's " book, **"A World Restored"** in which Ferguson postulates that balance is not a "naturally occuring phenomenon," and needed someone to preserve it, such as the likes of Britain in the 19th century, alluding to the fact that it is the U.S. that should be playing that roll in the Middle East.

The "book" was actually Kissinger's dissertation in political science at Harvard University that won him the Ph.D. A former classmate of Kissinger, John G. Stoessinger, questioned him about his mining of 19th century European history for a political science dissertation. Kissinger was interested in political stability. The peace that ended the Napolonic Wars lasted a hundred years without, as we call it, a world war, until 1914. The agreements worked out in the peace agreements at the Congress Of Vienna 1814/15 held secrets to maintaining stability that intriqued Kissinger, leading him to believe that order could only be achieved through realism, and he had little respect for American moralists such as Woodrow Wilson or John Foster Dulles who in his view both failed, the first with the failure of the League Of Nations. Dulles divided the world into good guys and bad guys and considered anyone on the fense as immoral, and it was his influenced that led us directly into the Vietnam war.

Kissinger saw the world as more complex than a battle between good and evil. In fact, in international affairs, it is often difficult to even know who is right and who is wrong. Most of the time there is only a choice between two rights or one wrong and a worse wrong. And as Albert Camus has written, " not to choose was also a choice." And if you wait too long for all the facts to come in, it is no longer a foreign policy choice, but history.

So his study of 19th century European history led him to develop a doctrine that is laid out very clearly in the " World Restored, " upon which his policies were later based, and had such an impact on the world during its most dangerous years of the Cold War.

1. For a peace to be secure it had to be based on a negotiated settlement, with all sides in equilibrium, instead of victor's peace, leaving everyone a bit unhappy but no one completely unhappy.

So the relative insecruity of each guarantees the relative security of all. This way the parties do not go to war with one another again.

2. The one who wins the war does not try and annihiliate the looser, but co-ops it, bringing it into the established order, giving the looser something of itself, hoping to diffuse the defeated of his revolutionary fevor and encourage him to develop into your image.

3. In the absence of a globally controlled system a balancer is essential. The objective is "equilibrium," which in itself maintains the peace. In the face of conflict, it is not who is right and who is wrong; but who is weak and who is strong. The balancer will throw its weight on the weaker side to maintain that equilibrium. The key to Kissinger, is that Peace is nothing more than a bonus of successful balance.

Ladies and gentlemen; this is the prism through which Ferguson wants the U.S. to view the world; with America as the balancer. The are two probems here. One is that Kissinger's approach may have made sense during the Cold War in dealing with nulcear stand-offs, but does not address today's conflicts, that have more to do with civil wars, ethnic conflicts, revolutionary demands for political change, and global public awareness that people can affect change in their societies.

What Ferguson, the historian, does not do is lift the cover to the historical period that so informed Kissinger's political theory. It was not all just geopolitical game playing with Great Britain actling as the balancer, there were revolutions going on all over Europe, uprisings that in many ways mimic the restlessness we witnessed in the Arab Spring, in Venzuela, and the Ukraine. In 1820 a revolution against King Ferdinand I ended in a constitutional monarchy, encouraging a revolt of the Carbonari in the north in 1821 that also resulted in a new constitutional monarchy. Austria sent troops to crush both rebellions.

The Spanish, supported by a large part of their military, demanded and recived a liberal constitution from King Ferdinand VII, until 1922 when 100,000 French troops invaded and reinstalled the absolute monarchy. In 1821 Greek revolutionaries fought for independence from the Ottoman Empire, and there were insurrections in Portugal and even Russia lead by Russian army officers.

All the insurrections were brutally put down by the powers that had signed the peace at the Congress of Vienna. So it follows that in Ferguson's mind the U.S. should not only have a grand strategy and use its power as balancer, but should intervene in wars such as Syria, the failure to do so as Ferguson claims, has been " one of the great fiascos of post WW II American Policy." Perhaps, the noble laureate in economics Paul Krugman may have been correct when he said that Feguson has no wisdom; and that he is all style, with no comprehension of substance. This all may sound cruel, but nothing is crueler than having thousands upon thousands of American men and women die in unnessary foreign wars often inspired by the writings and advice of brilliant men like McNamara, Bundy, Rostow, Kissinger, Pearle, and others too numerous to name.

It is not just a matter of opinion, it is a matter of life and death for those in uniform who have to enforce stupid decisions, often influenced by the writings of scholars who have access to the White House. Take for example the 2012 book by Robert Kagan, **"The World America Made,"** in which he misses the whole point of globalization and the need for diplomacy to prevent nuclear terrorism by insisting that America must throw its weight around, otherwise the United States would be committing "preemptive superpower suicide." This comes from a guy who was fully supportive of the 2003 Iraq invasion and and by 2014 saw the Ukraine crisis as a Cold War renewed, but what makes him dangerous is the unspoken access he has; his wife, Vitoria Nutland, has been a State Department spokesperson, appointed by Hilary Clinton. Kagan's brother Fredrick, a military historian, has been mentioned for his influence with the decision in 2009 to "surge" 30,000 U.S. troops in Afghanistan. Former Secretary of Defense Robert Gates in his recent book **"Duty"** admitted that he was persuaded by Frederick Kagan to order the "surge," whose mission of changing the strategic direction of the war turned out to be a complete failure. Over a thousand U.S. families lost a loved one during that 2009 fisaco. Never since the influence of the Dulles family has we had such influence on American Foreign Policy from a non-elected single family. These intellectuals, as well as other neocons, have rarely served in uniform, nor do their children. It would be okay if these two brothers were not just like other academics writing that eleventh book after reading ten others; these guys have "access," and are therefore dangerous to the well being of our troops in the field. Robert Kagan, whose perceptions of the world he writes about are distored by his prism of ideogical beliefs recently declared himself a "realist," as does Senator John McCain. You judge.

CASE STUDY: It is March 1, 2014: Russian/Ukraine …& American policy Political Realities.

The first reality that must be considered is that there are lines now drawn in the sand between Russia and the Ukraine; which means there is no going back to before this crisis began. The second reality is that, at all costs, there must be an agreement on both sides to freeze all military operations, to avoid war. This second reality is extremely important due to the very nature of these societies, for it is very difficult for them to back – off : in their blood runs warrior spirits of Viking, Tartar, Slavic genes whose ancestors filled the saddles of Cossack horses fighting the Golden Horde and centuries of combat with one another. During nearly a decade at the United Nations I spent so much time with Russians and Ukrainians that several U.S. government security agencies requested I work for them, which I declined, for I was on a scholar's journey, not a spy, just seeking to find out how they think, so I could understand them better. And one thing I learned; is that they find it very difficult to back-off once they have made up their minds, and the friction created by this can blow up into violence too easily. There is nothing that can over emphasize this importance, to not let the first shot be fired, less there will no end.

The first reality is something that Europeans and Americans had better accept, for none is going to get all the marbles for themselves. There is going to be pain felt by all, for to be resolved, only diplomacy and statesmenship will succeed. Realism and geopolitics take center stage here. Geopolitics: like an animal stakes out a territory, a nation defines its; just think the U.S. and Central America, Cuba, and the Monroe Doctrine. It becomes embedded in the psychology of the nation, an expectation that it be natural, our influence there, our buffer here, like five thousand years of Chinese history. In this situation one must point first to ethnic and cultural differences, but the wise statesman knows to focus first on geopolitics, it precedes everything and everyone, it shapes the everything and everyone, from childrearing to economy to defense. As I have written elsewhere, put all of China's people in the U.S. and all the American people in China and their foreign policies will mirror today's. I suspect the Americans now ruling China would still want to keep Tibet and know that someday Taiwan will again be under Chinese control; and that the Chinese running the U.S. will not only have a Monroe Doctrine, but would this time keep Cuba within its shadows again. When you spend more time in a place than tourists, and listen, and listen, you come to understand just how much place impacts itself on those who live in it, not just psychologically, but passed on from generation to generation in their bodies, in their bones. It was not just that Castro had Russian nuclear missiles pointing at us, it was happening just 90 miles away, in our neighborhood. The only time in American history that every one of us would have been killed, or left to die in the aftermath of a nuclear war. When thinking "

71

Crimea, " think basic stuff first, the land. Every people have an instinctive idea of what comes under their protection.

The Russians have their's, and Crimean naval bases are not on the table, for Russian control goes back to the 18th century when "Catherine the Great" defeated the Tartars to establish a naval base there (in 1944 Stalin brutally deported the Tartars from Crimea). True, Khrushchev gave the penisula to the Ukraine in 1954 (there must be a deeper story here, for Khrushchev was from the Ukraine), but then it made little difference for all were part of the USSR, and Soviet psychology prevailed everywhere, sameness, sameness, saveness. Then 1991, and the end of the Soviet Union, and an independent Ukraine emerges, with the historic Russian naval base in their country.

What can we call this conflict: A Civil War?

The unprovoked invasion of the sovereignty of one country by armored troops of another sovereign nation: classic act of war according to international law going all the back to 17th century, one of the basic principles first written by Hugo Grotius, the father of international law. If Russia crosses the borders outside of Crimea, we are going to have a great deal of bloodshed. Unless, there is some deeper and imaginative responses that will prevent this blood letting. It could be viewed as a Civil conflict, hopefully not a Civil War between Western and Eastern Christians.

I say Civil War; for it may be western Ukranians, who rightfully woukd view this as a violence against their sovereignty, have to recognize that the state of Russia, the sources of harsh Soviet politics and an undesirable cousin, rule over a people who are their spiritual, cultural, and historic brothers and sisters In this regard, the Russians and Ukranians have more in common than Rebels and Yankees of America's Civil war ever had. They share the faith symbolized by the cross atop the catheral of Saint Vladimir in Crimea who brought Christianity to both peoples in 988, the source of deep religious beliefs among both Russians and Ukrainians. Their culture is interwoven here in Crimea where Tostoy once served as a sailor and Anton Chekhov wrote " **The Cherry Orchard** " in Yalta where his passion for nature was inspired by the forest in Ukraine.

The decision of 1954 should take second place to 988 and the shared culture beyond Dostoyevshy, Gogol, Puskin, Turgenev, Pasternak, and others, who speak both Russian and Ukrainian. What should prevail here is not only a people power to oust a President but a people power to avoid bloodshed. To recognize each other not just as Russian or Ukranian citizens, but comrades in culture. The people came before the modern states and they will remain beyond the modern state system we know today. Let me quote a contemporary Russian author whose statement I use in the introduction to my recent book of poetry and stories from around the world. The author, Mikhail Shishkin: " Free men have no use for boundaries." The people must look beyond their leaders and their boundaries, less their children and their loved ones will perish; and for what?

As one who understands that violent passions lie in the hearts of many in this situation, as exemplified in a Reuter's dispatch on March 3rd, where a Russian businessman living in Estonia, that has its own Russian minority, claimed: " Putin is doing the right thing. To get things done, you have to use brute force, like Stalin did." This is an attitude I learned a long time ago while traveling the region or dealing with Russians and Ukrainians at the United Nations. This choice just goes to show that even in such times of globalization and instant access to world news, the bottom line remains the animal and irrational within us.

But in Washington even U.S. Senators who should know better have viewed the Ukraine crisis with the same ideological fervor as professor Ferguson with Syria. John McCain has claimed that Crimea must be the place where America "recognizes the reality and begins to restore the credibility of the United States as a world leader," and ends a NYT op-ed piece with a cry for strength, leadership, and…"realism." Realism? Again, you be he judge.

As I complete this chapter many Americans view Russia with such alarm, political leaders calling for a new Cold War approach such as sending weapons and men into Eastern Europe. I do believe that it is time for all to strenthen the Security Council's role in not just this near crisis, but to recognize its important role in our 21st century so as not to repeat the misperceptions and miscalulations of the previous century. The violence of the 20th century began a hundred years ago this coming summer, in 1914. It is my judgement that the current crisis over Ukranine should never had occurred if President Obama's administration had taken a realist's approach toward Russia. The effort to move the economic benefits of the European Union further east was one thing; but, with not just Obama, but previous administrations began a policy to not just move NATO further east, but the development of missile defense systems, it has opened a deep strain in the Russian national psyche that few in the West understand. Our failure to understand the reality of this psychology has brought us to the tensions of 2014. Here I insert a journalism piece I wrote in 2012 and upgraded after Putin's speech upset so many in the U.S. This is the position of a global realist.

RUSSIA & THE NEW GEOPOLITICS

Written in 2012

The United States should seize the moment, just as we did with China in the last century, turning ping-pong diplomacy into a reformulation of geopolitics to counterbalance Soviet power in the world. America needs Russia and we need not only to accept this reality within the growing shadows of Chinese influence and power in the world; but we had better understand what makes Russian leaders tick.

I am amused by not just the responses of politicians and journalists throughout America to Putin's essay in the New York Times, but the conclusions draw from his remarks. It reminds me of coming back to America from Europe at the end of the Cold War and lecturing in political science departments at various sophisticated east coast universities when professors where teaching about a future where democracy would become the norm, and one academic scholar even wrote a book called "**The End of History**," implying that this new era had come at the end of the world's final truth, within an Hegelian new world, with all democratic countries. The Cold War U.S. military officers I taught in Europe; fighter, aircraft, and bomber pilots; submarine officers and commanders, and those whose fingers were on the buttons of the short range nuclear missiles, most often rejected my views on Russians in a spontaneous knee jerk reaction, understandably for they were being trained to fight the Russians. Then when back in the states, professors cringed when their students related in their classes my view that we should not expect Russia to follow in our enlightened democratic way, for culture is culture, and Russians will be Russians. They want strong leaders, and anticipate power to be centered in the government, just like their ancestors who dealt with autocrats and centralized control, whether Czars or the likes of Communist's such as Lenin or Stalin.

I taught Russian history and politics to generations of university students as well as those combat military officers, learned a great deal as a graduate student actually sitting in Moscow courthouse trials in the early 1970s; but the learning curve expanded for me with spending nearly a decade dealing with members of the Soviet delegation to the United Nations in the 1970s, at a time when most of them were members of the KGB, Putin's brothers in arms. Their mindset was different, just as is Putin's today.

Made no mistake about it, Putin, as where those KGB guys and gals of earlier periods, is very knowledgeable about American history in all of its many twists and turns (knowing more than most young Americans today in high schools or universities), our culture, and pride in our political system. Just like the CIA during the Cold War had all new recruits study Marxism as a political ideology, Leninism, the history and culture of Russia; the KGB educated its agents on American history, culture, sacred documents like our Constitution and others. So it should not be such a surprise to some, an insult to others, that Putin has used the language we use to describe ourselves. My specialty at the UN was the Chinese, so the Soviets were spying on me and I knew it, for they were often very clumsy. I would bring them to my classes at Hunter College so my students could debate them and show the Commies how free young American students thought about the world. At first I was shocked at how easily my guest lectures' were able to turn the arguments with their questions about American history and politics that my students often stumbled with, and they would lead them toward their favorite conclusion: That America was not a Democracy, but an Oligarchy. "Oligarchy?" maybe in 2012, not 1970s. These kids at the City University of New York were from the diverse neighborhoods of the city, whose families were struggling to hold on to their apartments and homes, jobs, and dignity in a tough 1970s economic landscape, would be in rapture of these strange men talking about health, education, and welfare. They were always seduced, and my teachings about bread lines and scarcity and gulags in Russia did little to break the grip in their minds that maybe something was not as it should be in our Democracy. When I drank with the Russians at the UN bar and local East side bars it was not the domestic issues as with the students they wanted to talk about, but foreign policy issues such as Central America, Africa, Cuba, Latin America, and how right they were and how wrong we were. They loved to talk and they never, except for a few Ukrainians, admitted that the USSR ever made any mistakes or abused its power. My main interest was not winning discussions or arguments with them, but how they thought. At the same time I was studying for a Ph.D. in political science I was in a two-year program studying clinical psychiatry at Mt Sinai Hospital School of medicine so I was after deeper understandings than politics or ideology.   I was asking them questions about their relationships with their mothers, fathers, family, neighborhoods in which they grew up, if they worked odd jobs as a kid, basic stuff. With enough vodka they would open up and give me what I wanted, an inside view of their personal lives since childhood, in addition to another side of their minds influenced by their marvelous Russian writers and poets: Puskin, Tolstoy, Dostoevsky, Pasternak, Chekhov, and others whose artistic and flamboyant brilliance they learned as children, and whose lessons they carry with them as adults. I never met a dumb Russian at the UN, but I have met some dumb Americans. This deep influence of Russia's revered poets, artists, writers, has given them not just an anchor into their culture, but common ground upon which to deal with threats and invasions over the centuries from both east and west. Their Indians, with whom they shared a continent, the Mongols, once beat them and ruled them for over two hundred years, and there neighbors, unlike our neighbors, invaded them: Vikings, Swedes, Poles, French, and Germans and Germans again.   More Russians died in the World Wars one and two than any other nation.

We learned in WW II what great allies they can be, and it looks as if we need them again. Geopolitics demands it. And though we claim to like the give and take of politics, we had better get used to our ideals being tested against realities as perceived by Russians and not just ourselves. Syria is one case in point. The other: I believe history will prove Mikal Gorbachev to be the greatest peace maker's of all time; he ended a Cold War that could have ended all life on earth. Not a surrender in the face of the Reagan military build-up as some claim, but a "swords into plowshares" moment rewarded with a Nobel Peace Price in 1990, a

77

moment despised by today's President Putin. In dealing with Russian statesmen, we deal with contradictions.

Back to text

America's finest citizens, the best of us: U.S. military men and women

The sad part of Senator John McCain's position on the Crimean situation is that he should know better having experienced war first hand in Vietnam as a prisoner of war. At the same time I sometimes laugh at my own changing views of America based on a great deal of various experiences that brought me to the conclusion that the best of us are now in uniform. We are all concerned about the future of our country not only in terms of how we are viewed by others, but whether or not our economy is going to provide meaningful work for not only those in the work force today, but those born into it today.

So the question that must be asked, who is going to lead us? The American public is slowly becoming aware of how the power of their vote has deflated in value in direct proportion to the awesome control over our laws and regulations by the big money that pay for the re-elections of those supposed to be representing us. Since 2008 many bankers, Wall Streeters, and corporate guys and gals have shown us what they will do if in power. To protect their profits, they would send our military anywhere in the world. If Iraq had no oil, would Bush and Chaney have pulled the trigger to war? Are these people whose interest will determine when and how our military will be sent in harms way?

For those of us who work at it, learning, experience, and years on this earth can bring a certain wisdom to our judgements. I think of a young guy I once taught who has been so successful that his photo and has been on the front page of the Wall Street Journal several times. Then I think of young men and women I taught who have risen in rank all the way to Commanders, Admirals, and Generals; such as Admiral William J. Fallon whom I briefly taugh history at Villanova University, whom President George W. Bush appointed as Commander of the U.S. Central command (CENTCOM) in 2007, the first naval officer to hold that position. In 2009, his alma mater Villanova University granted him an honorary Doctor of Military Science. I doubt that Admiral Fallon remembers me, but while he was the commander of CENTCOM he made many public statements about China and Chinese perceptions of the world that let me to believe he may have read my 1982 book, **"China's Perception of Global Politics."** The first guy of the WSJ was about personal glory and wealth; the second was about devotion to country.

As a younger man I would have put my money on the business guy; but experience has taught me different. I did not learn this during my four years of active duty military service, but only years later working on U.S. military bases in Europe and Asia. As a realist, not as a patriot, I came to understand what an amazing character the U.S. military produces: not just in terms of a patriotic spirit but in terms of intelligence, commitment, judgement, empathy, management, and skills never before perfected in the entire history of the world. In the meantime I watched the guy on the cover of the WSJ, the businessman, become not just a very wealthy man, but a very selfish, narrow minded, elitest bully who represents thousands like him in this new America of ours. He, like many others are disciples of Ayn Rand, are the ones with the big bucks who get the wrong people elected. They are what I call the "Ayn Rand Gestapo," like Congressman Paul Ryan and Eric Cantor, neither having served in the military as with my former student.

This is not just an opinion, think: It was Eisenhower the president who nixed General Lemay's desire to drop nuclear weapons on China. If Kennedy had not been assasinated he most likely would have pulled all our advisors out of Vietnam (perhaps, why he was assassinated, as both Leo and I belived). Secretary of State Colin Powell found himself surrounded by weak men like Chaney and Pearle who wanted a war so badly they lied to him about Iraq's WMDs, undermining his credibility as he stood before the world at the United Nations. Chuck Hagel as Secretary of Defense brings his Vietnam war scars into his perceptions of current conflicts. Secretary of State John Kerry whose own Presidental asperations were stymied by the "Ayn Rand Gestapo" who attempted to denegrade his own wartime experience in Vietnam, took on the most difficult of all diplomatic missions in history, Middle East peace in our time, in exhausting but futile attempts to change the course of this bloody history.

What concerns me is that those of this Ayn Rand Gestapo class of Americans will have the power to again send our military guys and gals into conflicts that have nothing to do with our vital interests. With the military now a professional army few Americans have any contact with it, understand it, or even care about it, no less tha the extra thousand body bags that were flown into Dover Air Base in Delaware after the 2009 "surge" in Afghanistan.

History has recorded the last days of American involvement in Vietnam with people clinging to the underneath of Helicopters flying off the flight deck of the American Embassy in Saigon, but the end of Afghanistan is yet to be written. The policy decisions with regard to Afghanistan are mind bloggling when we review the decade of discussions by American politicians about the goal of a new democratic country, and bringing the light of truth upon reality.

This reality was brutally highlighted in late March 2014. The most secure place in all of Afghanistan where not just journalists, staff members from international organizations, foreign dignitaries, foreign business people, but successful Afghan families gathered, revealed, in a most grissly manner, the future. The Serena Hotel in Kabul with its heavy fortifications, high walls, and armed security was considered a safe haven until gunmen opened fire in the high scale resturant killing a Paraguayan diplomat there to observe the coming presidental election, a prominent Afghan journalist, a Canadian, two Bangladeshi nationals and several others.

A Mr. Ahmad, a reporter for Agence France-Presse was shot along with his wife and three children, a baby and a 4 and 5 year old. As reported by Rosenberg and Ahmed, the terrorist, a clean-cut looking guy, stood in front of the family as the mother begged: "Take my life, but please don't kill my kids." He shot the children first, killing the four and five year olds, then he killed the parents. The Taliban took responsibility for the attack but rationalized the horrible killing of the family by claiming that many Afghan mothers and their children have died in raids on their homes or from drone attacks.

With this book a few days and hours from going to printing press, American foreign policy is engaged on two dangerous fault lines, one in Asia, one in Eastern Europe; with President Obama engaged with Japanese leaders in discussions meant to calm their fears that America may not back them in their dispute with China over the islands conflict, but to calm these fears, Obama has gone so far as to maintain that the 1960 US/Japan security treaty is incllusive of the islands in the East China Sea. The US has not taken a position on the highly combustable "sovereigity" issue, but the Chinese are responding not only with words, but increases in naval and air activity in a show of strength during Obama's visit.

On the other side of the world Vice-President Joe Biden was in Europe to show support for Ukraine and NATO members of Eastern Europe, backed by 150 US paratroppers from the 173rd Infantry Brigade Combat Team stationed in Vicenza Italy to conduct military exercises with Polish troops, followed with later joint exercises with troops in Estonia, Latvia and Lithuania. The Ukraine crisis has most freightened Poland, with the polish foreign minister, Radoslaw Sikorski requesting NATO deploy upwards of 10,000 troops on Polish soil. As discussed through this book history has a way impacting itself upon current politics, and few in the west can fully understand Poland's suspicions of the Russians. Under Joseph Stalin's orders in 1940, Russian troops shot and murdered every captured Polish officer, over 22,000 of them in an attempt to wipe out the entire officer corp. Known in Poland as the "Katyn Massacre" of 1940, it continues to hold a dominate space in the collective consciousness of Polish people. Biden addressed Ukraine's parliament assuring not only that the US would "assist" them against Russia's "humiliating threats," and claimed that the US would never recognize Russia's "illegal occupation" of Crimea.

"These are the times that try men's souls." The opening lines of the pamphlet written by Thomas Paine in support of the revolutionary war against the British. I am afraid we are there again, for it is times like this that even the realist understands that that right and wrong, cause and effect are not so simple to define. When this book leaves my hands these two events above will evolve in ways I have perhaps not even considered, for I am like you, the reader, just trying to understand; as did Leo Brophy and myself in collaborating on the Gamble book.

At one time I did beieve that some of my ideas may have some impact on world affairs, for the good. I have no idea; but I was able to put both the Gamble for Survival and Chinese foreign policy books in then Senator Biden's hands, as well as sending some of my journalism to his Senatorial office. In 1997 then Senator Biden and then Secretary of State Madeleine Albright came aboard a ship discharging fruit from Central America in the Port of Willmington Delaware as some sort of publicity for international trade. I was the Ship Agent for the vessel, is was either the M/V Dole Costa Rica or the M/V Dole Honduras, and I member Captain Scotto, who was from Italy, for he was not too pleased that the Senator and Secretary had not shown him the proper respect by following protocol by requesting permission of board the ship, nor had they made the request through me, the Agent. As his Agent, I told the Captain I would ask the two of them to leave if he wished. I remember the control of emotions flashing in his eyes as he lit a cigarette and shook his head no. He would not make an incident over it.

But as they were leaving the ship Senator Biden said hello to me, for I knew him slightly through a relative of mine who had once coached him in high school football. Upon seeing that, one of Dole Fresh Fruit's executive staff also working the ship, ran to me with the two books he had requested me to loan him a month before, the Gamble and China book, and yelled out to Senator Biden to wait a moment as he shoved the books into my hand, nearly pushing me down the gangway to the dock. I ran the few yards from the docked ship and the Senator graciously took the books and told me to say hello to John, my relative. At times like this I often wonder if my writings about the Russians have any place in Biden's mind when dealing with such matters, or that perhaps he passed on to President Obama that case study on the South China Seas that you will read in the next chapter. There just might be something there that reveals the complexity of the China Seas issues, for the President surely has advisors that know much more than I about these disputes. I do not write this with pride; for as a writer the energy in my heart and soul remains married to my poetry and novels. You judge.

I would like to humbly conclude this chapter by reciting a few lines from one of my poems published recently in **"Poetry in Green: Poetry & Stories From Around the World,"** this poem was written in 1983 at a time when President Reagan was determined to increase America's nuclear and military might throughout the world, including a naval fleet of 600 ships. The poem is titled:

AMERICA AMERICA

America... do not get old
And fail to grow in wisdom's way

America... do not expect so much
Of a world not as secure as ours

...the world cries for your leadership
without Marine-style diplomacy

We are so great, so why act so small?

Give the refugees shelter...again
For today's tough food is tomorrow's strength

America, America, Blessed art thou among nations

Do not lose your soul,
For great nations only give, of themselves

America America Be father, mother
Sister and brother....to all our universe.

84

Chapter Two

American Foreign Policy

&

China...The Two-Headed Dragon

The history of the 21st century will be determined more by China than any other nation on earth. The problem is, we most often project our own understanding of the way the world works onto how this future will play out for China. At the heart of western democracies is the concept of "the consent of the governed;" meaning it is the people who give the power to the rulers. When you read the *"Constitution of the United States"* the first words you see are "We the people of the United States." We like to think we can throw the bums out. And that as China becomes more Capitalist and prosperous, democracy will follow...and democracies are less likely to go to war.

The biggest problem with this way of thinking is that it does not take a hard enough look at the reality that is China, and how China sees itself and the world. For some ideas on this subject see *"Game of Chinese Mirrors"* (appendix: Journalism). At the heart of any attempt to understand China's future, the Chinese culture itself must be put under a microscope, which we will look at later. In America, our history and our experience bred a culture of deep distrust of power; so much so that we are afraid that too much power in the hands of the rulers is dangerous. What jumps out at you when you read the U.S. Constitution is not only how we divide power among the executive, legislative, and judicial branches; but the constitution begins with the powers of the legislature, Article I of the constitution is the peoples branch of government. This is no accident. It is reflective of our American culture and history.

In China, today as well as throughout history, the separation of power is between those in power who control the political, military, and major economic decisions; and society as a whole. This is why I call China the "Two Headed-Dragon," the one China of the general population, the people, a wonderful culture based on respect, family, community spirit, spontaneously generous and happy people. The other China is the political sphere. This China can be ruled by cruel sub-human Emperors like the first one, Ch'in Shih Huang-ti. In the twentieth century, Mao Tse-Tung may have caused more deaths than any ruler in Chinese history, all for the sake of his personal power. Jung Chang and Jon Halliday write in their book **"Mao: The Unknown Story"** that during Mao's Great Leap Forward more than 38 million people died from being worked to death or starvation. Secret work camps for "special" prisoners still exist in 2014, though denied by Communist party spokesmen.

And there were extremely enlightened emperors who took Chinese culture to new highs and ruled a well fed and productive society. But this political head of the dragon is dangerous because it has more unchecked power and authority at its disposal than anything we understand in the West; and this degree of absolute power would corrupt God himself. The societal head of this dragon has a heart and soul that will blend peacefully and successfully with modernization; the political head, that includes the Communist Party and the military can never be fully trusted, for they are most often motivated by ideas generated by old men and ideologues who never did believe in compromise. When Western statesmen open dialogue with Chinese equivalents they assume there is a parity of mutual respect that will allow a dialogue for negotiations. But to the Chinese statesman, just your acceptance to discuss an issue, is interpreted to mean you will agree with their position.

This political dragon head is as stubborn as the bureaucracy that carries out its orders. It is incapable of allowing deviations from the group psychology that is China; the First Emperor,

Huang- ti, would not allow South China its isolation thousands of years ago, nor does the contemporary leadership respect Tibet. It is often overlooked that China's current leaders have been very heavy handed, finally quashing any hope Tibet would be spared the dragon's might. This is why it may be that no degree of cross-channel plane, ferry, and commercial investment ties will prevent the leadership of the PRC, at some time in the future, from taking the same control over Taiwan that the First Emperor and current leadership have exerted over both south China and Tibet.

The other head of the dragon is often flexible and quite capable of change, having centuries of experience surviving their own rulers. If things are going well in society, those at the top have nothing to fear. Chinese history is full of revolutions and dynastic failures; but never when there is "order under the heavens." Group psychology is also powerful with families, clans, and regions. The idea that increased wealth and prosperity will somehow inspire the Chinese to throw out their communist leaders is more of a wish than a reality. If China had a great economic depression with the failure of its own State branded Capitalism, then we would see a change in leadership that may change the Communist Party's grip on power.

In China, there is no check on the power of the CCP, the Chinese Communist Party. Therein lies the dilemma for the future. Even when there is an apparent change in leadership in China it is not really a change at all. The power lies behind the throne. The group psychology that is so central to most Asian cultures is most astute here at the center of political power. For example, in September of 2004 an important leadership change was announced; President Hu Jintao replaced Jiang Zemin as military chief, Jiang was the former president who held onto his control of the military. Thus, Hu Jintao commanded not just the government and the party, but the military as well. From Hu to Xi Jinping in 2014 the President continues to command the government, the party, and the military, but: there are shadows within the leadership that no one can penetrate. Deep inside the Communist party's

Central Committee is a small group of old communists who hold the ultimate power to make vital decisions, its called the Standing Committee. The power of the Chinese Communist Standing Committee from 1949 until our 21st century has no equivalent anywhere in the political world today.

To challenge decisions of the Standing Committee is dangerous. Let me give a few examples. Many Western observers were optimistic back when Mr. Hu's stepped forward, reflecting a new direction where the economic liberalism would soon be matched with some political liberties. The results seem to indicate even more repressive policies than before the transition of power.

A journalism professor at Beijing University, Jiao Guobiao, one of several arguing for more freedom of speech, and whose writings are not only a frontal attack on the Chinese government's Propaganda Department during the Cultural Revolution, but has argued that U.S. forces should have gone all the way to Beijing during the Korean War and ousted Mao as they had Saddam in the second Gulf War; the result would have been a modern successful country like South Korea, Japan, Taiwan, and Singapore. The Chinese people would not have had to wait all this time for the economic freedoms they now enjoy, and the hope this engenders. Professor Jiao Guobiao's publisher was ordered by the government not to print his books, two of which were scheduled for publication. A short time later the professor was informed he was no longer allowed to teach at Beijing University. He was detained by the Chinese police along with several other critics of the lack of free speech and press; including literary personalities Yu Jie and Liu Xiaobo and the political theorist Ahang Zuhua. It warms my heart that in March 2014 , The American President's wife, Michelle Obama , touring China, addressed thousands of people on what freedom felt like when people are allowed what she called " Human Rights," the rights of free speech, free press, and free assembly. A few blocks from where I went to high school in Philadelphia there is a street named after Tom Paine, our Babe Ruth of politics, from whom our DNA demands liberty, for he is called the " Father of the American Revolution." But I am afraid even though millions of Chinese took her words to heart and smiled, and smiled; nothing will change after she flew home to Washington. Maybe she should have left behind some copies of Paine's book, " **Common Sense.**"

The American public see an amicable smiling Mr. Jiang, or Hu, or Xi dressed in black business suits and ties, walking along with American Presidents in the Rose garden and assume their faces are the same as thousands of images of millions of Chinese in the prosperous cities of modern China. It is like comparing a housecat to a tiger. Even those who hold power locally are Party members who do not respond well to any criticism or calls for justice.

So, what do we really know of this new force in the world we call China? How does China perceive itself and the world, how does China negotiate with others in obtaining what it wants, what really motivates China? It is only by attempting to answer these questions can we even hope to understand this future.

Nearly a half century ago the eminent historian C.P. Fitzgerald in discussing the goals of China wrote a tidy little pamphlet entitled, *The Chinese View of Their Place in the World,* that the major aim of China was "to regain the full territory and standing of the Chinese Empire at its peak." Is this true for today, in the 21st Century? Strange, that Fitzgerald was then thinking not just about Chinese culture of which he was an expert, but about disputed territories with neighbors, particularly India and the Soviet Union. Some argue this is an outdated concept in our new global economy. For example, as discussed before, but Fitzgerald's ideas remain relevant. The New York Times journalist Tom Freidman in " *The World is Flat,* contends that China's aim to achieve power through its economic miracle has connected China to the global economy to such an extent that any disruption of the interlocking production and financial arrangements holding everything together would be destroyed by a war over territory. That the old geopolitics of past centuries has been replaced by a new geopolitics based on the inter-connectivity of the worlds economies; and that this is our best hope of avoiding wars in the 21st Century.

Freidman asks, why would China disrupt its success with war? Japan for a long time imported more from China than the United States and China has now replaced Japan as the world's second largest economy. By 2010 China's economy became double that of the world's third largest economy, Germany. Most astounding, for years China's economy doubled every eight years. No economy in the history of the world has ever done that.

Just the physical changes in Chinese cities tell a big story. When I wrote of the changing Chinese economy during the early stages of liberalization in the early 1980s, it began with letting farmers sell their surpluses at market, and at that time Shanghai had one skyscraper on its coastal horizon. Today, Shanghai has well over 400 skyscrapers with dozens going up or planned each six months. The port of Shanghai in the early 1980s looked more like a fishing village port than an industrial port; and today it is the second largest port in the world after Singapore, which it has recently overtaken (what contributes to Singapore's traffic is its position as a hub for containers going in and out of Asian ports).

But, when looking at China's economic growth demography must always be calculated in the equation. One out of every eight people in the world live in China; and sixty percent of them remain on the farms. Rural China has some of the poorest people in the world. The Chinese government strategy aims to shift populations from rural areas to new industrial places like Shenzhen. But this will necessitate creating close to 20 million new jobs a year. This also means rebuilding an entire infrastructure with new roads, houses, railways, sewage systems, schools, and the power plants to keep it all going.

Development on this scale demands resources that China does not have. We have already discussed Africa, but China has also invested in mining operations in Australia and Brazil to ensure supplies of iron ore, bauxite, zinc, timber, manganese, and soybeans, Bolivia for tin, Chile for copper. They are really going after increasing their oil investments in Venezuela and Canada, the later taking Canadian oil from U.S. pipelines; and have signed contracts with Kazakhstan for eight dollars a barrel for oil in the ground, meaning the Chinese have to pump it out and ship it.

Demography presents many problems to China's future. A new book has looked closely at the effects of new technology that allows prenatal sex selection in a society where historically boy babies have been preferred over girls. In some area in China ratios are so skewed, 150 boys for every 100 girls. This comes on top of decades on the "one-child" per family rule. Millions of young men, often unemployed, have little hope of finding a spouse and raising a family. V.M. Hudson and A.M. den Boer co-authors of the book, **"Bare Branches: The Security Implications of Asia's Surplus Male Population,"** speculate that not only is this unprecedented in human history, but could produce several unpleasant outcomes. Unemployed young men with no girlfriends or wives can not help but fuel a great deal of social unrest, such as has taken place in many places, and is still happening in 2014. Even back in 2004 alone there were around 78,000 riots. This social unrest is most always in the countryside; rather ironic, for the countryside is where this Capitalist revolution began in 1978. But this time, the train has left for the cities; Capitalism has gone urban, leaving its birthplace in the Chinese villages, and taking the youth with it. The phenomenal 9.5% economic growth of China's economy for years after 2004 brought little relief to these rural areas. These "bare branches," as the authors call them, pose not only an internal security threat, but a government that recruits them into the military in order to occupy them, may be creating a huge army that will pose a threat to the security of Asia and the world.

I sure do hope Tom Freidman's analysis is correct, that a prosperous global economically wired-in China will be less likely to go to war; but the test to this theory is Taiwan and the stubbornness of their positions on control of the islands. In private, people from Taiwan will tell you that they are a separate country. That China is China; and Taiwan is Taiwan. China does not see it that way and never will. The stark reality of the facts are sobering. China has over 500 missiles pointed at Taiwan. Back in 2003 Taiwan's national legislature called on China to remove these missiles, and described the threat as "state-sponsored terrorism." It should be noted that these are supersonic cruise missiles that were purchased from Russia; the same lethal missiles that used to be pointed at Western Europe and American forces by the Soviets. Of concern to the US is the purchase by China of several "Squall" missiles that were developed by Russia. The widely respected Jane's Intelligence Review claims that no Western navy has anything as deadly as the "Squall." The "Squall" rocket-propelled torpedo can travel 230 miles an hour underwater. This is five times faster than anything in the U.S. fleet at that time. U.S. naval commanders have said that it is impossible to protect ships against this kind of torpedo. With the U.S. committed to protecting Taiwan in the advent of an attack from China, these are not realities that can be ignored because of the hope that Chinese economic successes will make it very counterproductive to use force to put Taiwan back under its control. This old geopolitical game continues to play itself out as reflective in the U.S. 2005 decision to put a new nuclear powered aircraft carrier in the Sea of Japan, the first time Japan has allowed anything nuclear to position itself so near the hallowed grounds of Hiroshima and Nagasaki. Both nations decision speaks volumes of questions concerning the perceived 21st century balance of power in the Pacific.

So the "flat world" theory is that China's economic successes will tame the political dragon that we once witnessed unleashed at Tiananmen square or the brutality and force China uses in bringing Tibet in line with China's old Imperial perception of itself. In trying to understand China we often superimpose our own ways of thinking, leaving us unprepared to read and accurately interpret the various signals emanating from Chinese society. We are hoping they will think like us because their fortunes are tied up in our continued trade success.

I have believed that the best way to test the future winds of Chinese goals is to analyze Chinese behavior in regard to what they consider important to them, in particular the issues themselves. In my 1982 book *China's Perception of Global Politics,* I choose the issues important to China at that time... WMDs and military modernization, economic development, the Law of the Sea (China was interested then, now, and tomorrow in the oil and gas reserves of the oceans its shares with its neighbors), and Africa (for China was interested in exporting its Maoist version of economic "Self Reliance" to Africa, a flawed economic theory still employed by North Korea. I thought then, as I do now, that the best way to evaluate an individual is to try and comprehend what is important to them personally. Tell me what is important to you and I will understand you better.

But I may have been wrong in one important distinction. Nations, like individuals, do not always act on what is important to them. When looking at the broad issues of foreign policy, perhaps the keys are at a more fundamental level. For example, in this same book I drew upon an interesting study written by Harold Isaacs entitled, *"Scratches on Our Minds: American Images of China and India,"* in which he argued that Westerners are unable to comprehend how the Chinese deal with fundamental things such as " the implicit dynamics associated with the way in which the Chinese deal with conflict, authority, and the discipline of emotions within their society." Wow... so simple, but perhaps more fundamental and enlightening than the broader issues of international politics. Could it be that the historian, the psychologist, and the sociologist are better at understanding Chinese foreign policy than those who carefully study and analyze the economic and political dynamics. Seeds of identity, lie deep within an individual's personal history, and even deeper within a nation's history and culture; for an individual or national consciousness is not limited by space or time.

I think it may possibly be that history weighs more heavily on China than any other nation on earth. Do you think the United

States can be fully understood without it's history? Are there parts of us now that are rooted in our past as a nation? The early political experiments with Puritan theocracy, slavery, the American Revolution, The Civil War, WW 1 & II, Civil Rights, The New Deal, define who we are as a nation, and continue to have impact on American behavior in the world today. And we are babies in age compared to China, who experienced thousands of years of history before becoming "China," 221 years before the birth of Christ.

Let me tell a story. When I first studied China, I was mainly interested in trying to understand the thinking of the political leadership. Ten years later I found myself at the most convenient place to learn how the Chinese operated in the real world, where they had to take positions on all the political issues in the global arena, and their words and statements went into print for all to read. I could sit and listen to Chinese diplomats debate, interview those whom they debated, and get to know Chinese diplomats professionally and personally. This was the United Nations, and I was there before and after the PRC (Peoples Republic of China) replaced the ROC (Republic of China, Taiwan). I spent a lot of time with the ones who left and the ones who arrived; the intensity of the political differences takes books to describe. Perhaps like the difference between Mars and Venus. But, I was left with troubling questions about the culture that was the substance and roots of both political ideologies; an amazing convergence of shared culture. Are Chinese Capitalists and Communists cut out of the same cloth?

Since I was writing about Chinese diplomacy it was important to understand the thinking of the guy who gave all the major orders, Mao Tse-tung, the Communist leader. I knew that Columbia University library had one of the best Chinese collections, and quickly tired of all the heavy analysis of Marist/Leninist influence on Mao's thinking. Up to that point scholars had been writing about Mao the revolutionary. Even psychiatrists were trying to figure him out; Robert Jay Lifton wrote

"Revolutionary Immortality: Mao Tse-Tung and the Chinese Cultural Revolution," in attempting to explain how Mao's childhood and early life impacted onto his revolutionary personality. Other writers looked at the influence upon a young Mao who had read the 14th century classic novel, *"The Romance of the Three Kingdoms"* that begins with the ominous remark that "an empire is founded to be broken."

Then I came upon something interesting. Mao was fond of dancing and sleeping with young women, preferably two an evening. In one file were photos of Mao dancing with the young ladies, but in another file were copies of letters written by some of the young women who shared his boudoir. They spoke of the piles of books surrounding his bed, volumes and volumes about one man, the first emperor of China; the emperor who first unified China in 221 BC, not about Marx or Lenin. There was no "China" before unification in 221 BC, only thousands of years of Chinese culture, three major dynasties with many different states struggling for power.

Mao wanted to know how to rule a Chinese empire. Neither Marx nor Lenin could teach him this. Mao is said to have read everything ever written about Ch'in Shih Huang-ti, the First Emperor of China. There would be no Marxist "withering away of the state" or a Leninist Socialist State. Mao would be the Emperor of China. He wanted to learn how to bring all the power to himself. To centralize power at the center with him at the helm. Even the creator of modern Capitalist China, Deng Tsia-Ping, kept all the political power at the center, in his hands.

So I came to believe if I was to get a handle on China's future in this 21st Century I had to fully understand how the original Chinese state was put together. Can we understand our nation today without an understanding of all that preceded the American Revolution, its aftermath, and the political battles that went into the creation of our Constitution? There are stories of great American Supreme Court justices and senators who carry with them every day a small worn copy of the Constitution, for it takes a lifetime to fully understand the meanings within the U.S. Constitution.

I read all I could on the first emperor of China, for I wanted to know what it was about that experience that so interested Mao, and continues to inform the present political leadership in China. Perhaps history would teach me about the future. This deep history informs how the Chinese deal with conflict within their society; how they deal with authority; how they discipline emotions within the family and society; the relationship between families, clans, and the authorities that govern them. I was so moved by what I was learning I wrote a novel, *"Semineaux: Ch'in Shih Huang-ti & The Birth of China."* Whenever I teach a politics course on China at a university, I have my students read this novel first, to give them a grasp of a culture that so subtlety informs the present world- view.

Today, the news is all about the explosive economy of China and the excitement of young people who not only have little knowledge or memory of the May 4th 1989 Tiananmen massacre, but do not seem to care to think about it. The talk is about modernization and business; success and money. The world-view of both heads of the dragon is internationalist. But, with a Chinese twist. In this new world, as in the ancient, the rulers have always had a one world-view. It is, that China is superior to all others.

Make no mistake about it, China as a nation considers itself superior to all others. In my novel I bring the reader in to appreciate this attitude of superiority in the basic act of the "kowtow," a symbolic humbling of all who would come before the emperor, a superior authority. Emperors kowtowed before their own parents, for in the Chinese culture parents were superior to all their children no matter what their attainment of success, even after becoming the emperor of all China.

The kowtow is performed by an individual's dropping to their knees three times, each time prostrating themselves on the floor at full body length three separate times, touching the floor with their nose each time, for a total of nine prostration's.   It left no doubt who was superior and who was inferior. I write this for I believe that deep in the psyche of Chinese leaders, of whatever era or political persuasion, lies this ancient germ of symbolic superiority turned genetic. It makes no difference if the ruler is an Emperor, Chairman, or a President. Like the symbol of the ragtag farmer soldier of the continental army under George Washington standing behind the tree firing at a British soldier; whose modern counterpart is the Texas or Colorado "red-neck" with two rifles on display in his pick-up truck, even though hunting season is over. Deep in the American psyche is this individual defiance; played out by President George W. Bush with European leaders before the Iraq War.   The U.S. Constitution would most likely never have been voted upon if it had not been for the inclusion of the "Amendments" to the Constitution we call the "Bill of Rights." Specifically, Article two that ensures the "right of the people to keep and bear arms." Americans don't walk around with guns on their shoulders, and all Chinese political leaders don't expect humble deference from their American counterparts; but make mo mistake about it, these things lurk in the collective psyche, leaking out under times of stress.

You discover some of this psychodynamic power from the past in modern diplomacy. One thing I observed constantly during my years at the United Nations was just how much these shadows of the past projected themselves, mostly imperceptibly, into the arena of modern diplomacy, particularly during a crisis.   As I have argued, when under stress the real thing emerges. But we often can not even recognize it.

I have never viewed international relations in chess terms as do some others; to me it is more like a game of poker. Nations are identified by their space, geography; and this is the political reality from which we begin, like the available moves of the king, queen, pawns and others. But the politics and diplomacy between nations is pure Sun Tzu…like a game of poker. Keep the other guys guessing as to your intentions and motives. Bluff is often the name of the game in poker for you often have little to observe. The movement of hands, the glint in the eyes, breathing of the opponent is important, for you can not see the cards he or she is holding.

Case study: From the past, 2001
The EPSPA (EP spy plane affair)

.

In the Spring of 2001 a crisis in US/Chinese relations erupted when a U.S spy plane on a routine mission along the China coast was forced to land on Chinese soil. It came as a surprise to many Americans that this 1950's type mission was still being conducted when satellites, electronic monitoring, top secret technological spy systems, and traditional on the ground spies were being utilized making this type of intrusive mission obsolete. But, it was not a surprise to Chinese intelligence, or even fishermen on the South China Sea whose radar equipment on their fishing boats enabled them to detect such activity. I have personally talked with merchant ship captains who were also aware of this practice.

This case study is significant for it involves so many overlapping international issues, many still not resolved: disputes over seabed rights in the South China and East China seas involving Japan, Taiwan, South Korea, Vietnam, and the Philippines. Oil and natural gas claims test the fragility of the International Law of the Sea written in the 1970s, as all the nations in the area understand the relationship between their future well being and access to natural resources. Its possible that Japan's anger with the U.S. for keeping them from the oil they needed, contributed to Japan's rationale to attack at Pearl Harbor; and Hitler's fatal mistake of going east into Russia for oil were only blips on the map of WW II. But many believe George W's administration's motivation for invading Iraq was not the fictitious WMD's but a drastic attempt to seize control of oil production.

Story recap: In April 2001 a U.S. Navy EP-3 spy plane was 70 miles off the coast of China (think, a Chinese naval spy plane 70 miles off Atlantic City) when it was intercepted by two J-8 Chinese fighters that were sent from their base on the Parcel Islands (these are the highly contested islands involving oil in the South China Sea, why the Chinese have an air base in the first place). During the interception one of the Chinese planes collided with the spy plane killing the pilot and damaging the plane so badly it had to make a forced landing on Chinese territory, Hainan Island. The American crew of 21 men and 3 women were placed under custody in a military barracks while the plane was stripped and examined. The crew were interrogated at all hours of the day and night, and eventually moved to Haikou. The negations were very intense and the crew was held for nearly two weeks.

On very basic level this spy plane affair sheds light on Chinese and American differences in the style of diplomacy and negotiations. We see how the Chinese think about resolving conflict, and the very subtle difficulty of dealing with Chinese statesmen whom you know cannot deal and negotiate on their own, but must refer to the "group," or groups for confirmation. How Chinese and American negotiators had different senses of time. How the negotiations tested the very meaning of the law, agreements, and contracts. Perhaps, most important, the difference in psychology between the Americans and Chinese.

I wrote the following series as a case study for a think tank during the crisis itself, with the understanding that I disguise their proprietorship by sending them to a local paper. They will show the very complexity that lies at the heart all these disputes.

DEALING WITH CHINA IN A CRISIS

First of a series

For the Philadelphia Inquirer

We had better think through the implications of what the EPSPA (EP spy plane affair) has to teach us about China's perception of it's Interests in the South China Sea as well as the East China Sea, for this is not the last of the confrontations we will see. Just what is so important to China? What is important enough for us to fight a war there? In the South China Sea there are two serious disputes over the ownership of islands: one between China and Vietnam over the Parcel Islands; and the other among China. Taiwan, Vietnam, and the Philippines over the Spratly Islands.

In the East China Sea a dispute exists between Japan, China. Taiwan, and South Korea over ownership of the Senkaku (Diao Yu Tai) Islands. China's claim to the Spratly Islands is based on an old International Legal principle, "the right of prior discovery", which is this case is1282; and was never challenged until 1931, by the French then occupying Vietnam. The issue becomes very complex since Taiwan also claims the islands on historical possession by China from the Yuan dynasty (1279-1368) to the present, Vietnam claims then on the basis of possession by its former colonizer, and the Philippines claims they are within its archipelago seas as determined by the Law of the Sea.

And make no mistake about it, at the heart of *all* the parties motivation is "Oil." Oil has already been discovered off the Mekong in Vietnam and on the Reed Bank near the Philippines, the later area jointly claimed by China even though it is 700 miles from China. Both China and Japan have laid claim to the potentially oil rich Senkakus, or Diao Yu Tai, which lie approximately 100 miles northeast of Taiwan. China has determined it needs the oil beneath the sea beds for its 21st century modernization and is developing its deep water navy to project its power and protect what it sees as it Vital Interests.

What is often forgotten is that the area is a major trade and naval route that connects the Far East and Europe and the United States. During the Cold War the Soviets maintained a fleet in the north sector of the area around Vladivostok in the Sea of Japan and established fishing and refueling rights throughout the area. What we are seeing now is a low level cold war being carried on between the U.S. and China driven by America's military commitments to Taiwan, which could pull us indirectly into a war with China, which will be the second of a series of articles on China.

April 3, 200 1
Gloucester City, NJ 08030

THE PSYCHOLOGY

OF

THE "EPSPA" (EP spy plane affair) STAND-OFF

Second of a series

For the Philadelphia Inquirer

Why do the Chinese insist on an apology?   What do they want? What have we wanted since our plane went down?   The answer to these questions reveals the psychology that lies at the heart of the stand-off, the vast differences in Chinese and American perceptions, and last but not least it reveals what lies at the very core of the psychology of both nations.

First the Chinese side.   The hardest thing for the Chinese is to apologize. That is why it was such news in China last month when Prime Minister Zhu Rhongji made a nationally televised apology for the cover up story of a terrorist bomber responsible for the deaths of 38 young schoolchildren, they were blown up not by a bomber but by the fireworks they were forced to assemble as part of their school day.   To the Chinese an apology is not just I am sorry, or as we in America think just good manners; but a complete admission of guilt, and a submission to the punishment normally following an apology.   This goes deep into Chinese culture and remains part of the psychology down to the present day in the form of the strong Confucian value system that even Communism reflects, the respect for those in positions of Authority. Even in ancient China when emperors tried to rule as Confucian Sages from the power of Virtue rather than force; even then, there was no challenge to authority, as expressed in the full Kowtow. The Kowtow was only considered to be good manners but in essence it represented that acceptance of omnipotent authority and complete submission to it. To perform the Kowtow one had to knell three times and each time lie flat on the floor and touch your nose or forehead to the ground and repeating this three times on each kneel, adding up to a long process and a series of nine prostrations

103

Just considered good manners, but it left no doubt who was in charge   Even the Emperor would kowtow to his ancestors in the Heavens and to his own parents.   Somewhere, deep in the Chinese mindset, a verbal apology has the psychodynamic power associated with the Kowtow.   It is not just good manners, but complete submission to authority and acceptance of guilt.

On our American side. The hardest thing for us was the lack of communication. The first thing we wanted when the plane went down was for the Chinese to tell us if our men and women were safe. We wanted information on the status of the plane. We wanted communication and we were not getting it   We wanted out people back and our plane returned   We wanted them to talk with us.

What we wanted was communication. This is at the core of American psychology and best represents what we are about, the first Amendment of our Constitution, freedom of speech.   The hardest thing for Americans is not to speak out not to communicate; we did not invent poetry but we did invent the Internet. We hoped that the Chinese would comply with what we considered good manners. Not just to heap blame, but to speak with us and investigate the matter with us. So the Chinese psychology and the American psychology clash. Some China specialists and some Congressional leaders are in Washington advising the President if he issues a simple apology he will not be just admitting guilt in the eyes of the Chinese~ but ultimately an apology in itself will not be enough. Somehow, the Chinese will want to extract something symbolic from the United States. That somewhere down the line is a Kowtow, possibly leading to a change in the appearance of the power distribution between the US and China. Some advisors in Beijing think that their greatest leverage lies in not allowing open dialogue. This American land of free speech; dialogue will eventually lead to interviews, reporters, television cameras, exposure, all those things about the openness of American society they fear, the Jerry Springer effect. The American press is demanding accountability, information, voice recordings and radar track tapes. The Chinese press is demanding an apology and recognition of what we have done wrong.

The issues of apology and authority, free speech and diplomacy; and in the meantime we pray for the safety of our 24 brothers and sisters of whom our government has asked more than it should, to fly a mission that is unnecessary~ outdated, and provocative. But that is another essay.

April 4, 2001

Gloucester City, NJ

LESSONS LEARNED

CHINESE DIPLOMACY & THE CHINESE MIND

Third of a series

The EPSPA (EP spy plane affair) should teach us many lessons, some I personally learned having spent ten years watching, interviewing, and studying Chinese diplomats negotiating; while subsequently spending as much time talking with hundreds of negotiators and officials from two thirds of the world's nations who were on the other end of negotiations with the Chinese. Part of this experience I wrote up for a dissertation to earn a Ph.D., "China's Diplomatic Behavior In The United Nations." At a less intense level I spent several years in business dealings with the Chinese and believe whatever learned is not transferable to politics, for we must remember we are not dealing with Chinese Capitalists but Chinese Communists; a different mindset, a different agenda, often entirely opposite. When a crisis such as EPSPA occurs it makes me realize how much more I have to learn, for I don't think any American can truly know the Chinese, or what China will do, for they have always been and will remain an enigma.

Having said that allow me to make a humble attempt.
1. Two mistakes we made thus far. It was a Wonderful feeling for most Americans when President Bush came forward on public television but in doing that he prevented any quick behind the scenes agreement, for the Chinese leadership would have lost "face" if they had not responded as they did. We should have allowed those at a lower level to deal. Secondly, our Ambassador to China should not have issued a veiled threat that this might affect our decision on new arms to Taiwan. This was not the time to show muscle, it only hardened their position.
2. Chinese and American negotiating styles operate on totally different conceptions of time. We want answers, we are in a

106

hurry, we work by the clock, we consume time; the Chinese wait and they use time. To the Chinese time is quality not quantity.

3. The process and style of negotiation is quite different. We like to have clearly identifiable points upon which we can negotiate while the Chinese will take positions on non-negotiable principles; and while we are looking for concrete clues they look for subtle changes of attitudes, changes in tones, changes in wording.

4. The techniques are often opposite. We like to enter negotiations by focusing on common interests and good faith, anticipating that conciliation and compromise will lead to a common understanding. The Chinese see this not only as a sham and a weakness but deceitful, trickery, and a conspiracy to distract them from their agenda. The Chinese are not interested in bona fide negations but only in one outcome, complete victory.

5. Even facts and truth are viewed differently. The billions of dollars a year in trade and all the joint ventures with American corporations does not affect what China considers to be her obligations, and considers it normal and logical that they hold our 24 servicemen and women. The provocative behavior of the U.S. has changed the environment of Chinese/American relations creating mistrust and preventing immediate accommodation.

6. The Chinese will try and set the agenda and will demand two concessions for every agreement. They are usually tough and persistent in the early stages of negotiations. They assume that the acceptance of an issue on the agenda means that it is no longer one that is disputed.

7. We like tight legally binding agreements, but the Chinese will often want to conclude "an agreement in principle," deferring the disagreeable details till later while agreeing to disagree.

8. Making a concession to the Chinese is the most dangerous of all for the timing is very important; a move too soon is seen as a weakness. When to move from bargaining to negotiation is difficult because the Chinese are usually inflexible and stick to their positions, for a change demands a group effort on their side, beyond just those conducting the negotiations.

9. It is important for the U.S. to be clear and precise, examining every word to make sure that the Chinese equivalent means the same, and there is a quid pro quo where all compromises are reciprocal.

10. Don't try and outdo the stamina of the Chinese, for they want to wear you down.

April 6, 2001
Gloucester City, NJ

This crisis was resolved after a diplomatic apology, the crew was released but the Chinese kept the plane

Let me tell a story. I have lived and worked in many countries around the world and have always believed that the most important thing that can be learned is how people feel and think. The only way you can do that is to get to know them as best as you can. Often, pride prevents some people from ever really getting to experience intimacy with a people and its culture. I have watched many important and wealthy people who because of pride never open their hearts or their being to others, thereby missing out on the most important lessons to be learned about others. Some of these lessons are nearly impossible to even explain, for you have learned them intuitively. Like when you know how someone in your family will react in a given tense situation, when no one else in the room would have any idea of what is coming. This ability, or power if you will, can at times be very important in diplomacy. There comes a time when you need to give space, and times when you need to be firm. Having the wisdom to know the difference is a blessing, a gift.

Again, I was so grateful to have been privileged in spending years United Nations, for nowhere else in the world could I have mingled with so many different cultures in such a small space. And what made it interesting was that these Chinese diplomats were first from Taiwan, the ROC (for this was 1970), and I knew that it would not be long before the Chinese communists from the mainland, the PRC, would take over their offices and positions. That United Nation's vote to oust the ROC and bring the Communists in took place in 1971 and the following year we had an entirely new delegation representing the Chinese people.

Before and after this transition I gained considerable insight into what I personally call the "True Wall of China;" the wall that outsiders can never penetrate. I came to know many of the Chinese from Taiwan who represented China in those years, and I came to know many of the Communists who took their positions. In fact, when the new diplomats came to the United Nations in the Spring of 1972, I developed a very special relationship with members of the first delegation. I reached out to them, for that is what I was writing about, China in the United Nations. It made no difference to me whatever political label they attached to themselves. I was one of the first Americans who had access to members of the Chinese Communist delegation. I may have been the first, but I do not want to make that claim, for I have no proof of that. But, they did come to my apartment in New York City, six to eight at a time; all dressed in the same Maoist blue suits, both men and women.

My wife and children were quite honored to serve as hosts. Our neighborhood and neighbors were quite excited by their presence as if they were from Mars. Afterwards I received phone calls from not only China specialists but intelligence agencies and others wanting to know what they said to me on those visits. Richard Holbrooke, of the Bosnian peace negotiations fame, was particularly interested in his then State Department capacity. (I did not know of Holbrooke at that but was instructed to take his calls from my boss at the United Nations, but later came to respect him very much, even at the end of his life. Before going into surgery in December 2010, from which he would not recover, the last thing he said to the surgeon, according to news releases; "You've got to end this war in Afghanistan." At the time he was Obama's point man in Pakistan and Afghanistan). But back in 1972 I had little to report, for I too was learning something very interesting about the Chinese mentality. It is a closed shop, open only to their immediate family or clan. On the contrary, during those same years I got very close to Russians at the UN, for they were spying on me because I was so close to the Chinese.

But the Russians were quite different from the Chinese. You could never get a member of the Chinese delegation alone for very long. The Russians would not be always confined to the group like the Chinese. And when they drank, they opened their souls and talked a great deal about their childhood, family, and young friends; quite a contrast from their sober behavior when they never, and I mean never, deviate from the party line. The Soviet Union never made mistakes, etc, etc. The Chinese always had at least three other people with them while talking on even a personal level, the by-standers to the conversation listening to every word, and smiling, always smiling. Now I am talking only about political people, that head of the dragon I spoke of. And this head, no matter who speaks for it, is driven by an ancient authoritarian heart-beat, that considers itself superior to all, and expects total obedience to its will. There is no breaking of the ranks. There are none among them who opens up like the Russian on white vodka. They are part of a group-think whose lowest ranking civil servant is as unlikely to open-up as the Chairman or Prime Minister himself. As Mao studied the first emperor of China to learn how to rule; Western nations had better study the behavior of China's ruling class with the same precision our scientists study the planets. For in the long memory of known human history, China has the deepest universe of experience when compared to the 190 plus nations we share the planet with; truly, the most inscrutable of all nations on earth.

My guess is that primitive man's first sketch was of a circle; that form that entranced him at night in the heavens with moon and stars, and warmed him in the day with the sun, allowed him to depict life with its repetition of the seasons. All Chinese thought, philosophy, life, art, science, draws on the circle of the yin/yang, perhaps the first people on earth to give the circle intellectual meaning, that all life and experience is cyclical. Everything is in motion, and everything changes as do the seasons. And as the sun radiated out from a prosperous Japan in the late 1980s and 90s, China will have her day.

China will have her day, but which head of the dragon will emerge? In maintaining theoretical consistency, history gives us the best tool by which to answer this most important of questions. As I have argued, my political science cap leaves me very

111

suspicious of the awesome power available to the Communist Party. On the other hand, my historian cap tells me that China will ultimately become politically more pluralistic; groups competing for power at the center; but not the open democratic environment prevalent in the West. Western cultures with "me" at the center of individual psychology produced those political systems; China's culture with "us" at the center of individual psychology will produce its own liberal political culture. Of course there is the respect and distance from authority in China as compared with our American distrust of power; just look at the large numbers of Americans who normally distrust the President, no matter who he is; in China, the kowtow to authority is as sure as the rising sun. The pluralism will be behind the scenes; like in Japan where the Liberal Democratic Party (LDP) remains in power, for the fights are all behind closed doors. Many writers see economic liberalization, technological advances, modern communication, and the inabilities of the Communist Party to withstand the pressures an open economy forces upon their autocratic power.

The historical lesson that leads me to see this future is somewhat more basic than the above forecast based on the idea that wealth will somehow trickle down into the political arena. This reminds me of the Cold War "détente" argument that the more and more economic and cultural contact between East and West, the more chance there would be for the undermining of Communist regimes. Perhaps, this is so, and that is how it will happen. But what number to lay your money on is a different matter. The only sure thing to me is China's history.

This time about a hundred years ago the Chinese leaderships frame of mind was about the same as it is now at the beginning of this 21st century. They knew then that there was no alternative to modernizing. Then, China had been humiliated for over a half century by Western powers, while Japan had adopted Western modernization and even its constitutional type of governments. By doing so Japan had not only saved itself from Western colonization and humiliation, but in the year 1905 the Japanese navy defeated one of the most powerful navies in the world, the Russian.

But Japan was never to be occupied until 1945 with an "Unconditional Surrender" to the United States. The deep humiliation that comes from being occupied by even one power has been well substantiated throughout history, most notably by the writings of those who suffered directly from Colonialism, as we discussed with Frantz Fanon's *"The Wretched of the Earth,"* describing how he, as a black psychiatrist in war torn Algeria witnessed the impact of violence and its role in effecting historical change.

China, on the other hand, was occupied by so many Western powers that Sun Yat-sen called China a "Hypo-colony," making it worse off than a mere colony because China was not just the slave of one country, but the slaves of all countries. China's national humiliation was recognized by International Law in the "unequal treaties" of 1842, 1844, 1858, 1860, 1995, 1897-98, 1901, 1915. On a more basic level, one that would have interested Dr Fanon, was the infamous sign that hung over the entrance to a park in Shanghai, "Chinese and dogs not allowed."

China began the last century by sending its young people to some of the finest universities in Europe and America to learn about those technological and scientific ideas that could strengthen China; in fact it was called the "Self-Strengthening" movement. This was the time of the last Emperor of China and the powers at the time thought they could have their cake and eat it too; so they sent chaperons with the young people to make sure that they were not contaminated by Western liberal ideals.

Now, at the beginning of the 21st century China again wants its young people educated in the ways of Western science and technology, except this time, they do not have to send their young people abroad. This time around they have the money to bring the brains to China to teach the new generations. And again, the young Chinese are very nationalistic, but this time around they are not motivated by stigma of humiliation, but have great expectations for their future as a great power in the world. At the same time, the ruling class has not changed in a most important regard. They still do not want their young people to be contaminated by western political liberalism. The ruling class failed, for Western education produced a Dr. Sun Yat-sen and millions of young Chinese who wanted a new China modeled after what they had learned in the West, and after the fall of the last emperor it seemed as if China may be headed into becoming a parliamentary democracy.

The irony of this story is what makes it interesting. The ruling class feared democratic ideas, but their fears were ill-founded, for events took China in a totally opposite direction. The May 4, 1919 episode turned China toward the other new model in the world, that of the Russian Revolution of 1917, and Communism. The "May Fourth Movement" started in 1919 as a protest again the Versailles Treaty's awarding the German colony in Shantung Province to Japan instead of returning them to China. This was the final humiliation, and the May Fourth Movement turned China's youth, professionals, farmers, and workers away from ideas of Democracy, many of whom quickly absorbing Marxist ideas and writings.

Today's ruling class, the CCP, will also not be capable of preventing the contamination of young minds with Western liberal ideas, or a future not yet envisioned. Thousands of Western teachers have been working in China for years, and more are being recruited to teach in higher education. When once only about one and a half percent of college-aged Chinese were enrolled in higher education, by 2005 nearly 20% attended college. But today's young people are not interested in learning about liberal democracy and political theory; they want to learn computer science, engineering, and other sciences that will enable them to get good jobs and make money.

And to accommodate Chinese students Western professors are being brought into Chinese universities. For example, the NYT reported that Qinghua University in Beijing hired one of the top computer scientists in the United States, Dr. Andrew Chi-chih Yao of Princeton - university in its drive to make Chinese universities into great research universities like Princeton and Harvard. But...and this is a big but; only in the area of science and technology. They are less interested in Western professors of politics, history, or economics; subjects that demand questioning of truth and fact. China's Leninist ruling authority does not even allow public discourse, no less than an open classroom debate.

But, China's authoritarian leaders may be shooting themselves in the foot. The basic problem being that innovation does not come out of discipline and memorization; but out of a culture of conflicting ideas, critical thinking, and a liberal educational environment. Inventors are quirks; just look at the young Einstein dreaming he was flying on a space ship...oops, relativity theory.

But my concluding point is this: Chinese college students may not be very interested in rebellious ideas at this time, and Chinese authorities keep a close watch on college and university campuses, but make no mistake about it: in spite of the students themselves and the efforts of the Communist Party, the new generation will become more liberal and free-thinking, eventually changing the system. The current leadership is no more capable of controlling minds than were their ancestors at the beginning of the last century.

The timing of this change is difficult to predict, and may have a long way to go. As one professor of genetics at Fudan University was quoted in the NYT, "We need a new revolution to get us away from a culture that prizes becoming government officials. We must learn to reward real innovation, independent thought, and genuine scholarly work." Perhaps it is my faith in young people to change things that I believe that day is soon approaching, despite the controls and fears of the bureaucracy in power, the young people of China are the future, and they will change it. Rather than invading Taiwan; they will want to purchase second homes in Europe or America.

CASE STUDY: From the future, 2014 &
Beyond: U.S. & South China seas

How strange that it was a hundred years ago, in 1914, that the Emperor Francis Ferdinand sat in his summer palace in Bad Ischl Austria and signed the orders for the army to march into Serbia to punish it for a lone gunman who had shot his son, the heir to his throne; igniting the worst World War in human history over the actions of one man with a pistol.

I say "strange," for here in 2014, there is an even more insidious situation that could trigger a war in Asia over something not even the killing of an important figure, but few land outcroppings and rocks in the ocean not even sustainable enough for human habitation. Except, this time there need not be armies involved, but nuclear weapons.

In 1914 the Emperor's orders to march drew in other powers such as Germany who had committed themselves in alliance agreements to come to their defense, triggering other alliance members such as Russia, France, and England to oppose this action. Thus, a man with a pistol sparked an avalanche of military mobilizations and war.

No one at the time really believed such a war that followed was possible; for all were quite conscious of the civility of life that the Industrial Revolution had produced with its abundance that economic success had allowed and the sophistication of the civilization, like the Golden Ages of Chinese, Persian, Greek, and Roman civilizations of past history. It couldn't happen. There would be too much to loose by war.

Today, we have the delusion that "The World is Flat" and China would not do anything to upset its history breaking economic success. In the previous chapter we looked at the smugness of many after the break-up of the Soviet Union with expectations of a era with "The End of History" with former Communist countries becoming Democratic nations in this new world. As I write these words the situation in the Ukraine is still evolving even after Russia's annexation of Crimea to the extend that U.S. military personal and American aircraft and weapons are moving into Eastern Europe to reassure our allies and fellow NATO members that we stand behind them. The big question: will we see a new build-up of U.S. ground forces sent into Europe? Western Europeans have again seen the eyes of the Russian bear, the animal they had not seen since the end of the Cold War.

In Asia, we are also seeing strange irrational fears arising from within the national psyche of Japanese, Koreans, and other with several Chinese recent moves. In late 2013 China declared an "air defense identification zone" in the East China Sea over what Japan calls the Senkaku Islands and China call the Dialoyu Islands. Japan controls and administers the islands but China claims them. To China, the new zone gives it the right to identify and possibly take military action against any military aircraft near the uninhabited islands.

In Feburary 2014 the director of intelligence for the United States Pacific fleet declared that China was training its forces to be capable of carrying out a quick victory campaign over Japan in the South China Sea. U.S. military aircraft deliberately fly over the islands to reassure Japan of its position of the issue, but President Obama has warned civilian aircraft to divert their flights so as not to fly over them.

In April 2014 U.S. defense secretary Chuck Hagel made his first trip to China and met with defense minister General Chang Wanguan who asserted that china had "indisputable sovereignty" over the islands and would "make no compromise, no concession, no treaty." Then added: "The Chinese military can assemble as soon as summoned, fight any battle and win."

A second development: every two years all the countries that border the Pacific Ocean conduct joint naval exercises in what is called the "Western Pacific Naval Symposium," and are joined by other members such a the U.S., Chile, Australia, Canada and other Asian countries. The host country organizes this international review of the fleets and in this year, 2014, China is the host. It invited all the countries in the symposium, except one, Japan.

Just as Eastern European NATO members want assurances that the U.S. will be behind them in the advent of further Russian threats; Japan wants assurances that America will live up to all the treaty obligations it has fostered with Japan since WW II.

I wrote a case study of these island disputes in my 1982 book on Chinese foreign policy within the chapter **"Chinese Perceptions of the Law Of The Sea,"** that is called **"Offshore Oil,"** that I was inspired to write after spending time in China with men from Zapa Offshore Oil who had been hired to test for oil reserves beneath the seafloor around the disputed islands. It just amazes me, that here we are in 2014 and this dispute could become a trigger to war in the Pacific just as much as a single man shooting a pistol provoked WW I. That is why I am including my thirty-two year old study into this mix. Here, you can see the tremendous complexities from so many different sides.

OFFSHORE OIL (1982)

The search for oil has reached frantic economic and strategic proportions in this last quarter of the twentieth century. It should be recalled that during the early stages of World War II, Japan launched its great offensive in the Pacific for the primary purpose of securing oil from the Dutch East Indies. In Europe, Hitler struck eastward to get control of the Russian oil fields around the Crimea. The present territorial disputes involving offshore claims in the East China and South China Seas may be roughly compared to the nineteenth-century colonial struggles over tin and rubber.

Directly related to issues discussed at the law-of-the-sea conferences, and probably crucial to China's economic growth in future decades, is the volatile issue of offshore oil. Extensive sedimentary deposits are known to exist in both the East China and South China Seas, and this points in one direction—oil

Oil has already been discovered off the Meking in Vietnam, on the Reed Bank near the Philippines (an area jointly claimed by China and the Philippines, which is 700 miles from China), as well as in the East China Sea.

In the South China Sea there are two serious disputes over the ownership of islands: one between China and Vietnam over the Paracel Islands; and the other, which is partly related, among China, Taiwan, Vietnam and the Philippines over the Spratly Islands. In the East China Sea a dispute has existed between Japan, China, Taiwan, and South Korea over ownership of the Senkaku (Diao Yu Tai) Islands.

Concern over the ownership of these previously uninteresting islands clearly arose in conjunction with UN negotiations on the law of the sea. Many parties anticipated a new ocean regime, which in turn prompted desires and demands of equitable shares of the sea's untapped potential.

Since World War II the entire area from the South China Sea up through the Sea of Japan has been under the umbrella of American naval hegemony. The Soviet Union, whose enlarged modern naval fleet has made its mark in such areas as the Mediterranean and the Indian Ocean, is just beginning to test its position in those most volatile of areas. The Soviets have consistently maintained a fleet in the north sector of the area around Vladivostok in the Sea of Japan: The 1978 Soviet-Vietnamese Friendship Treaty has given the Russians a rationale for naval probes in the southern sector of the area, the South China Sea. This naval maneuver by the Russians is not looked on with favor by either China or Japan; China because it anticipates modernization of its own naval forces, Japan because it has never been able to negotiate a post-World War II relationship with the Soviets.

Politically, relations among the countries of the area are frequently complex and awkward, the most recent examples being the protracted and agonizing wars in Vietnam and Korea. It is often forgotten that the area is a major trade and naval route that connects the Far East and Europe, and the pattern of marine geography with its thousands of islands is the most complex in the world. The area has the potential for being the most volatile of any that is involved with negotiating law-of-the-sea issues

In the South China Sea, most of the Spratly Islands, including Spratly Island itself, are occupied by Taiwan. Nanshan, Thitu, and Flat Islands are occupied by the Republic of the Philippines. The crux of the problem is that any one of these nations could legally place some of the sea lanes passing through the South China Sea in their territorial or archipelagic waters. This could be done by simply considering other islands across these sea lanes from the Spratyls and the Spratlys themselves as one large South China Sea archipelago. In the case of China—or of Taiwan, for that matter—these islands would be the Paracel Islands, Hainan Island, Dongsha Island, and Taiwan. The Philippines and Vietnam could lay claim to a great many islands in the area, and the justification for their claims would most likely be made on the basis of the concept of archipelagoes considered at the Third United Nations Law of the Sea Conference or by unilaterally declaring a 200-mile territorial sea. This interpretation means that territorial waters would not only include the waters between these islands, but also all waters extending out from these islands. This might establish a case where another nation's land was less than 400 miles away, halfway to the other nation's territory.[62]

The Paracel Islands, controlled by China, are less than 200 nautical miles from the first of the Spratlys. According to the informal negotiating text of the third session of the Third United Nations Conference on the Law of the Sea, 125 nautical miles should be the maximum permissible as the encircling base line of an archipelago. No matter what criteria are used, the main sea lanes through the South China Sea can be included within the territorial or archipelagic waters of either Vietnam or China should either nation possess all of the Spratlys and choose to assert itself.

The Spratly archipelago is scattered throughout the South China Sea with over a hundred reefs, rocks, and shoals that remain apart from the islands already occupied by states involved in the controversy. The United Nations law-of-the-sea conferences have dealt with archipelago claims of this nature, and the remaining areas might be considered "land" by whoever erects a light on them. Any nation that wishes to claim the Spratly Islands area as an archipelago must put in a claim to these rocks, reefs, and shoals, which leaves the Spratly Islands very much in the category of a contentious geopolitical area in the South China Sea.

China's claim to the Spratly Islands is based on the right of prior discovery in 1282, and their administration by successive Chinese dynasties. Chinese claims were never seriously challenged until 1931, when France, who had been occupying Vietnam, based Vietnam's claim to the Spratlys and the Paracels on historical precedent dating back to 1816. France, however, has acknowledged that when it occupied the islands in 1933 the indigenous population was Chinese. Japan also refused to recognize the French occupation of the islands as legal under the auspices of international law.

Japan renounced any of its claims to the Spratly Islands in the Treaty of San Francisco, which was signed after the end of hostilities in World War II. However, as a result of the ambiguities following the signing of the aforementioned treaty, the Philippines laid claim to some of the Spratly Islands, which in turn sparked a reaction from Taiwan, so that it along with South Vietnam landed naval units on the islands in 1956.[63]

Over a decade later, the Republic of Vietnam (South) retained units in the Spratly Island until they were replaced by Vietnamese Communist (DRV) troops in May 1975. In the previous year (January 1974), after having been driven from the Paracels by Chinese forces, South Vietnam occupied six of the islands and placed eleven islands under its jurisdiction as part of Phuoc Tuy Province. The DRVs (Democratic Republic of Vietnam) 1978 treaty with the Soviets adds to the complexities of the Sino-Soviet dispute in that the USSR had voiced support for Vietnamese claims in both the Spratlys and the Paracels.

The issue of claims to the Spratlys is extremely complex. Both the People's Republic of China and Taiwan claim the islands on the basis of historical possession by China from the time of the Yuan Dynasty until the present. Vietnam claims them on the basis of prior occupation by France, its former colonial occupier. Whether or not French occupation was legal due to Chinese presence on the islands does not change the fact that France did occupy the islands, and conquest is still a valid method of transferring territory under international law. During World War II, however, the Japanese conquered the Spratlys from France, even though they evacuated them after the war. Therefore, it could be argued that the status of the islands is undetermined, and since the United Nations has not acted on this question, the islands in theory are up for grabs. On the basis of these arguments the Vietnamese and Philippine governments have both built airfields on islands in the Spratly group, while China has built one in the Paracels.

Concerning the law-of-the-sea negotiations, the perceptions of both China and Vietnam further complicate finding a solution to the Spratly Islands. China has supported those states favoring a 200-mile territorial sea, presumably adhering to the median-line principle where 200 miles between countries does not exist. China also interprets the concept of the continental shelf as an extension of the natural land area of any given state. The question that Peking has yet to deal with involves the equitable distribution of the area of the Spratly Islands, some of which extend on to the Sunda Shelf or Malaysia and Indonesia.

Vietnam's position is even less clear, since the Democratic Republic of Vietnam only recently became a member of the United Nations and now is able to participate in the Third United Nations Law of the Sea Conference. The central question is dependent on Vietnam's concept of archipelagoes and the 200-mile territorial sea.

The Philippines' position will be linked with the Third United Nations Law of the Sea Conference, since her claim will be based on the conference outcome. The future of China's image among the Third World countries within the context of the law of the sea will be very much dependent on the manner in which Peking handles the exploitation of resources in the South China and East China Seas. If China should perceive it to be in its best interests to press its maximum claims to full acceptance, Peking would control the vast resources in both seas.

There appear to be three approaches available to China at this time. They are as follows:

1. China's continental shelf extends to Korea, Japan, and Taiwan. China's claims are not unique, since many states are acting on the assumption that they have sovereignty over their continental shelves as they extend into the sea. The Third Law of the Sea Conference may have an impact since it should eventually define a new international law of the sea.

2. China's second approach is linked with the relatively new growing assertion of the right to a so-called economic zone of 200 miles, whereby the adjacent state may exercise exclusive rights of exploitation and may share it only at its own discretion. This concept, which has been applied to Latin American states and has been recently enacted into law in the United States has substantial international legitimacy.

3. China must decide how it is going to approach its territorial claims within the context of the 200-mile economic zone principle. Peking's claims involve the Paracel Islands in the north; the Spratlys in the south; and the Macclesfield Bank in the east. All these claims could involve China in disputes with the Philippines, Vietnam, and Malaysia. In addition, both China and Japan have laid claim to the potentially oil-rich Senkakus, or Tiao Yu Tai, which lie approximately 100 miles northeast of Taiwan." -

China's image within the East Asian arc, extending form Korea to Vietnam, will depend on the way Peking negotiates its claims with all the states involved. In January 1974, China reacted militarily in its disagreement with non-Communist Vietnam concerning the Paracels, followed by Chinese press reports that reminded one of the coverage during the Sino-Soviet border disputes of 1969. In 1974 Chinese forces occupied the Paracels following South Vietnam's expression of intent to issue oil-exploration permits in the area. Heretofore, the Paracels had been partially occupied by both South Vietnam and China. The Chinese displaced the Vietnamese forces after fierce fighting which resulted in some deaths and several (tens) of casualties. This dispute became sharper following the Chinese-Vietnam border war in the spring of 1979. But during the war itself neither side utilized its naval forces, even when fighting approached the Gulf of Tonkin, a contiguous border area ripe for tension. In fact, all China's extensive seismic surveys and extensive exploratory drillings in the area have been strictly confined to Chinese territorial waters.

By 1979 it appeared as though the Chinese were in complete control of the Paracels. The Vietnamese seemed to have withdrawn from oil exploration, in spite of the fact that Vietnam had a promising field 214 miles south of Vung tan where Shell made a commercially valuable strike in 1974. The Vietnamese withdrawal was not entirely due to China's military presence. Several Western companies intent on developing offshore production became dissatisfied with "maddening" bureaucratic barriers and left for home. The Soviet Union did not seem to be of much assistance since Moscow's sea-drilling capabilities are limited to shallow waters; and, the United States had an embargo denying the Hanoi government access to oil-exploration technology.

Conversely, Peking has also displayed a conciliatory attitude in her perceptions of the Philippine offshore oil question. In 1976 the Philippine government announced that it had contracted with foreign companies to test-drill in the Reed Bank area near the Spratlys, whereupon Peking, Taipei, and Vietnam (by now the Socialist Republic of Vietnam) protested. Manila and Peking maintained a dialogue, and the resulting diplomacy avoided any military confrontation.

Chinese perceptions of its relations with Japan are reflected in the law-of-the-sea issues. For example, the possibility of vast oil reserves in the subsoil beneath the East China and the Yellow Seas has brought China and Japan into contention for the rights to the areas under question. The Senkaku, or Tiao yu-t'ai Islands are in addition claimed by both China and Taiwan as well as by Japan. Both Peking and Taiwan perceive their claims to be based on several factors.

First, they point out that geographically the islands are situated on the continental shelf which is contiguous to the China mainland and Taiwan, whereas the Ryukyus are separated from the Senkakus by the Okinawa trough.

Second, although the islands are uninhabited, they have traditionally been used by Chinese fishermen.

Third, the earliest writings to mention the islands refer to them as part of China rather than the Ryukyus.

Fourth, the Chinese maintain that when Taiwan and the smaller islands associated with it were ceded to Japan as a result of the 1895 treaty ending the Sino-Japanese War, the Tiao-yu-t'ai chain was also transferred. Therefore, when Japan surrendered to the allies in 1945 and agreed to the return of all Chinese territories, this included the Senkaku or Tiao-yu-t'ai Islands.

The Senkaku issue, like an earlier dispute between Turkey and Greece in the Mediterranean Sea, developed after the announcement of promising results from a survey of seabed oil prospects in the East China Sea. Ironically, this survey was undertaken under the auspices of the United Nations Economic Commission for Asia and the Far East in 1968. The purpose of the survey was to forestall competitive national rivalry in the East China Sea. The survey's optimistic assessment of oil potential on the East China shelf resulted in a rash of conflicting claims, exploration permits, and prospecting activities emanating from Japan, South Korea, Taiwan, and China.

The Senkaku issue appeared to strain relations between China and Japan in the early 1970s, but since 1972, both parties have been moving in the direction of reconciliation and normalization of relations. In September 1972, Japanese Prime Minister Tanska and Foreign Minister Ohira visited China and signed a joint statement pledging normalization of relations. As reflective of this trend, Vice-Premier Teng Hsiao-p'ing of China indicated in 1974 that the Senkaku controversy was quieted for tactical reasons, and by 1978-1979, China and Japan had entered into a close economic partnership. The Taiwan question, however, complicates the issue which could return to prominence at some future time. Of crucial importance within this context is the future of Peking's relations with Japan. By 1979, Peking indicated a degree of flexibility in defining its offshore claims in the East China Sea vis-a-vis Japan and Taiwan. This would entail cooperative arrangements in exploiting the seabed off the Senkaku Islands.

The question of oil and the continental shelf exhibits all the variables that might make this complex and explosive issue Peking's dilemma involving its entire law-of-the-sea policy. In the early 1970s Peking appeared to favor acceptance of the idea that undersea access be "apportioned by mutual agreement as done in the North Sea."" By 1973, Peking was formally protesting the exploration of the East China and Yellow Seas by American companies given approval by South Korea, stating that areas of jurisdiction for China and her neighbors in the Yellow and East China Seas have not yet *been* delimited. In 1974 Peking was objecting to an agreement between South Korea and Japan, referring to the agreement as an "infringement of Chinese sovereignty" that China "absolutely cannot accept." Peking then called for consultation with "the other countries concerned."[67] The "signal" that Peking was sending out was compromise.

The crucial variable in China's perceptions of the law of the sea remains the continental shelf and oil, which has extremely sensitive political implications, since the stakes will be high for all the regional states in the area for the next several decades. The energy needs of Japan, Korea, the Philippines, and Taiwan (and Communist Vietnam) will almost surely be greater than those of China, which possesses more underground resources. The reality of this geopolitical fact will test Chinese decision makers' abilities to strike the correct political balance among the Asian states involved. Probably these disputes will have to be mediated bilaterally, regardless of the treaty negotiated by the Third United Nations Law of the Sea Conference.

I would not have believed when I wrote the above, in 1978, that the US would be as involved as it is in 2014; and that we would see incidents that could possible trigger an escalation into conflict, as in 2013 when a Chinese Navy vessel cut within about 100 yards of the American cruiser the Cowpens that had been monitoring the Chinese aircraft the Liaoning in the South China Sea. Japan claimed that Chinese warships had used targeting radar on Japanese military ships and airplanes, radar only used for weapon use. The Admiral, Wu Shengli, commander of the Chinese navy omitted these actions took place near the disputed islands, and warned that tensions with Japan remained serious and the risk of incidents as sea could not be excluded. He even went on in an interview to say: "That's what we call accidental discharge when cleaning a gun. The gun is an objective fact, but what we need to study is how to avoid accidental discharge when cleaning a gun."

The US has not taken sides in the dispute over sovereignty of the islands, but when President Obama in late April 2014, while in Japan offered a security blanket when he said the US was obligated by a defense treaty to protect Japan in its confrontation with China, yes; and over a few clumps of rock in the East China Sea. What are know as the Senkaku in Japan and the Diaoya in China, could possibly be a "Pearl Harbor" moment for America.

The main obstacle to a solution may be Japan's unwillingness to even accept the idea that the "sovereignty" of the islands may be in dispute. And behind this is China's newly accentuated, or perhaps perceptions, that she is being hemmed in by American ambitions in the area; or just China's newly perceived insistence on demanding a recognition that she is now the big guy on the block, that all must accept.

It seems as if world events are preventing me from sending this book off to be published, for in the last week of April 2014 the Obama administrated responded to the Philippine concerns with Chinese aggression of their own island disputes and signed a 10 year deal allowing American troops temporary access to military camps in support of warships and fighter jets. The sight of US marines setting up camps in the Philippines is one of historic proportions, considering that the country was an American colony for a 48 years.

Geopolitics seems to be determining the direction of American Foreign Policy in the Pacific. So reader, for your patience in wading through my tedious case study of the islands and oil written decades ago, let me end with an interesting story, the cause of which is not geopolitics but, "geostrategic" proportions.

I remember meeting US naval and marine personnel on and around Rota Naval base in Spain who had been stationed at Subic Bay Naval Station in the Philippines and air force guys at bases in Germany and England who had been stationed at Clark Air Base there, both posts the largest American outposts in the Western Pacific, many of them with Philippine wives. Many confided their displeasure with growing nationalist Philippine forces that were demanding the end of US bases on their islands. It did come to an end in the 1990s, but in a very strange way, helped along by a volcano eruption, changed by a geostrategic event.

A book review by Simon Winchester in the WSJ of the book, "Tambora" by Gillen D'Arcy Wood about the 1991 eruption of Mount Pinatubo in the Philippines caused two "colossal institutional casualties:" Subic Bay Naval Station and Clark Air Base...both bases were buried in several feet of "choking silicate mud, and officials opted to close both of them down for good."

The aftermath is interesting with regard to our previous discussion. After the closure of the bases the Chinese "military began to sniff around a corner of the Pacific Ocean suddenly depleted of all the earlier squadrons of watchful American ships and aircraft. Chinese vessels began to raise their flags on disputed islands, to claim territories about which they had remained silent for decades, to threaten Japan, to rattle sabers."

So with Obama's new foreign policy of a "pivot" away from the Middle East after Iraq and Afghanistan, the Pacific Ocean is the new theater of global interest. But by now, China is no longer willing to stand by an watch a new American build-up.

The author of this book review amusingly writes: "If Beijing ever sails its gunships close by Pearl Harbor, or threatens San Diego, then seismic historians will reasonably argue that it was the eruption of Pinatubo that initially prompted China to imagine doing so. Pinatubo is a volcano that changes the geostrategic complexion of the new century."

I would like to end this chapter with one forecast and one news story, a piece written by a Chinese dissident's daughter: **"A Dissident's Daughter, on Rights and Reform in China,"** a letter published in November, 2013. First the letter.

"China's New Agenda" (editorial Nov. 17) highlighted several planned policy shifts by China, including important developments concerning human rights. As the daughter of a Chinese political prisoner, I welcome China's commitment to begin reforming it's abysmal rights record with much trepidation, as its continued refusal to permit fundamental freedoms of expression and dissent call into question the stability of any progress.

My father, Wang Bingzhang, was the founder of China's overseas Democracy movement. A medical doctor by education, he instead devoted his life to what he believed were basic freedoms long overdue to the Chinese people.

In 2002, my father was abducted from Vietnam, stolen away by boat to china and arrested by the Chinese police. He was subjected to a sham trial, where no evidence or witnesses were presented, and sentenced to life in prison. He has been held in solitary confinement ever since.

China recently committed to dialing down capital punishment, but is the torture of indefinite solitary confinement (I interrupt at this point, for only those of us who have had the unfortunate experience of being in solitary confinement, truly understand it as the inhuman brutal punishment it is, and ' indefinite ' is beyond any comprehension, perhaps worse than death itself) much better? The plight of activists like my father highlights the need to press further. Among all the promised reforms, nothing indicates that what happened to my father cannot and will not happen again to someone else."

Ti-Anna Wang, Montreal, Nov. 18, 2013

Now the forecast. The Chinese economy will implode in as early as 2015, it will happen fast. The Communist Party has not only put severe limits on the freedom and exchange of ideas; they have not allowed for a free market in capital. For millions of Chinese there are no financial capital markets. Plus, they are so fearful of inflation that while the People's Bank of China benefits from vast accumulation of foreign exchange reserves, they continue to use the Yuan to peg the exchange rate at predetermined levels, ignoring markets, and using excess Yuan in the hope of preventing runaway inflation.

The highly leveraged state banks, holding billions in debt backed with nothing more than CDOs (collateralized debt obligations), the same non-liquid packaged instruments that brought about 2008 in the West, along with massive debt from loans from state banks to non-state regional banks holding ever greater amounts of non-performing CDOs and loans to regional and local Communist Party powerbrokers without the ability to repay, for with local economies immediately devastated by the financial sunami, will force the government to bail out the state banks, just as Washington bailed out America's largest banks. But unlike in the West where inflation was kept from emerging, the entire banking system beyond those controlled by the Communist Party, will collapse, bringing about a demand side inflationary climate with people desperate for currency just in order to afford the basic expenses of daily life. Merchant ships normally active with millions of containers being shipped world-wide sitting empty in Chinese ports due to downturns in demand from emerging economies such as Brazil, where huge exports of raw materials to china have been drastically trimmed due to the slowdown in Chinese factory production, now unable to pay for Chinese consumer goods, resulting in a vicious cycle. The China envied by many in the west will come to be perceived as a paper tiger; and the Chinese will be forced to re-evaluate their commitment to the western style of Capitalism just as they were forced to re-evaluate their commitment to Communism in 1979. The outcome, will be a retreat to what China knows best and its source of strength during times of great distress: the value system steeped in the history of ancient China. While remaining a modern nation state; it will draw on this cultural capital, but sorry to say, moving further away from the ideals of western liberal political values.

Chapter Three

THE FUTURE OF TERRORISM

&

The Lessons of Iraq

I believe there are several things about terrorism that we need to address. First, that all weapons of mass destruction are terrorism. What else could you call it, for they terrorize as much as they kill? We must begin to declare that anyone; be it a dissident, freedom fighter, or head of state that would use such a weapon in a first strike is a "Terrorist." Is there ever a time, when a first strike with any WMD is justified? We must re-write the rules of war that are as out of date as their 17th century origins in International law.

Two, the history of terrorism goes all the back to antiquity; but by 2005, for the first time it has become something entirely new, terrorism is now an "Ideology," just as much as Communism or Fascism are labeled ideologies. We should use a capital "T" rather than a small "t" when referring to this violent ideology. The immediate cause of this change was the latest war in Iraq. As an ideology it is global and like others it has many faces whose momentum is motivated by different forces. For example Cuba's communism was motivated by different forces than say Russia's, China's, or the Marxists UNITA or MPDA of Africa's Angola. Terrorism as an Ideology will be more difficult and long lasting than all forms of terrorism facing the civilized world before the U.S. invasion of Iraq in March 2003.

The sixteen year-old female suicide bomber in Palestine may not be motivated by the same forces as the Egyptian and Saudi pilots who flew airplanes into the Twin Towers, but what makes them both part of this new ideological threat is modern communications technology in all its forms. Modern communications have enabled a global consciousness and awareness to develop, Iraq made it all come together. Ideologically, Iraq did for Terrorism what the Russian Revolution of 1917 did for Communism. Terrorists have always relied on news coverage to spread fear, but broad coverage of resistance to American occupation in Iraq, the ubiquitous cell phone, and most profoundly…internet web sites, have changed the mind-set of terrorists and would-be terrorists.

It is a psychological component that gives it its ideological foundation. It is a major shift in consciousness, but one somewhat difficult to quantify or even identify in its entirety. Let me explain this "shift of consciousness." In the early 20th century, China's nationalism was taking its lessons from Western democracies evidenced by Dr. Sun Yat-Sen's democracy movement and the thousands of Chinese students who went to study at American and European universities.

This Chinese democracy movement was called "The Three Principles of the People." The three principles are nationalism, democracy, and people's livelihood. A tectonic shift took place due to one specific event. China, who was allied with the Western democracies in WW I watched helplessly during the peace negotiations following the war when Japan, China's number one enemy who had invaded and defeated China in 1895 and insulted China with its "15 demands" of 1915, was allowed to take control over the former German concession of Shantung in China.

When word reached China from the negotiations going on in Europe on May 4, 1919, students, workers, and even business people rioted in the streets. Japanese businesses, consulates, and citizens were attacked. In one day, Chinese consciousness began to change. To many intellectuals, students, and workers; Western democracies had not only let them down, but had conspired with China's worse enemy, Japan. Confusion set in and within a year ten young men met in Shanghai to form the beginnings of the CCP, or Chinese Communist Party. The youthful nationalist movement would soon turn away from democracy and toward communism. The psychology of consciousness had changed. No matter how much the pro-Western Kuomintang struggled for the hearts and minds of its people, this change brought about the communist victory in 1949. There are some of us who believe that the unexpected consequences of America's invasion of Iraq had by 2005 changed the consciousness of terrorism. What Al Qaeda was unable to achieve before the invasion had occurred; Terrorism became a global ideology.

Why do I say this? My first experience with attempting to understand the minds and motivations of terrorists was in a special program in the Clinical Psychiatry Department at Mt. Sinai Medical School where we analyzed the minds of assassins and terrorists. Terrorist organizations have always needed assassins. But the assassins proved predictable to some extent for they could be linked to a particular political objective. Even most terrorists had political objectives: the IRA in Ireland, the Palestinians in Israel, and the Basques in Spain to name a few. This new Terrorism of ideologic dimensions comes more abstract, shadowy, and sometimes indefinable motivations of the now global "suicide bomber,"

It is possible to end the violence of many terrorist organizations, albeit not very acceptably by those being attacked; surrendering to their political demands may end the violence, such as independence for a breakaway republic. But this new terrorist is difficult to placate by what we have experienced in the past. Sometimes all they want is death; for themselves, you, me, and the small child next to you with her attentive grandmother.

Next on my journey to understand the mind and motivations of terrorists I began to subject myself to the tricky business of interviewing terrorists in their home cultural homestead. At first it was difficult because I have and remain disrespectful, unforgiving and in contempt of any person who inflicts terror on innocent women and children. Most troubling on these interviews, many

135

from these organizations were likeable people. For example, the Basques of northern Spain reminded me very much of the guys I had gone to high school with in West Philadelphia; lighthearted, down-to-earth and sincere, humorous, but resolute and focused on a belief system based on a loyalty to each other that somehow transcended the ideology that determined their responsibilities to the cause. My point is that most of these people, their organizations, and their recruits all worked toward a political solution, albeit one demanded by them and unacceptable to the governments they were fighting.

An example of this momentous change is the terror of 9/11. For over thirty years we have seen hijackings of the "take me to Cuba" variety or like the episode in 1970 when four airplanes flying from Europe to New York were hijacked by Palestinian terrorists. Hostages were released in the later crisis as well as most others. The suicide hijackings of 9/11 changed this forever.

How does one account for the fact that the 9/11 terrorists were graduates of some of the finest universities; and the lead suicide bomber on 9/11 had a Masters degree in Urban Planning from a German University. They did not come from economically deprived families or from families that have seen members killed by their perceived enemies.

What has happened? Decades ago I mistakenly thought that most terrorists were bred because of perceived economic or political injustices and if these could be resolved the terrorist would denounce violence as a way of achieving their ends. The ideal hope was that terrorists may some day take part in the peaceful pursuit of sharing power in a democratic setting. Such as the hope in July of 2005 when Sinn Fein, the political arm of the Irish Republican Army announced that the IRA was denouncing violence. In fact, some former terrorists in Germany and Italy, for example, now sit in parliamentary chambers making laws. The most dramatic possibility would be Hezbollah participation in the political system in Lebanon.

The new terrorists do not recruit as Tamils would in Sri Lanka, or Chechen, or Basques, or Uzbeks... all in the name of "freedom fighters." There is a new breed of market specialist and they use the internet to recruit. These web sites tell all. For they appeal to would-be terrorists whose motivations are far and wide. This is what makes the future particularly dangerous. The display of violence on these web sites appeals to a very wide range of young men and women around the entire world with varying motivations. We generally knew what the IRA wanted, or what was demanded by the "Red Brigades." Perhaps, the only motivation for some is to just kill U.S. Marines. Why? I am sure there may be a hundred different answers from a hundred different terrorists.

These new terrorist web sites reflect what is new since the invasion of Iraq and why I say Terrorism is now an "ideology." What is an ideology? Simply put, it is an idea that serves to organize concepts, plans, goals, and even feelings. The International Encyclopedia of the Social Sciences defines ideology as, "the more or less coherent and consistent sum total of ideas and views on life and the world (belief system, doctrine, Weltanschauung) that guides the attitudes of actual or would-be power holders or leaders...." When I studied ideology with the specialist, Professor Ivo Duchacek at CUNY, he taught that ideology is related to modern mass media and to the spread of ideas and propaganda. He was right on target with these new web sites. These terrorist web sites offer educational manuals on how to attack foreigners, U.S. Marines, those who cooperate with the formation of a new government, and anyone or any group deemed a target. They teach how to be an assassin, and specifically who should be assassinated in a given country or area. They offer the latest up-to-date ways to acquire the right materials to make a road-side bomb with suggestions for even more powerful ones.

Before 9/11 the major training camp was Afghanistan. Since 2005, web sites have been the major training camp; again, contributing to not only the global nature of it all but perhaps more dangerously, the decentralized aspects of the new threats. After

9/11 we were searching for bin Laden in a cave in the mountains of Afghanistan. Now web sites are showing the killing and torturing of U.S. Marines. They teach how to make weapons and ways to carry out more killings. They carry recruitment propaganda of photos glorifying suicide bombers' successful missions. If one web site is shut down, another one pops up the next day. It is a system that would have been envied by the Nazi propaganda machine in Germany.

After 9/11 the intelligence agencies talked about cells, some independent, others directed from a cave somewhere in Afghanistan. The internet has allowed so-called cells to proliferate, most alarming, beyond groups that would be normal recruits in this war against not just "infidels," but all that America and Western Civilization represents in the modern world. There are no longer wiry young men swinging beneath a horizontal ladder like monkeys and practicing assault techniques in the sun-drenched dry deserts of Afghanistan; they now sit in front of a computer or television screen and watch actual footage of insurgents destroying American vehicles and killing American soldiers, accompanied by the sound affects of glory and war.

What makes this a thousand times worse than before 9/11 is the enormous disparity in what motivates young men not just in the Middle East, but from around the world, to go join these insurgents. Iraq became a magnet for hate and training to kill. Young American men and women never in our history have been asked to perform a more difficult job than to police a war zone filled with urban guerilla fighters. I would like to see the film clip of Dick Cheney, Donald Rumsfeld, and Richard Pearle before the war suggesting that U.S. forces would be greeted like liberators by the Iraq population. One journalist suggested to Richard Pearle of let's bomb the Soviets during the Reagan administration that since he was so sure American "coalition" troops would be greeted as liberators perhaps he should lead the troops into battle himself; Pearle's normal snarling facial expression turning to shock..."that's not fair," he retorted. Chaney and Rumsfeld's denial reminds one of Robert McNamara's unrepentant rationalizations of his Vietnam bombing days.

Back in the first week of August 2005 the U.S. Marines operating in western Iraq sustained more casualties from roadside bombs than at any time since the war began. This is urban guerilla warfare in an age of Terrorism; and the toughest fighting force in the world today, the U.S. Marines, were initially being sent into combat without sufficient heavy armor. They were also dealing with other phenomena; we never seem to learn the lessons taught by Sun Tzu in his classic, <u>The Art of War</u>. This ancient Chinese text was being followed very, very closely by the insurgents in Iraq and Afghanistan utilizing not just hit and run tactics, but they do not fight unless they are assured of a victory. The insurgents define victory based on the American body count. It didn't matter how many insurgents die if enough Americans are killed. Even when heavy armor and more firepower were used such as with the surge in Iraq and the surge in Afghanistan, the insurgents, again taking lessons from Sun Tzu, found new methods of inflicting heavy casualties. If the marines can stop them; they will be back, tomorrow, next week, next month...and, stronger each time they change tactics, as with the March 2014 suicide attacking within Kabul in Afghanistan.

The main enemy of the United States in this battle with Terrorism is psychology. A psychology we have never faced before on such a massive level, people willing to die for their cause. We know the stories of Japanese kamikaze pilots, but they were not the entire military and their numbers were limited. In Vietnam Ho Chi Minh's army was armed with a psychological mind-set totally dedicated to driving out American forces as they had with the French in 1954; under, I might add, General Giap, himself an ardent student of Sun Tzu. When I taught U.S. Army, Marine, Air Force, and Naval officers during the Cold War I made them read Sun Tzu to understand who we fought in Vietnam; and I had them read the sacred Koran so they would understand something about the foundations of Islamic psychology. What

U.S. troops were dealing with was immeasurably worse than the Vietnam or WW II experience. The fringe of Islam that generates this hatred has become a global phenomenon. It is not just confined to one particular type of nationalism like with the Japan or Vietnam experience. It is that part of the Muslim world that hates America who declared war on the U.S., and they do exist, in spite of the consternation of millions upon millions of Muslims who denounce this violence.

A global Jihad had been declared against the United States, but in practical terms, this psychology of resistance fuels enough recruits to eventually far outnumber the number of U.S. military we are willing to commit. Each American killed incites more young discontents to join the war against the infidel. In October of 2005, the Pentagon released a special report showing that 312 foreign nationals had been captured in Iraq in one month that year, April 2005. What is startling is that they came from 27 different countries.

How to Win the War Against This New Ideological Terrorism

This new Terrorism cannot be defeated, but the war can be won. It can not be won militarily. I say it cannot be defeated because it has become not just a movement of isolated pockets of terrorism but it has become a global phenomenon of deep psychodynamic dimensions. Simply put, it has become a resistance psychology with ambiguous and wide-ranging appeal to not just Middle Eastern Muslims, but to anyone or group with malice in their hearts toward America. So we are fighting an idea. You can not kill an idea, only temporally slow it down with intelligence gathered by infiltrators; and only hope to defeat it with a counter-brainwashing campaign. It begins in the mind, and must be challenged in the mind; the psychology determines the life span of this new Terrorism.

On the other hand, there is no question that terrorists must be killed; particularly in cases where their potential attacks can be countered with just a little common sense, like the attack on the USS Cole. There is no other way to deal with terrorists on the front lines of today's global war as they continue to target the innocent, defenseless women and children. Even the Dali Lama has justified using violence to stop terrorists.

The war on terrorism will demand using all means to kill, particularly those groups that will never stop their violence, no matter what concessions are offered to them. For example, in Palestine there is some hope that with Hamas taking part in Palestinian elections it may one day assent to becoming part of the peace process; while the smaller Islamic Jihad terrorist group rejects all attempts to bring it in closer to this process, and offers Israel no other alternative than killing as many of its fighters as possible.

Attrition may be satisfying especially after a terrorist attack, but the more terrorists killed, the more recruits will volunteer. This is the dilemma we face, and we witnessed, particularly in Syria.

What must be understood is that we are dealing with multiple motivations on the part of terrorists who really have only one thing in common, hatred. It could have been spawned from an unhappy childhood of abuse and degradation. This hatred may begin with self loathing, a belief that it is the victim who is somehow unworthy. Individuals made to feel they are failures and it is their own fault. In psychiatric terms, a suicide bomber would be killing that part of themselves that had been humiliated and intimidated by oppression.

So many terrorist recruits themselves may have no memory or experience with former colonial rule; but nevertheless have lived under authoritarian oppression all their young lives. The authoritarian regimes that replaced colonial rulers were, and are, often crueler and more punishing than the colonizers had been. To site just a few: in Cambodia, Uganda, Zimbabwe, China,

Indonesia, Haiti and the list could go on. My point is that the end product of abuse is the same. It doesn't matter who inflicts the abuse, your father or your uncle, the colonialist or the present dictator. The damage to the human soul is done. These young people joining the global jihad will never be stopped with a military or police response alone. Their pain is deep, like the man or woman who has been beaten by a parent in childhood, or has been sexually abused by a priest. That hatred or pain will always be there; but it is not hopeless. There is no hope for stopping the violence in the future unless these people are able to see, understand, and believe there is an alternative to the hatred and warfare that is becoming their lives.

How is this done? The Bush administration believed that instilling democracy into the Middle East would transform this psychology of violence; for, as political scientists like to say, democracies don't start wars. But democracy is not born at the end of a gun. At the very heart of a democracy are the freedoms of speech, press, and assembly and the right to worship. When Muslims are in the majority such an open society allows them the path to power. This is often a one-way-street. Once in power Islamic parties often suppress what they see as subversive movements and impious writings or teachings. The fatwa issued by Khomeini against the novelist Salmon Rushdie for example. As Bernard Lewis has pointed out in his book, **The Crisis of Islam: Holy War & Holy Terror",** democracies are at a disadvantage because their "ideology requires them, even when in power, to give freedom and rights to the Islamist opposition. The Islamists, when in power, are under no such obligation. On the contrary, their principles require them to suppress what they see as impious and subversive activities." Thus, we witnessed recently in Egypt.

In 1989, Algeria established a multiparty system under a new constitution. One political party, the Islamic Salvation Front (FIS), appeared likely to win a majority of seats for the National Assembly in 1991. The FIS completely supported Saddam Hussein's invasion of Kuwait and his outright defiance of the

West, and wanted the Algerian military to assist him. The following year the military dissolved the assembly and established a dictatorship. A brutal struggle followed and over 8,000 people were killed. But once the FIS was in power there would have been no return to democracy. No Western capital protested. Al Qaeda blames America for the military takeover. We watched as the brotherhood gained power in Egypt through elections after Mubarak's overthrow, then refusing to share power, the military overthrew the newly elected government.

I think the answer has to be more fundamental than democracy. They have to be shown that there is hope for the future beyond killing westerners and being suicide bombers. The front line here is the propaganda war. Who controls mass media? Who has the power to profligate ideas around the world? Who has the greatest source of satellites and websites on the internet?

Who are the best marketing experts? All must be brought to the table to educate the millions of young terror recruits and potential recruits that there is an alternative to violence. Propaganda and education are the only hope. The psychology must be changed, and it will not be easy.

Let me tell a story. I remember a twelve year-old boy in Miami. I had just returned from teaching the US military officers in Europe I had spoken about, and was substitute teaching a very crowded seventh grade class populated with some children recently arriving from their war-torn countries in Central America in the late 1980s. In the middle of the class this young boy I will call Pedro, stood up and cursed me out when I asked him a question about the lesson we were discussing. This child reminded me of a few jockeys I knew whose bodies were hard and whose faces were lined from the sun and booze. This boy looked twelve going on forty. His eyes blazed with fury and fearlessness. When I feigned a look of astonishment, which I had to do for the sake of the other children, some of whom seemed appalled by language they only heard from a drunken parent, he cursed me again. When I walked down the aisle toward the boy he stood as if to fight me. He was not afraid of anything I would do to him. He had seen machine guns pushed into his face and his father, brothers, and uncles shot in front of him. When I approached him he looked as if he was going to take a swing at me. He was ready, but not for what I did next. I put my arms around that boy and gave him a hug. His body felt encased in steel, but he was trembling like a scared child. He began to cry and the class, at first startled, began to cheer and laugh. The boy followed me around all day and refused to leave my side. When other teachers complained to the principal that Pedro was skipping their class to be with me, the principal, a wise old Vietnam vet understood and allowed him to stay with me until the last bell rang.

I see the thousands of potential young terrorists around the world as Pedro's brothers and sisters. Young people abused by authority at many levels, witness to violence in all its hideous forms, educated in the belief that their natural young urges had to be curbed so not to be infected with the same un-God like evil behavior infecting the infidels. They had to resist the degradation and sexual debauchery seen in the exotic media of the West, and that this devil called Western culture had to be destroyed, to save a "pure" Islam.

I am not foolish enough to suggest that love would turn them around. What I am saying is that if we use all our power of persuasion by utilizing all the propaganda tools of the mass media, we can educate these potential terrorists that there is a better way for them to go.

These young recruits have to see other young people who are of their same ethnic and racial composition, not Westerners. They have to see and hear from these others that Islam has alternatives that can offer them another road. Perhaps a crude analogy, but it is somewhat like the star pro black athlete who goes into the inner city ghetto school to educate the children that there is another path than drugs and violence. It has to come from someone with whom there is a chance to identify. If China, India, America, Europe, Brazil and other capitalist economies can sell goods and services;

surely, there is the capability of selling a young terrorist or would-be terrorist that they can find whatever it is they want, without joining a jihad. A shift of what I like to call, a shift of psychodynamic proportions. Like when a young boy or girl reaches the age of puberty and they "discover" their sexuality. The little girl finds she really does like boys and Tommy no longer runs from the girls, but chases them.

Killing terrorists is necessary to protect ourselves, but this will never put an end to the war, and our insecurity. Only by converting the terrorist; through not just ideas but biologically, so they do not just think about change but feel it as well, feel that killing or being a suicide bomber is the wrong path for their lives, now and into the future. If we can build nuclear bombs and put a man on the moon; we can figure out a way to do this conversion. There can be no future for any of us or our children or grandchildren unless there is a hopeful future for the worse elements of our present world.

Let me tell another story. This from my maternal Grandmother's Iroquois roots, the Mohawk legend of Atotarho. Some of the most ferocious American Indians were the five nations of the Iroquois (Mohawk, Oneida, Onondaga, Cayuga, and Seneca). There were no limits to their cruelty in battle. Blood feuds erupted into cousins killing cousins. They conducted unlimited warfare as tribes tried to eliminate other tribes; women, and children were killed after all the warriors died or were put to death. The greatest obstacle to peace, so the story goes, was the Onondaga warrior leader Atotarho, whose mind was so twisted and evil that snakes grew out of his hair and his body was bent in seven places. His evil magic was so powerful that birds fell dead from the trees and dead fish floated to the surface in the streams and lakes when he was near.

In the legend, one day he was approached by Aiontwatha (who is today known as Hiawatha, or the one who combs) who sang a hymn of peace with such mystic sounds, Atotarho became so hypnotized and calmed by the hymn that Hiawatha was able to comb the snakes from his hair, straightened his body, and set him up as one of the Peace Chiefs. He became head of the Five Nations and thus created the famous "League of the Iroquois" that brought peace to the Five Nations for over two hundred years; long before the League of Nations or the United Nations.

The lesson of the legend is to take the worst and most violent and make them leaders. The evil energy is transformed into doing good. This conflict between good and evil is a favorite Iroquois theme. That some good lies somewhere in the worst of men. If you can find and nurture that good in the wild beast, that warrior quality can be used as a force for good, not evil.

There are thousands upon thousands of young Atotarho out there in the world. The challenge is to transform that energy into something good. If there is one thing that I believe we may have learned by now in the early 21st Century, is that in this global world we can not sweep a problem under the rug, or eliminate a problem by killing it. Call it persuasion and propaganda, call it education, call in brainwashing, call it marketing, call it anything... but call it necessary for the modern world to grow and thrive.

During the Cold War we had "Radio Free Europe" broadcasting messages of freedom and liberty into Eastern European countries behind the Iron Curtain. Despite communist-controlled countries physically imprisoning their populations, the desire to be free is strong as we witnessed when the Berlin Wall came down. Terrorists and potential terrorists will be more difficult to free, for imprisoned in their minds are beliefs warped in a mind-set of violence. This future conversion to change their thinking must employ not only all the sophisticated modern communication technologies available today and tomorrow, but the message has to be one that does not denigrate the pain, suspicion, and hatred that lies in their souls. How to do this I am not sure. An ideology can only be confronted with another ideology; and this new message must be compatible with the experience of those whose mind-set you want to change. You can not be in their face; but you must appeal to their humanity that lies beneath their beliefs and mind-sets. You may have to temporarily take their lives in combat; but in the long run their very souls must be changed if there is to be peace. We must use the written and spoken word to create a compelling visual presentation that is more powerful in this battle than all the grenades, guns, and bombs put together.

Chapter Four

THE FUTURE OF RADICAL ISLAM

I once stood with a Jew on a street in Seville, Spain facing one of the largest Roman Catholic cathedrals in the world; not just any church, but the one from which the Spanish church launched the Inquisition in the 13th Century, a sort of Catholic fatwa that punished, tortured, murdered, and burned Jews and infidels (Muslims) in an attempt to eradicate them from the earth. My Jewish friend, an intellectual who was deeply aware of the history of this monstrously elaborate church before us, quivered as if this had happened to his immediate family just recently. Jews, who were not only accepted but honored for their intellectual contribution throughout the Islamic world for centuries, were, in the Inquisition, to be hunted-down like animals by the storm troops of the Spanish government in the name of the Roman Catholic Church. I think that many people in Europe and America today are like my Jewish friend on that street in 1987: they perceive Islam as a direct threat to their security, existence, and life. I believe that this is an incorrect perception of Islam.

Why? We must step back and look at the historical record. Not necessary some would say; but how can one person be fully understood without some reference to his or her past? Our case histories are so important that they are coded into our driver licenses, passports, and often our security passes to enter the work place... fingerprints, age, addresses, etc. History qualifies us individually, collectively, and internationally.

The Bush administration had bought into the thesis of a distinguished professor from Princeton University, Bernard Lewis who perceived the struggle as a zero-sum game and wrote that, "For Islamists, democracy, expressing the will of the people, is the road to power ... but it is a one-way road ... on which there is no return … no rejection of the sovereignty of God." Once in power, Lewis argued, democracy is destroyed.

In all due respect to this distinguished scholar of Islam, as well as the distinguished Harvard scholar Samuel Huntington who wrote of a "clash of civilizations" between Christianity and Islam: there is another branch of Islam that may determine the long-term future of a faith whose history speaks of a civilized culture far superior to the barbaric and primitive beginnings of our Western culture during he Middle Ages.

This is the Islamic world few are aware of. An Islamic world that was so advanced and cultured that it gave Western civilization the most fundamental pillars upon which we now stand. They preserved for us the writings of the Greek philosophers such as Aristotle, Socrates, and Plato in Latin translations; the philosophical foundations of all Western political though. Islamic culture gave us algebra, cryptography, windmills, teaching hospitals, coffee, marching bands, and even the guitar, derived from the "oud." Most fundamentally, they gave us paper … discovered from China and without which the ideas of Western civilization could not be written down or conveyed to others.

Let me tell a story. I once lived in a small German town eight miles north of one of the most beautiful cities of Europe, Heidelberg, when it celebrated its 1,000 year history. I was born in an old American city, Philadelphia, which by contrast is but a baby in historical time. This town, Neckargemund, began its weekend celebration with a parade designed to depict the evolution of those 1000 years. Since this was in the year 1988, the first displays in the parade would depict life in the year 988. True to form for that period the people were dressed in clothing looking more like the harsh brown bags that are used today for potatoes…sacks. Their primitive carts with the round wooden wheels were pulled by oxen…this first segment of the parade looked very much like the primitive medieval times it was trying to depict. Peasants living in a Feudal system not much different in quality of life dimensions to 18th century American slaves. The parade evolved in time, and proudly displayed the technology produced at that time in West Germany.

My point is that in 988 when this little town looked like parts of rural Kentucky, there existed farther to the south of Europe an Islamic culture with cities that had hundreds of libraries and an environment that produced doctors, astronomers, mathematicians, musicians, poets, botanists, translators and other creative and scientific scholars. At the same time Europeans were confined to a primitive feudal life, these Islamic cities had paved and lighted streets, running water, and architectural structures of pure beauty. I suggest that to get somewhat of a feel for this aspect of Islamic culture one should visit the Alhambra in Granada Spain. You will be mesmerized and enchanted by the simplicity of the beauty. It is more of a poem to nature than a palace.

It is true that in the early 10th century a fundamentalist North African army attacked and destroyed much of this culture believing it to be far too liberal in its interpretation of the Koran; similar to the secular/fundamentalist conflict in the Muslim world today. But, it is my belief that the modern secular trends in Islam will prevail in the long run; for environment is the major determinate in all human development, and modernism in this global world will prevail.

Amir Taheri wrote a book in 1987 entitled, **"Holy Terror: Inside the world of Islamic Terrorism."** The conclusion was called, "The Future of Islam." In this pre-9/11 analysis he discussed the reaction to the first truly Islamic state imposed on the Sudan in the mid-1980s by Muhammad al-Numeiri, who believed that after years of false hope with socialism, Nasserism, Arab Baathism, nationalism, and pro-American liberalism, the Muslims of the Sudan would welcome the prospect of life under the shar'ia, or Islamic law. What Numeiri did not expect was the universal reaction when people took to the streets. The majority of the demonstrators may have been students, poor rural farmers, women rejecting being forced to wear the purdah, but a sizable number were from the professional classes and housewives. Their subversive chant was, "Down with the shar'ia."

In Egypt, long before today's crisis, intellectuals took on the Party of Allah at an ideological level. Nur Farwaj, a lawyer, wrote that "The shar'ia is a collection of reactionary tribal rules unsuited to contemporary societies." Faraj Fada, another lawyer, published a pamphlet, "**No To Shar'ia**" in which he boldly stated that "Islam has no policy suitable for modern society and should not be mixed with politics." The problem that these intellectuals had with Islamic law and politics was that politics by its very nature is about compromise in the face of opposing views. As James Madison argued in the "**The Federalists Papers**", politics is about allowing "factions" to work out their problems without resort to arms. If the Party of Allah came to power, there would be no power sharing, as we recently witnessed in Egypt. A fact brought home by the 1979 revolution in Iran when the clerics completely replaced the ruling class, not unlike the French revolution of 1789 or the Russian Revolution of 1917.

Taheri writes of the brutal pressures that the Islamic Holy War organizations exerted to change minds, such as throwing acid in the faces of women who did not show enough modesty. The widow whose husband had led the commando raid that assassinated Sadat (for making peace with Israel) revealed that her husband had been a normal guy. He smoked and allowed her to study at the university, but changed into a "different creature" after joining the fundamentalists. She had to wear a veil, could not watch television, and was not allowed to eat cucumbers or stuffed vine leaves as they would cause sexual arousal. Female doctors were encouraged to end their careers, wear veils, and become "good wives."

The unresolved political dilemma in the world of Islam is no different than it is in most other societies in the world. How does a society draw boundaries between a person's private and public life? Seventeenth century Americans left Europe to seek religious freedom and some ended up in a New England Puritan theocracy where the sleeping arrangements of a husband and wife were regulated. Liberty in these Puritan colonies existed only for those who behaved in the accepted light of the Lord. By the twenty-first century America is still sharply divided over the issues of birth control and abortion.

Taheri wrote that "Islam cannot ignore the fact that the Renaissance, the French Revolution, the Industrial Revolution, the dramatic technological progress of the past three centuries, and its own violent contact with Western colonialism have led to the creation of a global system in which it is virtually impossible for a single nation, or groups of nations to wall themselves in with the hope of shaping a separate destiny." Of course the Taliban would have other ideas; bin Laden and many in his movement including the suicide pilots of 9/11 had not only Western educations but were bi-cultural, and as we have learned, we have home grown British citizens blowing themselves up to kill other British citizens, and American citizens who blow people up at the Boston Marathon.

So the future of Islam can take several paths. The worst path would be the violence we have seen since 9/11. The second path, the quasi-theocratic revolution set up in Iran after the 1979 revolution that ousted the Shah and brought Khomeini to power. A third possibility is the Wahhabi fundamentalism exported by Saudi Arabia. Finally the fourth path could be the secular Islamic society set up by Turkey in the early Twentieth Century.

By Summer 2014 it appeared that the first and second of these paths was taking hold when fighters for ISIS drove Iraq's U.S. trained army out of Mosul in its declaration to set up the "Islamic State in Iraq and Syria," and as reported by Juan Zarate and Thomas Sanderson ISIS is "flush with funds," some from international donors intending attempting to help the refugees under now ISIS control, controlling banks, oil installations, granaries, and business in areas under their control in both Syria and Iraq. For example, they have stolen over $400 million from banks alone. With this, they pay their fighters very good salaries.

And as in Afghanistan with the Taliban, they control the drug trade.

Presently this fourth path is the least likely to emerge, but with 65 million people, Turkey today is the second largest Muslim country after Indonesia. What Mustafa Kemal Ataturk accomplished in the early 1920s was nothing short of revolutionary. As the British historian Arnold Toynbee wrote in his book, **"The World and the West"**, "perhaps as revolutionary a program as has ever been carried out in any country deliberately and systemically in so short a span of time. It was as if, in our Western world, the Renaissance, the Reformation, the secularist scientific revolution at the end of the 17th Century, the French Revolution, and the Industrial Revolution had been telescoped into a single lifetime and been made compulsory by law."

The dictator, Kemal Ataturk, realized that Turkey had to adapt Western ways or it would be exterminated. Turkey had been feared in the West more so than today's Al Qaeda. It had become embedded into the European psyche for centuries since the Muslim Ottoman Turks almost conquered Europe in 1683; the Turkish army had been at the very gates of Vienna preparing to conquer Europe. As recently as the last century, Europeans could see the Turkish crescent flag still flapping in the breeze on the east coast of the Adriatic Sea. The flag was visible from Italy only a hundred years ago, in 1914.

The reality of the modern world crashed in on Turkey in several ways. First, at the end of the 18th century they were decisively defeated by what they perceived as their inferior Russian country cousins who, centuries earlier, had fully accepted Western modernization under Peter the Great. Where the European Crusades had failed in their overland invasion of the Middle East in the 13th century, the Portuguese circumnavigation of Africa in 1488, the European transit of the Atlantic and Pacific Oceans, and the Western conquest of the ocean with their navies caused the Turks to feel they were being surrounded. By the beginning of the 20th century, Turkey was being referred to as "the sick man of

Europe," and the last humiliation came with Turkey's defeat as an ally of Germany in W W I.

Turkey had tried to survive by adapting Western military weapons and techniques. As Toynbee had emphasized, the truth is that technology alone is not sufficient for reform. A way of life, a civilization is an indivisible whole where all the parts sort of hang together and are interdependent. Like the Chinese who thought at the end of the 19th century they could send their students into the West to study science and engineering and help to use these skills in building the weapons needed to bring China into the 20th century. You can not compartmentalize knowledge. When they returned they had ideas of liberty, freedom, elections, and democracy. Japan, by contrast, understood that the science and weapons development was insufficient, and in 1868 completely revolutionized Japanese society by adapting American political institutions. Adopting the art of war alone will not work.

The Turkish Republic was formed in 1923, when the Turks, for the first time ever, called their country "Turkey." Kemal Ataturk disestablished the Islamic religion thereby creating a secular state. Women were emancipated, Western culture flowed into turkey, and they even adopted the Latin alphabet for the first time in their history. By 1950, Turkey moved from a one-party state into the consent of the governed. There was no bloodshed or violence. Today, the Turkish Republic is the only Islamic state that has organic democratic institutions allowing for a free society, a liberal economic system, and a political order that transfers power peacefully.

Chapter Five

INDONESIA: A Case Study

I have selected Indonesia for it is not only the fourth most populous nation on earth today, but the largest Islamic state in the world.

So the question remains: which path will Muslim countries take? An interesting case study is perhaps Indonesia, since it is at the type of crossroad that Bernard Lewis talks about when he writes of the "Crisis" in Islam today. What should first be pointed out, Indonesia was not converted to Islam by the sword as so many others, but over time Islam evolved peacefully, even absorbing influences from Hinduism, Buddhism, and Sufi mysticism. But as late as the 1990's Indonesian students were sent to study in Egypt and Saudi Arabia where for the first time they absorbed ideologies that were not only anti-Western and anti-Semitic, but denounced the tolerance that Sufism has infused into Indonesian Islam. What they learned was Wahhabism, of which a few words must be said.

The current form of Wahhabism was born out of a need for meaning in the larger Muslim world after the failure of pan-Arabism envisioned by leaders such as Abdel Nasser, and the failure of both capitalism and socialism to save them from the humiliation the modern world created in their eyes. In the West we labeled it "fundamentalism," a term gleaned from American Protestant churches that challenged biblical interpretation and liberal theology. There is no comparative challenge to the Koran in Muslim theology; but the term "fundamentalism" is now widely applied and accepted among Muslims as the school with uncompromising standards of authenticity and Islamic purity, denouncing not just Christianity and modernism, but Sunni and Shi'ite as well.

157

The founder of Wahhabism was Muhammad ibn 'Abd al-Wahhab, an Arabian theologian who lived in an area ruled by local sheikhs of the House of Saud. He preached the purification of Islam and in 1744 launched a crusade against what he considered the "distortions" of the authentic teachings. The Saudi princes embraced his teachings and began to spread his word by the sword. They sacked Karbala, the Shi'ite holy places in Iraq, and by 1806 conquered the holy cities of Mecca and Medina.

Those preaching Wahhabism viciously attacked both Sunni and Shi'ite, killing men, women, and children, destroying their holy places, burial grounds, and not only burning their sacred texts and books but killing those who preached or even those who wrote the books.

The expansion of Roman Christianity in Europe was very much helped by the conversion of Clovis to Roman Catholicism in 5th Century Europe as was orthodox Christianity in 10th Century Russia by the conversion of Vladimir. But unlike Europe and Russia, the political entity that gave Wahhabism protection was itself nearly eradicated. The Ottoman Turks, with the support of Egypt, destroyed the Saudi state in 1818 and beheaded the Emir. But the Wahhabi movement survived until another Saudi prince, with the help of Wahhabi supporters, re-established the Saudi in 1823 with a capital in Riyadh. Thus the bond between the Saudi royal house and Wahhabism that endures to this very day.

This is the brand of Islam that Indonesian students returning from Saudi Arabia and Egypt brought home, doctrines that had heretofore been rarely known in Indonesia. Next came not only Wahhabi teachers from Saudi Arabia but Saudi money to finance mosques and the education of millions of young Indonesians who had little access to education, for Indonesia has no compulsory public education system. Saudi money financed the building of thousands of boarding schools to be staffed with Wahhabi trained teachers from Arabia. It's much like the Christian evangicals who spread their gospels in many parts of the world today.

In Indonesia, the military is widely-respected and revered institution that had overwhelming support during the authoritarian regime of General Suharto which ended in 1998. The military's corruption is legendary. It allowed links between its officers and militant Islamic groups such as Jemaah Islamiyah, I askar jihad, and the Islamic Defenders' Front. Some of these groups were responsible for terrorizing nightclubs and bars in Jakarta and carrying out deadly attacks against Westerners in Bali in 2005. They have established their influence regionally; for example, even in independent East Timor in 2006 special police arrested women waiting for buses to get home from work. Police claimed they dressed improperly and charged them with prostitution.

After the fall of Suharto in 1998, the most extreme of these groups, Jemaah Islamiyah, had been driven into exile to Malaysia and ended up in Al Qaeda training camps in Afghanistan. They returned home to a democratic Indonesia. Their new bases of operation and planning of terrorist attacks became the boarding schools set up throughout Indonesia with Saudi money. The big change came after 9/11 and the American invasion of Afghanistan.

A new anti-Western ideology that had been imported from the Arab world was now being preached by respected Muslim scholars calling on all Muslims of the world to unite against the United States. To make matters worse for secular Muslims in Indonesia these same clerics called for the introduction of the harsh Muslim system of justice. As we saw in Iraq, many are insisting that this system of justice, called "shar'ia," be implemented. Surprisingly to a Westerner, many pushing for these conservative changes are highly educated men and women.

I chose Indonesia as a case study because I believe the future of its Muslim population is the future of Islam and the West. There is hope that moderate Muslims will over time prevail. If history is the guide the future can appear grim. It seems that it is always the extremists in most political movements who disrupt moderate factions over time. Such was the case with the Bolsheviks victory over the Mensheviks in Russia, Hamas as a challenge to the PLO, Hezbollah in Lebanon, and the radical faction of the ETA in Spain. Even in American party politics we have seen this occur, where moderates are attacked from both the right and left. Tea Party, fundamentalist Christians, and right wingers in attempting to turn the Republican Party into a force of obstruction with uncompromising positions on any issue they disagree with.

Thousands of years ago Aristotle warned of how difficult it was for moderate forces to prevail and "good" government to be maintained; a passionate minority, persistent and unyielding, can have political leverage far beyond their numbers or influence.

Indonesia is part of the explosive Asian economic boom that in itself necessitates peaceful solutions to old ethnic, racial, and regional hatreds. We have seen the thirty year old war in Ache province negotiated into a possible settlement after the disaster of a deadly and destructive tsunami. The newly accepted awareness in Ache that war and terrorism only begets more war and terrorism, and everyone loses, and that modernization is not necessarily Westernization, and Islam can flourish in a culture that adapts to changes in the global economic system.

There are strong moderate forces in Indonesia. The late Muslim scholar Nurcholish Madjid wrote nearly forty years ago that Islam can thrive and grow in a modern democratic society. He expressed this in his 1968 work, **"Modernization is Rationalization Not Westernization"** applauded by many moderate Indonesians while at the same time he was attacked by conservatives as advocating a too liberal interpretation of Islam. When Jakarta was in the midst of anti-Suharto demonstrations in 1998, it was Mr. Madjid who visited the general at the presidential palace and suggested to him that it was time to give up power. The following day, President Suharto announced his resignation.

Nurcholish Madjid was perhaps the best known of all moderate voices in Indonesia where millions of Muslims reject what the extremists are advocating, and moderates are in the majority. The internet, television, and mass communications provide extremists with images they co-opt to inflame the impoverished masses who can see how unfair the world may appear. Most Muslims are more interested in a better life for themselves and their families and in spite of some hatred preached in their mosques are uncomfortable with the violence being perpetrated in the name of their religion. This very theme is at the center of Abou el-Fadl's book, **"The Great Theft: Wrestling Islam from the Extremists.".**

Since 9/11 Islamic scholars from around the world have argued that Islam was a religion of peace and had nothing to do with terrorism. The persistence of terrorists who say they act in the name of Islam, such as the 2005 London bombings committed by young British Muslims born and educated in England, killing other English people in the name of Islam; as happened in Germany and in Boston, leaves many distrusting of this argument. What are we to make of this?

I think there are two areas here that need clarification. The first is the idea described earlier: the new "ideological" aspects of the Iraq and Afghanistan wars. The ideology allows people who have very little hope for better lives to plug themselves into something larger than their bleak lives. Like the Chinese masses in the 1950's who had scant resources following the decades of war beginning with Japan's invasions in the early 1930's, WW II, the Korean War, and the Chinese Civil War between the Kuomintang and the communist culminating in a victory in 1949; or the impoverished Soviet citizens who suffered approximately forty million casualties in two world wars and domestic hardships during the Communist period. This new ideology of terrorism created by the American invasion of Iraq gives disconnected young men and women from Asia and the Middle East and beyond something above their futureless existence to plug into. This is not about Islam. It is about the desire to fight against Americans for many reasons that are deeply psychological yet expressed in simple ideological terms.

Secondly, and more importantly, how can we begin to understand the phenomena of the suicide bombers who say they act on behalf of Islam? To begin with, suicide bombers are not always brainwashed automatons going happily to their deaths in the belief that they will end up in paradise with 79 virgins and all the pleasures of the flesh denied them on this earth. Nor do they all die for Islam. They do not die for some mystical afterlife, nor do they die for their religion. It is like arguing that the Crusaders of the 13th Century marched to the Middle East motivated to liberate the birth place of Christ. Rape, pillage, and more rape and pillage had little to do with Christianity.

What the lead 9/11 pilot who flew the first plane into the World Trade tower and other suicide bombers had in common is a deep sickness inside their souls. They are not brainwashed. They are sick human beings. If we could study the case histories of all these bombers we would find a deep sense of humiliation or helplessness that developed in their lives. Many of us feel humiliated at times in our lives or sometimes feel helpless in the face of overwhelming problems, but we do not want to kill ourselves or others as a result. In the case of suicide bombers, you would discover that in many of them the humiliation and helplessness became pathological. What triggers the pathology is when the humiliation (perceived or real) or helplessness degenerates into shame.

Now what is "shame?" Sigmund Freud talked about the destructive aspects of "guilt," but guilt can be overcome much easier than shame. In trying to explain this to students I ask what they feel guilty about, and they will often relate their guilty feelings and it opens up discussion, even bringing laughter into the equation. There was a skit played out on the "Tonight Show" when Jay Leno got audience members to divulge secrets about what they have felt guilty about. Right there on television, they talk about things they did in the past and never related before. They win a prize and everyone, nearly everyone, laughs. We can somehow rationalize our guilt. Like the German soldier who said he was just obeying orders. Shame, is an entirely different thing.

Shame is something we very rarely reveal to even our best friends. It is something very deep and personal that we have internalized, even to the point that it has become subconscious in many people who do not think about it, but yet, it affects their lives in most profound ways. I ask students to understand its uniqueness by suggesting that male students relate to their mothers and females to their fathers, their sexual fantasies. Of course, they are horrified at the suggestion. For these are things they are often ashamed of. Guilt you may relate, but shame is often your private hell. Things you do not want anyone to know. Shame diminishes us in our own eyes. Like the shame a girl carries with her all her life because an uncle has sexually abused her or the forty year-old man who was sexually abused at twelve by a clergyman, teacher, or the sexually impotent man who physically abuses women. The millions upon millions of people who were physically or verbally abused by parents in childhood and go through life feeling a sense of shame inflicted upon them for being worthless, unable to give fully of themselves, even to their own children. Then you have the extremes like the serial killer whose sickness may be rooted in his shame from an abusive childhood. This is also acted out on the world stage. Then there is the dictator responsible for millions upon millions of deaths because he is acting out the shame in his soul; Hitler, Stalin, Napoleon, Ceausescu, Mao ... most likely shame from their childhood in some distorted and sick twist.

The suicide bomber often uses religion as a rationalization to act out personal misery. In many of their cases, it is the shame that has sickened their soul. It has little to do with Islam. If not Islam, then some other cause, like those jihadists who have gotten caught up in an "ideology of terrorism." It is hatred for America and the modern world with all its confusing messages and unreachable and unattainable things.

If there was one thing that tilted this tug of war toward the extremist in Indonesia, as well as other Muslim communities, it is the American-led war in Iraq. Richard A. Clarke sums this up most appropriately in his book, **Against All Enemies: Inside America's War on Terror** when he says that, " because the U.S. apparently believes in imposing its ideology through the violence of war, many in the Arab world wonder how the United States can criticize the fundamentalists who also seek to impose their ideology through violence." The Bush administration's war in Iraq made it very difficult for moderate Muslims in Indonesia, as elsewhere, to turn their young men and women away from the messages of hate and revenge.

In conclusion I want to be optimistic. Can America take the positive images such as its assistance following the tsunami and Pakistani earthquake catastrophes and use these images to begin to repair the damaged perceptions that millions of Muslims harbor as a result of the Iraqi and Afghan wars? What is interesting to me is that today's terrorists pose more of a direct threat to the security of the American homeland than did either Japan or Germany during WW II. Think? Should not the talents of America's marketing specialist; the Madison Avenue guys who have sold Coke, McDonalds, Pepsi, and thousands of American products around the globe have been enlisted, or conscripted, to sell what this window of American compassion displays when we come to aid peoples in distress? Is it too late? President FDR must be rolling over in his grave, for during WW II the talents of corporate executives were utilized over and over in the war effort against both Nazi Germany and Fascist Japan. If Madison Avenue could connect with the reality that terrorism is bad for profits; perhaps, they might begin to put more of their creative resources into enhancing the positive, such as what young American military men and women have done to save peoples lives in both Indonesia and Pakistan in times of nearly unimaginable tragedy. Can Madison Avenue marketing executives be patriotic enough to give their best in selling the big-hearted, uncelebrated American military response to these soulful human tragedies to a world-wide Muslim audience?

I am also optimistic that we are not alone in our fight against terrorism. Think for a moment. How many early 21st century nations, in addition to the U.S. have so much to lose to the threat of terrorism? On the front line, Saudi Arabia has its very existence on the line. China may have more to lose than anyone since its economic miracle future depends upon a world that is stable. Egypt's very existence depends upon a resolution to terrorism. So here we see the wealthiest of all Middle Eastern countries, the most dramatic Capitalist economy in Asia and perhaps the world, and the most populist country in the Middle East; all having a most vital stake in seeing the violence of the terrorist movements constrained.

Chapter Six

IRAN: A Case Study

Enter Iran: I have selected Iran; for no other country presents a more compelling picture of both threat and hope. One cannot talk about the future of Radical Islam without a close analysis of Iran, whose version of Islam rules the state. Iran is, unlike Iraq who was signaled out as a terrorist supportive state by the Bush junta prior to the invasion, is truly a supporter of terrorists; having been a financial and adversarial backup to Hezbollah since its birth. Hezbollah are the terrorists who killed the 241 U.S. Marines in 1983 Lebanon, the deadliest single-day death toll for the U.S. Marines since WW II's Battle of Iwo Jima; and in 1996 killed 19 Air Force pilots and crews at Khobar Towers in Saudi Arabia.

Iran has called for the destruction of Israel and has been working hard on its nuclear weapons program. Since the Bush administration destroyed Iran's two most threatening enemies with regime change in both Iraq and Afghanistan, Iran stands to be a superpower in the region. The perception of some is that we are witnessing a Shia revolution orchestrated by Iran, using Hezbollah as its military spear head, and that the capturing of two Israeli soldiers in 2006 and the rocket firings into Israel were without question either ordered by, or encouraged by Iran. Hezbollah did not act alone in July 2006. Not too long after Sunni Hamas captured Israel soldiers sparking the Gaza war; Shia Hezbollah replicated the act sparking the Lebanon war.

How do we deal with Iran? How can we understand what motivates Iran? To begin, Islam defines Iran; and only in Iran is Shia the official state religion, and where Shia constitutes the majority. Most Muslims throughout the world are Sunni. "Shia" means partisans or followers; Shia are followers of Ali, whom they claim is the true successor, or caliph, of Mohammed who was assassinated in 661. Shiites are more fundamental than Sunni Muslims, and interpret the Koran differently than Sunni.

In Iran rulers have tried to modernize as we have discussed in regard to Turkey and Ataturk. But Ataturk was different in one major aspect; he installed a republican form of government with a parliament and slowly pushed his reforms through the legislature. His Iranian counterpart in the 1920's, Reza Shah (Shah meaning king) rejected these democratic reforms and believed only an authoritarian king could modernize, as did his successor. The failure of the Shahs to build political institutions would haunt Iran down to this very day, and led to the success of the Islamic revolution that came from within the state in 1979. The United States was still so blindsided with communism at the time that it failed to see the revolution coming; no less the storming of the American embassy in Tehran on November 4, 1979. It began at mid-morning when a large mob of young Iranians broke into the embassy compound, surrounded the chancery building, set fire to part of the embassy, ultimately knocking down the door of the political officer who was on the phone with Washington. Her last comment was: "We are going down," as one of the Iranians with a picture of Khomeini pinned on his shirt pulled the phone from her. They then blindfolded the sixty-three American embassy personnel and led them into captivity (this was a skeleton staff of personnel that had been scaled down from the thousand plus members during the Shah's time). America was in shock and this "hostage crisis," as it was to be called, would eventually bring down the President of the U.S., Jimmy Carter.

Let me tell a story. When the American embassy was attacked in 1979 there was a major backlash against Iranians living in the United States, many fearing for their lives. It may seem remote now but it was no less fearful for anyone from Iran at that time. In our history, German-Americans became suspect and Japanese-Americans were relocated and interned during WW II. These things happened and it can be frightening for the majority who are innocent. At the time of the Iranian hostage crisis I was teaching at a University in South Florida and there was an Iranian friend working at the library who had dozens of threats on his life within a few days of the hostage crisis. He was such a gentleman and when I saw the fear surface on his face I offered him refuge in my home. Americans became very confused by Iran when President Ahmadinejad suggested that Israel should be "wiped off the map" and then went on with development of a nuclear weapons capacity (which is why, by the end of 2013, I believed that Israel has every right to oppose President Obama's insistence that Israel be patient with the diplomatic developments begun in Geneva, for Israel demands to see the suspect facilities dismantled and shipped out of Iran, as was accomplished with Libya, before any sanctions are lifted). We saw blindfolded Americans being humiliated and threatened. What was it in the Iranian psyche that hated America so very much? That was my question to my new house guest. It's when another level of my education about Iran began.

My friend said that most Iranians were young people and they loved American culture with its movies and music, then went on to explain how the psychology toward all outsiders as a result of being invaded so many times; by the Greeks under Alexander The Great in the 3rd & 4th century B.C., the Arab-Islamic invasion and conquest in the 7th century A.D., Turks in the 11th century, the Mongols in the 13th century, and Russia, Britain, and the United States in the modern period all attempting to model the great Persian culture to their own.

Persia was renamed Iran only a few years ago in 1925. The Persian culture, like Chinese culture, is very old and feels itself superior to all others. Like the Chinese, Persians watched over the centuries as all the invaders were swallowed by the very culture they supposedly defeated. Like China, Persia experienced being forced into a semi-colonial and humiliating relationships. It made no difference if it was Russian Cossacks or The Shah's brutal secret police, the SAVAK; humiliations and crushing power had the same effect. Iranians knew the United States just about created and armed the entire military infrastructure of Iran under the Shah, a fact that was completely separate from this love affair young Iranians had with American pop culture.

Thus, Iranian's perceptions of America were wrapped around the entire history of Persia, and American's perceptions came from a TV showing their countrymen and women being led like animals, blindfolded. These images became America's perception of all Iranians, pictures of mad looking uncivilized creatures. Why do they hate us so, was the question on Americans lips?

My friend spoke of the deep soul of his culture that Americans at that moment in time, and presently in this early 21st century, are mostly in complete ignorance. He spoke of the tolerance of Persian culture as expressed by the Persian poet and founder of one of the oldest orders of Sufis, Rumi (1207-1273); the mystical side of Islam with its popular "Whirling Dervishes." Rumi's **"Masnavi"** is a Sufism work considered by Iranians to rank in importance with the Koran. In **"The Teachings of Rumi"** he wrote a piece entitled "The soul of good in things evil, evil only relative," in which these lines appear:

> "In the world there is nothing absolutely bad;
>
> Know, moreover, evil is only relative.
>
> In the world there is neither poison nor antidote
>
> serpents poison is life to serpents
>
> To the creatures of the sea, the sea is a garden
>
> To the creatures of the land, it is fatal."

And then we have the 11th century Persian poet, Omar Khayyam, who wrote of the shortness and mystery of life and the need to make merry while it lasts. In his book **"Rubaiyat,"** he wrote these lines:

171

"For "Is" and "Is-not" though with Rule and Line

And "Up-and-down" by Logic I define,

Of all that one should care to fathom,

I was never deep in anything but - Wine."

My Persian friend argued that these poetic and spiritual seeds lie at the heart of every educated Iranian, and although the leadership may be authoritarian, be it the Shah or the Mullahs, the middle class population are liberal and seek modernization; but not at the expense of "our national pride." It just so happened that President Carter had just allowed the deposed and hated Shah to come to New York for treatment of his cancer and his presence in the United States evoked memories of 1953, when the CIA staged a coup (Operation Ajax) against the democratically elected Mohammad Mosaddegh,, followed by the Shah's flight from Rome with his triumphant return to the throne. In November 1979, my friend argued, many Iranians feared that the United States was about to back another coup and again restore a Shah.

He then suggested we look closely at a map of Iran in order to visually feel its vulnerability to the world around it; surrounded by Iraq and Turkey on its west, Afghanistan and Pakistan to the east, and central Asia to its north. Millions upon millions of Iranians have been killed over the centuries from Iran's wars with its neighbors. Now within the context of recent history, Iran's leadership sees U.S. military forces on both its major borders, in Iraq and Afghanistan, in Uzbekistan to the north, and the U.S. Navy in the Persian Gulf and the Arabian Sea to the south.

As my friend said years ago, "Persian leaders often make outrageous statements that echo through the world and give the impression that Iran is lashing out and threatening. When in reality, he said, "we are like the lion that is cornered for the kill; he roars in order to keep others at a distance." We have been invaded and attacked for centuries. If we stand firm, and sometimes boldly, perhaps we can bluff." I wonder if my friend from 1979 would have considered Khomeini's fatwa against the writer Salman Rushdie in 1989, and President Almadinajad's statement in 2005 about wiping Israel off the map as just a lion's "roar." By 2013, and into 2014, this is an existential question that demands an answer.

An analysis of what makes Iran tick must deal somewhere with supporting terrorism, developing nuclear weapons, denying the Holocaust, and threatening to wipe Israel off the map. It is fine to speak of the vast majority of middle class educated Iranians who are farther from power and influence then they have been in thirty years. Many believe that if the U.S. and Europe come down too hard on Iran with sanctions, it will be even longer before these potential liberal forces will ever come into their own. It is a dilemma, the stakes are high, especially for Israel.

First, the United States must deal with Iran like it dealt with an emerging Soviet Union in the late 1930's, recognizing that it is not going away and that the exportation of its ideology has far-reaching appeal; in fact Iran's influence and control of Hezbollah would have been envied by the Russian "Comintern",: the instrument used to export Russia's brand of communism around the world. Even Cuba must take notice, for Che' Guevara's death in Bolivia reflected Cuba's failure to export its brand of Communism at the time. Even Castro could never have predicted that in early 21st Century Socialist governments would be democratically elected throughout the Americas, in part as a backlash to United States sponsored globalism with its exploitive "free markets," with the U.S. even helping to overthrown a populist elected government in Honduras in 2009 (I was in Honduras during the military takeover and all the poor hardworking people I spoke with knew their populist President was taken down with the support of America) . Oh, the unpredictable nature of international politics!

The Hezbollah-Iranian connection is a rather unique alliance not seen before in international politics. States have supported revolutionary/terrorist groups with money and arms, but never has such a revolutionary/terrorist group been elected into office and held ministry positions in a parliamentary government. They have built a state within a state primarily by supplementing the existing inadequate health, education, and welfare programs of Lebanon. They have built an armed militia more powerful than the state military, with only the militia capable of defending the nation against an outside aggressor. This process was very much encouraged by the United States pushing its own beliefs that open democratic elections are essential of a free society. Thus, as with the electoral victory of Hamas in Palestine, then the Muslim Brotherhood in Egypt.

With this having been said there is a more basic variable that must be considered in any analysis of Iran. Iranian journalist Maziar Bahari has written that Hezbollah may very well make decisions "independently of Iran," and pointed out that Hezbollah is fundamentally "an indigenous Lebanese armed resistance group that owes its popularity to Israel atrocities, biased American policies and corrupt Lebanese politicians." Bahari argues that "when the U.S. and Israel try to portray Hezbollah as an Iranian proxy, they are pointing the finger in the wrong direction." In Bahari's analysis, Hezbollah has in reality become a liability for Iran.

If Maziar Bahari is correct, why is this so? First, it may be that the war in Syria proves him incorrect. Iran has not only sent arms to Hezbollah in Syria fighting in support of Assaid but Iranian military commandos as well. Only by looking at this relationship in purely political terms can we understand the analytical truth. The political factor has to be isolated and distinguished from other factors far removed from how many would like to see it. The difficulty lies in the fact that isolating the political factor is not easy because human nature is complex. Hans Morgenthau, the father of 20th century realism and one of the most brilliant political minds of the last hundred years, expressed it this way: "The political realist maintains the autonomy of the political sphere, as

174

the economist, the lawyer, the moralist maintain theirs. The economist asks: 'How does this policy affect the wealth of society,' the lawyer asks 'is this policy in accord with the rules of law?' the moralist asks 'is this policy in accord with moral principles?' the political realists asks ' how does this policy affect the power of the nation.'"

Secondly, the United States must recognize a new geopolitics in the Middle East, much of it made possible by the 2003 invasion of Iraq. Iran has emerged as a regional Superpower with nuclear potential, deepening ties with Russia and China in their quest to control Central Asia with its resources and strategic importance, the Hezbollah factor, its championing of a Shia revolution, and the enormous support from both Shia and Sunni Arabs throughout the world for its support of Hezbollah's war with Israel beginning in the summer of 2006, and its defiance of Western pressure to put a cork on its nuclear weapons program and enrichment processes.

The U.S. backing of Israel's demand that Hezbollah be disarmed as part of any cease fire or peace agreement flies in the face of the reality not only on the battlefield, for Hezbollah is Lebanon; and they blend into their environment as " fish in water" (if I may quote Sun Tzu), indistinguishable from ordinary citizens, from whom they are recruited, particularly after their perceived heroism and success against Israel's powerful modern army and air force in the first three weeks of the 2006 war. Saddam did not have nuclear weapons and was not an immediate threat to the region; Iran has been working hard to become a nuclear state and has become the dominant power in the Middle East, rendering meaningless any democratic gains made in Iraq, Lebanon, Tunsia, Libya, or Egypt. Iraq and Afghanistan failures has weakened the U.S. bargaining positions on both strategic and tactical levels, which has made Secretary of State Kerry look like Sisyphaus in Camus' novel. The U.S. support and arming of Israel during the siege of Lebanon in 2006 has contributed to destroying a sixty year-old U.S. "honest broker" image, thereby diminishing its diplomatic leverage. An "honest broker" nation is one to whom all parties are willing to engage in diplomatic dialogue, that had something to do with Secretary of State Kerry's inability to succeed with the peace negotiations in 2014.

On the international level, the United Nations must put Iran in its cross-hairs like it did with Iraq before the Bush administration decided "containment" was insufficient, and invaded. The invasiveness of U.N. inspectors in Iraq before the invasion would be the ideal scenario with regard to Iran, allowing inspections of its most secretive locations. The emergence of a strong liberal middle class seems to be something more of a Western wish than an Eastern reality, and I see something else on the horizon that may be more important; a process that goes back to Persia's first oil concession with D'Arcy in 1901, series of oil deals that could not only change the geopolitics of Asia, but will tie Iran in closer with nations where stability is king, for with it goes their upcoming economic fortunes following the disastrous impact of the sanctions.

Japan was granted a contract to work on the largest new oil discovery in 30 years with a potential twenty-six billion barrels of reserves. China signed a contract to be supplied with natural gas for 30 years and the Chinese oil company Sinopec has purchased a 50% stake in the Yadavaran Oil Company. Iran is negotiating with Pakistan to build a pipeline through Pakistan in order to pump Iranian gas to India.

It is imperative that Russia and China, with strong developing ties with Iran, continue to be engaged with attempting to mitigate Iran's threat to world stability. This is not a naïve thought, for the essence of geopolitics is often wrapped in a riddle seemingly detached from reality, as in regards to China not seeming to act responsibly with North Korea's nuclear threats, nor Russia's hesitation with regards to Iran's nuclear ambitions. Together with Europe and the U.S., the hope is that Iran can be persuaded to act in a responsible manner. Many believe, here in 2014, that diplomacy is the only option in regards to Iran. Perhaps, and once this crisis subsides, and Israel no long feels threatened, the poetic soul of Persian culture will emerge; for Iran could be the most important player in the geopolitics of the Middle East in this 21st Century.

The 2013 international conferences in Geneva attempting to end the nuclear stalemate with the U.S. being joined by China, Russia, France, Germany, Great Britain negotiating with Iran in anticipation of a settlement was a failure; Iran said not now. Like an ancient Persian emperor pulling up their tents and leaving neighboring Arab tribes blinking into the desert winds, wandering; what just happened? Iran's seemingly continuous position, right up to 2014, is that it has the right, under international law, to enrich nuclear fuel for its industrial reactors, and has no intention of building bombs, so it claims.

No intention of building bombs? The history points in another direction. Taking Uranium 235 which has a 0.7 level of radiation and cooking it in hundreds of centrifuges taking it up to 3.5%, and presently calculated at 20% is enough to make observers suspicious. True, to make a bomb it has to be enriched up to 90%; but that distance can easily be reached in a short period of time, as we have learned from North Korea, who now has bomb producing Plutonium.

The problem, is that while many accept the smiling face of the new leadership as representing the cutting edge of political decision making, Ayatollah Khomeini retains the power, and uses it, despite his and the foreign press denials to the contrary. And it is Khomeini, as recently as 2013. who has demanded that Iran has drawn " redlines " against pressure to stop enrichment of Uranium and has claimed that they will not step back one inch from "our rights." While he has not threatened to wipe Israel off the map as with the previous administration, he refers to Israel as, "untouchable dogs."

Ayatollah Khamenei may claim that Iran's enrichment rights are protected under international norms; but Iran violated these norms when the former President Mahmoud Almadinejad threatened to wipe Israel off the map, thereby loosing it rights under international law; for international laws are written explicitly to prevent such threats. There is no proof at this time that Iran is not constructing a nuclear bomb as I write. It is one thing for me to lay out different aspects of Iran's history and behavior as I have above; but Israel's Prime Minister Benjamin Netanyahu has no alternative but to keep a realist perspective, for if he miscalculates it could result in the end of Israel as a state and an inhabitable place to live.

In conclusion, lets look at two opinions; the first of ones who should know better, and the second from one who does know better. The first is from the editorial board of the NYT who wrote that the sanctions and diplomacy seem to have lead to a sufficient level of inspection authority giving hope that Iran will recognize its responsibilities in not developing weapon capabilities.

In the April 26, 2014 **"Meaningful Progress With Iran,"** the editorial board's analysis argued that "Iran promised to dilute half the enriched uranium to a grade that is less susceptible to proliferation and to convert the rest to oxide for use in nuclear reactors...Another potential bright spot is a proposal by Vice President Ali Akbar Salehi, head of the Atomic Energy Organization of Iran, to redesign Iran's heavy water reactor near Arak to use low enriched uranium and limit the amount of plutonium the facility can produce."

The analysis did recognize that "the most alarming feature ...has been its ability to enrich uranium to 20 percent purity, which is a short technological hop to the higher level needed for nuclear bomb-grade fuel;" and even recognizing that "Iran began producing this grade fuel in 2010."

My question; what is it about the Iranian regime that has changed that much since 2010 that leads the board to trust that this time they really mean to comply, and may give up having a nuclear weapon?

Perhaps, the board, like many others, see the new Iranian president Hassan Rouhani as behind the progress they hope for. But the reality, that this new, smiling, and kind face is of a man who was and remains part of the same political mafia that beat, killed, and jailed students during the protests of 1999.

The second, one who does know better, Reuel Marc Gerecht, a former Iranian-targets officer for the CIA who wrote in the April 26, 2014 WSJ, that western observers, Obama administration officials, those believing economic sanctions are leading to successful inspections and compliance, and many Iranians themselves are in denial of the real intentions of the ruling cleric, and main decision maker, Ali Khomenei. Gerecht believes that "Mr. Khomenei's republic will endure great economic hardship to realize its dream of becoming a nuclear power."

At the heart of the West's current denial is the confusion and uncertainty of recognizing the insidious nature of Tehran's denial of the Holocaust, for in denying that Hitler killed 6,000,000 Jews, the Holycaust can be labeled " a narrative spun by Jews to engender guilt and special advantages over Muslims and others. In that light, Holocaust denial is both moral and politically essential."

The second reason, Gerecht contends; "Doing so implicitly negates the need of Israel's existence...if six million Jews didn't die, then Israel has no excuse to exist." He goes on to argue that it is not credible to consider that the "Jew-obsessed" Iranian leadership would cease its thirty year old aim to obtain nuclear weapons just because "Mr. Khomenei now wants hard currency-which is the essence of our sanctions policy and the primary leverage in the nuclear talks," for we must remember that the Supreme Leaders goal is the creation of an Islamic bloc, with the ability to turn back Judeo-Western imperialism, with Iran leading the way.

The NYT editorial staff reflect the naïve perception of European and American negotiators with their technical vision of trying to find the correct verifiable limitations on uranium enrichment, "heavy-water plutonium production and ballistic missile development to ensure that Tehran can't develop a nuke."

The Iranian perceptions are based on a totally different set of perspectives, a much larger religious conflict. The Supreme Leader does not just see the murder of six million Jews as just a "fiction," but a "devious way...for 'cultural vandals to inject doubt and atheism...hedonism and decadence' into the faithful Iranian people."

In conclusion, Gerecht writes that; "the Iranian regime is unlikely now to be humbled by Western officials – those diplomats who are so well-briefed in their nuclear dossiers, so hopeful that economics is the universal religion, so discomfited when their negotiating partners start railing about Jews and the Holocaust.

With diplomacy failing, as far as Israel is concerned, and Netanyahu's lack of leverage with the U.S., he has fallen back to a move that would have been admired by Sun Tzu, a geopolitical move: in December 2013 Netanyahu visited with Putin in Moscow. With its survival perceived to be in jeopardy, Netanyahu's moves are purely that of a realist. He must strip away all abstract ideals and concentrate on what the truth of Iran's behavior reveals. The difficult decisions, are acting upon what is believed to be this truth.

This is why I have dedicated this book to Elie Wiesel, for his position that "Iran must not be allowed to remain nuclear."

Chapter Seven

American Foreign Policy & the 800 Pound gorilla
Nuclear Proliferation

A case study: Japan's nuclear industry, 1980 – 2014

2014 Marshall Island lawsuit against 9 nuclear-armed nations

A History Lesson

I have always believed proliferation is best defined in systemic terms meaning that we have to look not only at the arsenals of nuclear armed nations and those attempting to develop a nuclear capability, to terrorists who want to acquire nuclear weapons, and the 439 nuclear power plants used for producing electrical power worldwide. (by 2013 there were 59 new reactors under construction and plans for 149 more). For an enemy that wanted to do damage, blowing up these plants would be close to dropping bombs.

The deadly elements of radiation are by their very nature systemic, for today's Plutonium, 239 Americium, 241 Iodine, 129, Uranium 235, Radium 2261, Strontium 90, and Cesium 137 will outlive the next 20 generations of today's families throughout the globe.

Nuclear proliferation today in 2014 is systemic in that it is indivisible from our planet earth's biosphere. The weapons, the power plants, the wastes, will affect what we breathe, eat, and drink. Proliferation has to be addressed in all its forms in order to perceive the totality of present and future threats. The most obvious area of proliferation concerns the staggering build-up of nuclear systems by the rogue states such as North Korea and Iran. The upgrading and modernizations of nuclear arsenals of the known nuclear powers are the second concern. The third concern is the market availability of non-nuclear countries to purchase nuclear weapon technologies, if the price is right, example Pakistan. The fourth concern is that the increase in the selling and proliferation of nuclear reactors for electrical power is the one sure way of threatening health and life in the event that we can prevent war itself. The sixth concern is that terrorists will use the knowledge available to construct nuclear weapons; or use money to buy nuclear weapons that can be purchased.

If the powerful nuclear states deal with their proliferation developments, the 3rd, 4th, 5th, and 6th concerns expressed above, could be dealt with. Every discussion of nuclear proliferation must begin with the main players. Let us simply look at the facts of proliferation to put the issues in perspective. The U.S. exploded its first atomic bomb in 1945 and the U.S.S.R. in 1949, followed by Britain in 1952, France 1960, China 1964, India 1974, Pakistan 1998, North Korea 2006, and Israel (unknown or 1967).

The U.S. developed its long range strategic capability in 1948 with the first intercontinental bomber, followed by the USSR in 1955. The Soviet fired the first successful ICBM in 1957, followed by the U.S. in 1958. China is the only other country with long range ICBM capabilities .

The U.S. produced the first SLBM in 1960, followed by the USSR in 1968, thereafter followed by China, Britain and France. MRV's were first developed by the U.S. in 1966, followed by the USSR in 1968. The first in ABM's was the U.S.S.R. in 1968 followed by the U.S. in 1975. In 1982 the U.S. had the long range cruise missile, and in 1983 the neutron bomb. The Soviets have developed both weapons. By 1984, both superpowers began to push ahead with programs to develop anti-satellite and space war weapons.

The bomb dropped on Hiroshima contained the equivalent of 15 tons of TNT; the MX missile is equivalent to 5,000,000 tons of TNT. The B-29 bomber traveled at 360 mph at a maximum distance of 4000 miles; today's MX travels 8,000 miles on its own power and can be accurate within feet of its target. Each MX missile carries 10 warheads which make it 300 times more powerful than all the American bombs dropped in WWII.

By 1984, both superpowers had a combined total of over 50,000 nuclear weapons capable of destroying the world 50 times. In 1945, the U.S. had the only three bombs in the world. Today, an artillery shell can now deliver more explosive nuclear force than these 1945 bombs. A bomber can carry a dozen cruise missiles, each being able to travel 1500 miles on their own and have a destructive force 13 times more powerful than the 1945 weapons. One U.S. Trident submarine has the destructive power of 5,000 Hiroshima type atomic bombs.

By 2014 the deployment of strategic nuclear weapons is real and profound: USA 1,922, Russia 2,484, UK 160, France 290, India 80-100. The total inventory of states holding nuclear weapons are: USA 7.352, Russia 4,484, UK 225, France 300, China 250, India 80-199, Pakistan 90-100, Israel 80-200, North Korea 10.

Think for a moment about the threats posed if electrical nuclear power plants are blown in any country, and the cross border tensions that exists in 2014. Russia has 33 nuclear plants and the Ukraine 15; South Korea has 23, India has 21 and Pakistan 3. Or for terrorist concerns in the US, that has 104 reactors.

The 1968 Non-Proliferation Treaty bans the transfer of weapons or weapons technology to non-nuclear states. The treaty requires safeguards on all nuclear facilities, and its philosophical intent was to commit the five major nuclear powers to halt the arms race. One hundred and nineteen states signed the NPT, but in addition to China and France many states have not signed the 1968 NPT treaty. For example, India, Brazil, Argentina, Israel, Pakistan, South Africa, and Chile have not signed.

India's entry into the nuclear club in 1974 can be used as a prototype of proliferation in today's world. India's perception of global politics changed as did her position on nuclear proliferation resulting from the felling of powerlessness India experienced in dealing with China, Pakistan, and the United States. India's painful war with China in 1962, the Conflicts with Pakistan through the 1960's culminating with a United States/Chinese supported Pakistan during the Bangladesh war of 1971, the experience of seeing the nuclear-powered American aircraft carrier U.S.S. Enterprise with its supportive task force, sailing into the Bay of Bengal during the 1971 crisis, all contributing toward India's desire for a nuclear deterrent.

Argentina found itself confronted with nuclear weapons of the British Navy during the Falkland War. Argentina has not signed the Treaty of Tlatelolco or the 1968 NPT treaty, but the British violated both treaties by bringing nuclear weapons into Argentina's waters. Both the United States during the 1971 Bangladesh war and Britain during the Falkland war should have displayed prudence by keeping "anything" nuclear out of the theater waters during the conflicts.

It was three years after the 1971 conflict that India detonated its first nuclear bomb; In 1991 Argentina and Brazil ratified a bilateral inspection agreement to verify both countries pledges to use nuclear energy only for peaceful purposes, and in 1995 Argentina acceded to the NPT as a non-nuclear weapon state.

The United States does have leadership options in dealing with proliferation in Latin America, and elsewhere. The hemisphere is not doomed to proliferation. Cuba is a stumbling block for the U.S. The Treaty of Tlatelolco is easily implemented for it only addresses weapons; but the N.P.T. is the most desirable, for it bans the entire nuclear threat. Iraq signed the N.P.T. in 1967, but it surely did not impress the George W. Bush administration. Israel knocked out Iraq's nuclear reactor in 1981, which rather than curtailing Iraq's nuclear ambitions, probably fueled them. If Iraq used chemical weapons against Iran in the 1980s, the later thought was what would Iraq do with a nuclear bomb? In addition to the N.P.T. treaty there have been many agreements which aim to curtail proliferation.

Many of these agreements, protocols, and treaties bear little resemblance to the world they are addressing. If nuclear technology cannot be neutralized politically, its devils will take much life from this earth. Governments must address the nuclear future as if they would defend their own borders, for borders mean nothing without life. What happens when your ecosystem begins to signal that radiation from nuclear power plants are damaging to life?

WHAT IS PLUTONIUM?

Plutonium is a man-made element that did not exist in nature until 1940. It was created at the University of California by a team of scientists whose director later recalled storing all they produced, then the world's entire amount, in a match box in his desk. At this time in the early 1940's workers noticed the eerie phenomenon of plutonium oxide in a tray, "breathing" as it were, with a life of its own. Known as plutonium 239, when it emits what is known as an alpha particle, it becomes uranium 235, "whose most spectacular property is also exhibited by plutonium 239: the ability to sustain a chain reaction." (10)   It was soon obvious to insiders that plutonium 239, like uranium 235 would be potential raw material for constructing a nuclear bomb.   Plutonium does not exist in nature.   It is manufactured in uranium-fueled reactors.   For example, a large light water reactor produces about 500 pounds of plutonium a year. If plutonium is extracted from used fuel, it can be used in another reactor, and substituted for about 1/4 (one-fourth) of the normal amount of uranium.   Plutonium's potential use in breeder reactors makes it a serious threat as a major fuel of the future, since it is highly toxic and can be used to make bombs. Plutonium extracted from the waste during reprocessing can be used in weapons; as India displayed in 1974 by exploding a nuclear "device", but vowed at that time to never to make nuclear weapons.   By 1983, Indian officials declared a lack of sufficient storage space for its radioactive waste compelled reprocessing. India's nuclear power plant in question was American built, but shipments of enriched uranium, and spare parts for its obsolete engineering, were banned by the US in 1978, even though President Carter approved the sale of 38 tons of uranium in 1980. Later, President Reagan and Prime Minister Indira Gandhi agreed to allow France to supply enriched uranium, while West Germany and France were to supply any spare parts not supplied by the US.

HEALTH EFFECTS OF NUCLEAR RADIATION FROM POWER REACTORS (LONG BEFORE JAPAN, 2011) NUCLEAR WEAPONS TESTS

Industrial nuclear reactors such as those used to generate electricity are the most insidious success story of "scientific" salesmanship ever perpetrated upon mankind. Many "scientists" proclaimed nuclear reactors were safe, the "economists" claimed they ought to save money; ultimately they will not save money, and they will always be a threat to the environments surrounding them, and then some. Thus, Three Mile Island, Chernobyl, and Japan 2011.

Once referred to as "Peaceful Nuclear Reactors," industrial reactors globally numbering close to 439 in 2014 are capable with alternate degrees of conversion, of producing between four and eight thousand nuclear bombs a year. Basic engineering problems, some recently uncovered and perhaps more yet to be discovered, reveal that (As I quote from my 1982 book on China) "all nuclear reactor cores presently operating and under construction will eventually leak, bringing unprecedented problems to future generations." I wrote this for these leaks will be caused by the failures of support systems such as values, cooling failures, or human error.

The waste from these industrial reactors must be disposed of since the wastes remain deadly to living organisms for hundreds of thousands of years. So it appears that if the military technology of nation-states doesn't do us in, peacefully-intended technology will.

The diplomatic complexities must be dealt with above the state level for there is no leader capable of having such vast global influence. International *organization and* global politics presents the only level at which nuclear threats can be dealt with. Whether loved, hated, respected or disrespected, the U.N. better be made to work on nuclear solutions and alternatives in our politically unstable world. The United Nations is the most logical political forum to investigate and report threats of industrial reactors, and to debate and negotiate solutions to the problems unmasked. Disarmament and Arms Control issues have commanded increased attention at the United Nations over the years in terms of energy, time, publications, and financial expenses. This is a positive development since addressing the long term threats of industrial reactors *can not* be de-coupled from the more immediate threats of nuclear weapons. The United States must take the lead for it is in America's vital interest; and with "Three Mile Island", it has engineering and scientific experiences that could be used in teaching the world to de-atomize itself, excepting for medical purposes. No plutonium ever existed before scientist in America produced it. The United States therefore has the responsibility to lead the issue of nuclear proliferation through the global structure of the United Nations.

Some history:

The U.N. could ultimately use its good offices "in some agreed upon procedure resembling a muted peacekeeping force" to deal with nuclear proliferation of industrial reactors. Consistent with United Nations peacekeeping efforts, it will be the host country deciding to accept U.N. personnel, in the form of inspection teams, or dismantling crews. Once the problems associated with industrial nuclear uses are recognized, there will be tremendous global pressures for some agreed upon procedure to deal with these most deadly man-made time bombs.

By the mid-1980's major concern remained focused on nuclear war technology while most of the world remained unconcerned with any future threats from industrial nuclear equipment guaranteed by many scientists, engineers and politicians as "safe." By 1983, the U.S. had 140 nuclear power plants operating or under construction; and the U.S. Supreme Court encouraged further proliferation by ruling that the Nuclear Regulatory Commission (NRC) "need not consider the environmental consequence of nuclear waste disposal as a factor in licensing individual nuclear power plants." Some communities have nuclear wastes others do not. Some states in the U.S. house more radioactive waste than others. The Nuclear Regulatory Commission rule concerning nuclear active wastes assumes they can be stored without damaging the environment. The U.S. Supreme Court has ruled that this NRC rule is constitutional and the majority opinion written by Justice Sandra 0'Conner implies that licensing of a new nuclear plant does not have to be contingent on the environmental effects of nuclear wastes.

Radioactive wastes from experimental laboratories, hospitals, and factories are a major problem alone, but waste from power reactors place the waste in a problem area not yet part of public concern. Congress decided in 1980 that low-level radiation (by whose standard?) wastes were the responsibility of the individual states. For may years Washington and South Carolina have served as dump sites for other states. The courts contend that if any state belongs to a compact with other states, it can exclude dumping to outsiders. For example, ten Northeastern states presently dump their nuclear wastes in South Carolina. As of 1986, South Carolina will have the authority to turn away such waste deposits. Some states such as New Jersey contend that it should not house nuclear garbage because of dense populations and flooding problems. When states agree to join a compact with other states; they must agree to eventually be host to nuclear garbage, since every 20 years a site will be closed and a new site in a different state will be opened. Any state that decides to go it alone will have to bury all its nuclear garbage forever. It is unlikely that states like Maine that have a small waste problem, would wish to bury the nuclear garbage of New York, Pennsylvania, and Massachusetts which produce huge amounts of wastes.

By 2014, on the global level, there are close to 100 known graveyards for nuclear garbage, in addition to unknown deposits having been dumped into the oceans of the world. By the year 2020 there could be more than 1000 nuclear reactors globally producing nuclear garbage that remains deadly for hundreds of thousands of years. Surprisingly enough, China in 1984 was negotiating with West Germany to bury Bonn's nuclear garbage in China for $514 billion; with the implication that China may consider burying much of the West's nuclear garbage, a decision that would pale in comparison with damage done to China by Western nations in the 19th Century. Any state in America or any country that houses these wastes must consider the dangers to its environmental future. It must also be considered that these "wastes" are materials for bombs.

Ireland does not have its own nuclear industry, but must deal with radioactive contamination of the Irish Sea caused by British plants. One plant called "Windscale Works" on the northwest coast of England has dumped plutonium wastes into the Irish Sea over the three decades. The plant with its four nuclear reactors has put more radiation into the Irish Sea than all previous discharges into the world oceans excepting perhaps the Russians. Each day the Windscale plant pumps 1.2 million gallons of radioactive water into the sea through a 1.5 mile pipeline. Windscale is the oldest and largest nuclear recycling plant in the world; the stuff comes hotter than a desert's sands at noon, and is chemically processed to make different types of plutonium, some of which has been sold to the U.S. for bomb production. One of the wastes from this reprocessing is Cesium, "an element produced as a by-product of decaying uranium fuel." The contamination from radioactive Cesium was 250 times the normal in local seas, and traces were found as far away as Norway and Greenland. Accidents at the plant have been linked with radioactive driftwood, metal beer and soda cans, seaweed, and many other contaminated materials and living organisms found washed up on beaches. Windscale had a nuclear accident 22 years before the 1979 "Three Mile Island" that was "40 to 400 times more deadly in radiation than that released in Pennsylvania. In 1957 a reactor used to make atomic bombs caught fire and radiated the skies over England. We can expect that it will be a long time before a global consciousness is activated to address the problem because Britain and America are unwilling to accept the fact of future threats to the environment. With close to 400 industrial reactors operating or under construction, what will the problems of nuclear leaks, contamination, and waste become for the 21st Century?

The waste nightmare will continue since each nuclear reactor in the world only uses less than 5% of the uranium it is fed. So reprocessing plants recover the valuable plutonium residue from the partly used uranium. This plutonium is used for some power reactors, and bombs, while the additional wastes are disposed of again for almost, forever. There are reprocessing plants in Japan, India, and France. The U.S. has a government-operated plant in Hanford, Washington, and the Reagan Administration built a commercial reprocessing nuclear plant in South Carolina. Radioactivity is eventually washed from the land; but how can it wash from the ocean? The harm to the lowest levels on the life chain of the sea is presently difficult to measure, for the greatness of the oceans makes measurement of radioactive threat inaccurate for now. Perhaps, when the whales die, we will understand that our seas are irredeemably soon to follow, for radioactivity seems to live forever when measured against the lifespan of human generations. By 2014 there are 16 nations who never had nuclear power or pledged to stay that way; and seven pledging to phase out nuclear power, which includes Petra Kelly's Germany.

CASE STUDY: BOMBING OF NEVADA, UTAH, MARSHALL ISLANDS.

"We live in interesting times," so the Chinese Curse puts it. Most Americans trust their government to not just provide security from foreign threats, but to pursue policies that enhances the health and welfare of our nation and its people. But a close study of atomic testing tells a questionable story. In 1946, not long after the last shot of WW II was fired the U.S. began testing new atomic and hydrogen weapons by bombing the island of Bikini in the South Pacific Marshall Islands (within a twelve year period the US conducted 67 nuclear tests). Tests were conducted in the summer of 1946 after the explosions of several atom bombs and the results of the tests were published in a study in 1948. The radioactivity measured was considered so dangerous that any method of decontamination attempted would be useless. The conclusion argued that there was no real defense against dangerous levels of nuclear contamination, no medical or sanitary safeguards a population could rely on in preparing for such an event, and that the land and its people would be affected for centuries.

Between 1951 and 1962 the American government detonated over 100 atomic bombs at the nuclear test site near Las Vegas, Nevada. Skeptics of all political persuasions failed to speak out about the effects of radioactive fallout, in spite of evidence tracing deadly components of nuclear fallout through the living chain. For example, an element called SR- 90 was found in milk children drank, having found its way through the food chain in grass contaminated with Sr90 which cows ate. Sr90 "is one of the most biologically harmful elements of radioactivity and the main determinant is agricultural land contamination."

In 1963, in what may have been President John F. Kennedy's greatest achievement, a nuclear test ban treaty was signed with the Soviet Union, relegating testing to underground. The controversy over threats to human health continued. How many children developed leukemia or brain tumors as a result of those test between 1951 and 1962? Perhaps we shall never know, for the broken hearts of parents of victims whimpered silently and often alone, far removed from the thunder of the political arena.

In the early 21st century research doctors in the Mid-West who had been collecting the teeth from Children who lived during these periods of testing found deadly levels of Sr90 in these teeth.

Most studies of cancer deaths from the Hiroshima and Nagasaki bombings dealt with survivors' health from direct radiation. Few of these studies measured the radioactive fallout in relation to exposure and health. Few studies of "downwind" contamination affecting local population exist. In March of 1954, a 15-megaton hydrogen bomb explosion on Bikini Atoll yielded little warnings concerning fallout threats until confirmation by medical authorities. The 1962 study on the fallout effects *on* the islands of the Bikini Atoll mistakenly concluded: It could be generally agreed that all of the radioactive products of all the test detonations to that time had produced a total human exposure that was small compared to the exposure to natural background radiation.

By 2014 these statements were proven to be false and is part of the arguments and indictments presented with the April 2014 Marshall Island law suit against 9 nuclear armed powers

In 1977, a University of Utah cancer specialist began testing the "theory" that the tests resulted in cancer, which he at first skeptically dismissed as "overheated *environmental hysteria.*" After a year of examining death certificates, confirming diagnosis and conducting medical studies, the cancer specialist changed his opinion; *and* concluded "an association" between fallout exposure and higher-than-expected incidences of childhood leukemia in Utah.

In 1979, the specialist Dr. Lyon, published the findings of his study in the New England Journal of Medicine testifying that the average incidence of leukemia deaths for all children born throughout Utah from 1951-58 increased by 40% during this period. During that period of intense testing, calculations of expected deaths from leukemia would have been placed at 13. The number of deaths was 34. In Utah counties closest to the test site, they were 3.4 times higher.

By 1983, threats from industrial nuclear reactors became the new health debate while the U.S. government continued to deny its irresponsible policies of the 1950's and 1960's. In the 1950's, entire families in small towns like St. George, Utah would climb the surrounding hills in the early morning hours to view magnificent flashes of light. These people thought they were witnessing history, and the government authorities who had sufficient warning from scientists, rarely warned anyone. Dr. Knapp a former operations analyst for the Atomic Energy Commission and later with the Defense Department testified in court that the downwind fallout might have been up to "1000 times what government monitors reported". He revealed that one of the "dirtiest" tests in 1953 code-named "Harry" could have killed half of the 5000 residents of St. George (100 miles north of the test) if a thunderstorm had washed the fallout into the city. Dr. Knapp further testified that personnel responsible for monitoring public health threats ignored knowledge that contradicted government perceptions skewed by overwhelmingly myopic concern with Russians catching up. Some Atomic Energy Commission officials even deleted information on government reports of individual blasts; many of which were conducted without warning, subjecting patriotic, god loving, hard working, heartland Americans to health risks beyond their rights of awareness, a privileged sanctuary in a democracy respecting "life, liberty, and the pursuit of happiness."

A dramatic article appeared in the Professional Journal of The American Medical Association (JAMA) on January 13, 1984. This traditionally cautious journal took its first position on the dangerous life threatening effects from both radioactive fallout and the venting of underground nuclear tests. For example the 15 megaton bomb that destroyed Bikini Atoll in 1954 caused radioactive damage to the populations on islands such as Rongelap, which is located 180 Km. from Bikini Atoll. In 1959 the U.S. sent a medical-biological survey team to Rongelap. The team called a meeting and informed the people of Rongelap that all was well.

At the village meeting the main questions centered on the necessity for continued medical treatment for people who were generally in good health. It was difficult to explain to them that, though they appeared in good health and to have recovered from the acute effects of radiation, very little was known about the possible late effects of radiation, and continued examination was essential in order to detect and treat any untold effects should they arise. The coconut crab problem was brought up again. It was explained that fish poisoning had been going on in these islands for years and was not connected with radioactivity. After much discussion, it seemed that the people were satisfied with answers to their questions.

By 1984 the reports on Rongelap were quite different from the 1959 assumptions. The medical journal brought out that 77% of the children of Rongelap, younger than ten years at the time of the explosions, later required surgery for benign and malignant thyroid nodules. The children of Rongelap were the greatest victims, since the younger they were, the greater amount of radiation absorbed by their bodies. But it was not until 1964 that the benign and malignant thyroid tumors in the children of Rongelap began to appear.

Bikini, Rongelap, and Utrik are as mythic entities to many Americans, but Nevada and Utah hit home; and the JAMA study brought the discussion to American shores. What is most interesting in this study is the fact that Utah had the lowest incidence of cancer in the nation. The researchers attributed this to the lifestyle of the Mormons who comprised about 72 percent of Utah's population. The Mormons are urged to abstain from alcohol, tobacco, drugs, tea, coffee. Mormons normally had a cancer incidence that is 23 times below the national average; while non-Mormons in Utah have had a cancer incidence 16 times greater than that of Mormons. Even those Mormons living outside of Utah have reported a low incidence of cancer.

In 1951, the first of 600 nuclear bombs were tested in Nevada and through 1962 one hundred and eighty three of these tests were exploded in the atmosphere. These tests were normally exploded when the prevailing winds were not blowing toward Las Vegas or Los Angeles, but a "swath of radioactive fallout" fell over Utah. High explosive tests were made to study the dispersion of plutonium or uranium from nuclear weapons, contaminating northern Nevada and Utah. The populations in Nevada and Utah were not sufficiently warned to the possible threats and one area was contaminated with a plutonium concentration of 9.6 picocuries per square centimeter (p Ci/59). A picocurie of a radioactive isotope of an element is a quantity sufficient to produce 2.2 disintegrations per minute. These disintegrations release ionizing radiation. There are eight important isotopes of plutonium, but 239 PU is the predominant isotope and has a half-life of 24,390 years.

Estimates of radioactive iodine dosages to children less than five years old in St. George, Utah in 1953 were between 500 and 2,500. These were greater than the dosage of RAD's inflicted on the children of Rongelap. RAD is short for the word radiation, and is defined as a unit of absorbed dose of ionizing radiation equal to an energy of 100 ergs per gram of irradiated material. In Utah, as in Rongelap, it was the children whose bodies absorbed the most radiation. Animals absorb even more radiation than children. Following the 1953 tests, 4,000 sheep died in Utah. It appears that the weakest elements in the life chain are the most affected by radiation. For example: the children absorb more than adults, the animals more than the children; and the fetal lambs of pregnant sheep which in the 1953 aftermath received 20,000 to 40,000 RAD to thyroid glands. The mothers of these fetal lambs received, by comparison, only 1,500 to 1,600 RAD to their intestinal organs; while their external bodies were estimated to have received only 4 RAD. We can conclude from this that radiation is hundreds of times more damageable to the internal organs than any external machine or device could measure.

In other areas of Utah that were not as closely monitored such as the Southwestern portions, follow-up studies show a high increase in leukemia in children, 14 years after the nuclear tests. In 1984, more than 30 years since the first exposure, citizens of Utah were still being exposed to radioactive isotopes of every trace element. Radioactive gases in the air, contaminated soil, contaminated food and water are all cumulated in the body tissues. Results reveal an excess of cancer in Utah test cases between 1958 and 1966; and, an even greater excess between 1972 and 1980. The greatest incidence was leukemia and thyroid cancer, followed by lymphoma and breast cancer. There were excesses of cancers of the stomach, colon, brain tumors, bone, and melanoma. Between 1972 and 1980 Utah Mormons suffered 30 times more cancers than a decade earlier. Leukemia was preponderant early and persisted later, compatible with a prolonged period of exposure to radioactive fallout during 1951 through 1962 and afterward from the venting of 11 underground nuclear tests (1962-1979). This is in contrast to the peak of leukemia deaths in about 5 years among the Hiroshima-Nagasaki survivors after one exposure in 1945.

The JAMA article pointed out that Plutonium workers have a greater ratio of brain tumors than expected, eight times higher. The essence of the report is the admission that the Utah fallout is not only attributable to the evidence of excess incidence of cancer; but the largest increment of cancer in Utah was yet to come in the 1990's. In all, the figures of the JAMA article speak for themselves: exposures in southwestern Utah to radioactive fallout (1951 through 1962) from atmospheric nuclear detonations at the Nevada Test Site (NTS) were followed by smaller exposures (1962 through 1979) from venting of underground nuclear detonations. The cancer incidence in a 1951 cohort (4,125) of Mormon families in southwestern Utah near the NTS was compared with that of all Utah Mormons (1967 through 1975). There were 109 more cases of cancer than expected (288 observed/179 expected). Leukemia was most prominent early (1958 through 1966), with 19 cases, five times more than expected (3.6). The excess of leukemia persisted into the later period (1972 through 1980), with 12 cases observed, 3.4 expected. There was an increase in lymphoma. Excess cases of thyroid cancer appeared early and a notable excess appeared later (14/1.7). An excess of breast cancer was noted later (27/14). There were more cancers of the gastrointestinal tract than expected. There was an excess of melanoma (12/4.5/0, bone cancer (8/0.7), and brain tumors (9/3.9). A subgroup with history of acute fallout effects had a higher cancer incidence. That these cases can be associated with radiation exposures is supported by a comparison between groups of the ratio of cancers of more radiosensitive organs with all other types of cancer.

ONGOING DEBATE

One generation faces images of bombers dropping weapons and digs itself underground shelters. Intercontinental missiles of unstoppable quantities and qualities numb another generation into negative acceptance of luck or inevitability. Decentralization of nuclear potential globally creates anxiety among all nations. If these external manifestations of proliferation are not enough, the very existence of reactors sharing spaces in communities of families, completed the total, continual, and systemic threats posed by nuclear energy to all life on earth. The public threat today and upon many tomorrows remains beyond public awareness, as did yesterdays threats from above ground nuclear explosions. A nuclear reactor engineer who had worked for the Atomic Energy

Commission's Division of Naval Reactor, states the problem directly: "So called 'hard' scientists (physics, chemistry, astronomy) often criticize the 'soft' scientists (economics, sociology, political science) for taking positions on questions considered beyond their understanding. The 'hard' sciences yield precise answers whereas the 'soft' sciences yield ambiguity and uncertainty. Science has given us answers to many complex problems. Pasteur presented us with the germ theory of disease; the Augustinian monk, Mendel, discovered the laws of inheritance. Darwin gave us evolution theory. Newton, the father of the scientific revolution, set standards for those who followed his 17th Century discovery of the law of gravity. He left scientists with suggestions for humility and open-mindedness often forgotten by today's reductionists."

The urge to "reduce" every problem to the predictive pattern of physics is often too myopic in a world as complex as today's. Scientific "reductionism" has revealed how life is transmitted through the molecular blueprint we have come to know as DNA (deoxyribonucleic); but what are the answers to the affects of low-level radiation, dioxin, , food additives, bad air, polluted air and water? Overly confident scientific experts differ so frequently over these questions that they leave little ground for public confidence, much less any hope of intelligent conclusions, generally agreed upon. Hard scientists criticize the social scientists for their lack of predictability and failure to yield precise answers. But social scientists deal with the most complicated of all subjects, for the laboratory is man's culture and human psychology. Einstein claimed that physics was simple in relation to the complex changing nature of politics. Even the scientific standard bearer, Newton, believed that nature was ultimately opaque to human understanding. Human nature is unpredictable, and since science fails us in being unable to live up to its own announced strength of predictability, it is imperative that the public study and help decide its own future. There is much common sense among the masses, and sufficient public wisdom to influence policy-making political decision, intelligently.

Scientific research may often be controlled, but creativity works best in ways only it knows. Newton's great discovery of the law of gravity had a humble beginning. He saw an apple fall from a tree and wondered if the same force reached the moon. It was later that he discovered how gravity acts between any two heavenly bodies. Today, we have facts and questions dealing with our most perplexing problems of survival itself, and what we basically need to do is think. We must think, and believe in the intelligence of our conclusion.

By 2000, new scientific studies on ionizing radiation, considered the most dangerous type, suggested that all previously held theories of health and radiation had to be dramatically re-evaluated; radiation is now believed to produce cancer 4-20 times greater than were judged in the past. America and British veterans who observed close up atom bomb tests in the 1940's developed cancer at much higher rates than was expected; the common cause was ionizing radiation.

Radiation from nuclear sources has sufficient energy to kick loose some electrons that are embedded in molecules of human tissue. This breaks down the numerous and varied structures in human cells, leaving the molecules from which they are torn to produce chemical reactions that would not normally take place. This translates into cancerous tumors and leukemia. The British epidemiologist, Dr. Alice Stewart, writing in the April 1983 medical journal, The Lancet, revealed that the British veterans of the 1950's South Pacific nuclear tests suffered an unusually high incident of cancer. An American epidemiologist, Edward Radford, studies the affects of "very low" doses of radiation from a uranium dump in Pennsylvania. This low level radiation appears to have more than doubled the rate of thyroid abnormalities in the local population.

The most dramatic source of experience on the health effects of ionizing radiation are the 80,000 survivors of Hiroshima and Nagasaki. Scientists since 1945 have been carefully evaluating the types and numbers of cancer cases. A 1982 report by scientists at the Japanese-American Radiation Effects Research Foundation has challenged original estimates of the number of cancer victims among the survivors. The Japanese studies are important and indicate that the risks are twice as deadly as previously reported. Cooperative Japanese/American studies continue to probe away at the most horribly unique case study resulting from American bombing of two Japanese cities.

Nearly sixty years after radiation exposure to the people of Hiroshima and Nagasaki statistics continue to be evaluated by the medical profession. In JAMA, in 2006, reported a continuation of increased risk of thyroid cancer. The average age of the subjects (4,000 survivors) was 70 years and 67 percent were women. The findings: 32 percent of the men and 51 percent of the women had evidence of thyroid disease. Thyroid cancer was present in 2.2 percent of subjects. Radiation was thought to account for 37 percent of thyroid cancers. These Japanese paid a price with high rates of cancer.

Japan is unique, and for this reason was selected by the author as a case study.

JAPAN: A CASE STUDY   1980-2014

Japan was chosen as a case study for three reasons: One, it is the only nation to have experienced massive atomic destruction as a result of war. Secondly, Japan is the only nation with so many nuclear reactors on unstable geography like volcanoes. Thirdly,

Japan is the only modern-industrialized nation so reliant on imports for its energy needs. Japan, smaller than California, supports a population over one-half the size of the entire U.S. soon to near the 120 million mark, with one of the highest density problems in the world, with over 800 people per square mile. Japan is poor in the resources needed for a modern industrial society. She must import 80% of her energy raw materials and 99% of her oil needs. In light of these realities the temptation to go nuclear was persuasive. (This case study ends with the 2011 Fukushima disaster and its aftermath).

In April 1981, Japanese scientists examined samples of mud from the sea-bed of Tsuraga Bay. They discovered radioactivity in the samples to be ten to one-hundred times higher than normal. The radioactivity did not date from 1945, but was a direct result of the leaking of a nuclear plant. In light of Japan's experiences coupled with her volcanic geography, why had Japan taken the nuclear route? Japan's primary motivation for going nuclear was economic and financial. A succession of postwar conservative governments placed "Increase Production" as the motive-image motto for all Japanese. It would in time significantly change an entire world's perception of Japan and its people. It stood as a rigorous example of a nation regaining respect in a grudging world. Japan has had nuclear facilities within its community since 1950 and by 1983 over 25 nuclear power plants provided power for what was proudly referred to as "Japan Inc."

Japan became addicted to the idea that its continued economic growth is crucially dependent on the expansion of nuclear power. Seeing nuclear power as the key to the future could take Japan's industrial power source down a costly long-term and predictably dangerous trail.

On the subject of nuclear weapons, Japan unilaterally professed that it would not build, possess, or allow nuclear weapons, and has additionally signed the multilateral NPT treaty. Japan's non-nuclear stance on weapons thereby reflects a "nuclear allergy" resulting from her victimization in WWII, but deep problems remain to be dealt with. Most Japanese perceive the NPT treaty to be an "unequal treaty" Japanese political parties and business interests have often criticized it. In fact, when the NPT was being formally accepted by other nations, the Japanese waited until the last moment to sign, after debating signing for 1 1/2 years.

Japan's participation in the NPT was often taken for granted in a world perceiving Japan in the 1980s primarily in images and models of economic success. Fundamentally, the NPT does not present a barrier if Japan decides it needs nuclear weapons; for the treaty in itself contains no built-in guarantees, and the Japanese surely have the capabilities to convert peaceful technology if they ever arrive at that crossroad. But, this depends on the global political environment. Japan remains concerned with the fact that China is not a signatory of NPT, and the 21st century conflict over the islands in the China seas raised new questions for Japan.

Years ago the Japanese became aware of the gap between consecutive American administration rhetoric of non-proliferation, and America's actions. They are reminded of the non-proliferation "intentions" of the Johnson, Nixon, Carter, and Reagan administrations, and the concomitant arms build-up during those administrations. As discussed earlier, it was the U.S. that kept raising the nuclear threshold by its near-paranoia in demanding nuclear superiority over the Soviet arsenal. The Japanese accepted America's "deterrence" concept by allowing over 100 American military installations on the islands of Japan, that continues to this day in 2014, evidenced by President Obama's April visit welcomed by Japanese leaders.

Yet energy consumption in Japan has grown at a faster rate than any nation in the world. By 2011, nuclear power plants produced 30 to 40 percent of Japan's electricity. In spite of recently politicized public opinion, signs of future radiation safety problems, especially after Fukushima, the government ignores.

The problem is that the Japanese government has decided on a nuclear energy future. These are developmental projects for advanced converter reactors, enrichment of uranium, reprocessing of spent fuels, and work on breeder reactors and nuclear fission, at a time when problems with older technology have not yet been sufficiently solved. For example, a nuclear fuel reprocessing plant began operation at the Tokaimura nuclear plant back in 1981, and immediately problems arose:

The jet pump for the melting furnace broke down. Operations resumed, but there was a malfunction in the acid recovery unit, two more accidents - a leaking steam pipe and a small fire ignited by sparks from a welding machine - followed in quick succession. In spite of such problems a second reprocessing plant was completed in 1991. In March 1982, the first uranium enrichment pilot plant began operation, then the construction of a commercial enriching plant that opened in 1990 . A liquid metal fast breeder reactor was developed, which is much more sophisticated than the converter reactor that gave Japan its first completed nuclear fuel cycle in 1980. A fast breeder reactor allow for approximately 70% more efficient in its use of uranium than light water reactors.

The lessons of the 1979 Three Mile Island accident in the United States were not lost on the Japanese who sent their own investigation team to study what had gone wrong. Protest movements picked-up momentum in Japan, and the government responded by changing its sales technique to the Japanese public. Whereas nuclear power had been sold to the public as economically necessary for continued prosperity, nuclear power was then being portrayed for its safety features in the Japanese press.

The 1981 accident as the Tsuruga nuclear plant was difficult to cover-up, particularly with the tremendous increase of radioactivity discovered on the Tsuruga Bay seabed as described earlier. Investigations had discovered 21 earlier unreported accidents, but the "Tsuruga" accident of April, 1981 was the most telling, until 2011. A holding tank had overflowed for three hours dumping forty cubic meters of "Radioactive sludge" onto the plant floor. The cleanup crew swept the sludge into plastic buckets which were emptied down an illegal drain into Tsuruga Bay; all of the resulting from a simple failure when a man failed to close a valve. Later, a worker failed to turn off the automatic warning signal, and no alarm was sounded to warn everyone of the accident. Investigations revealed that it was common practice to discharge water used to clean the radioactive treatment facilities through a "secret manhole" which emptied into the bay. Research indicated many other nuclear mishaps at other Japanese nuclear facilities. The Mihama plant, for example, had a history of problems determined serious enough to close the facility in 1974 with a steam generator accident, and in 1977 when a nuclear fuel rod snapped and went unreported. The Mihama accident occurred in the Summer of 1981 with a leak of three tons of radioactive water and released radioactive gases; both of which, the company claimed, presented no harm to the public.

Japan must dispose of its nuclear wastes for other uses, but it has yet no policy. Hundreds of thousands of drums containing nuclear wastes are being stored until a policy is decided upon. Meanwhile, the Japanese public is aware of accidents that have even occurred in storage areas. It is said in Japan that, "We have built a house with no toilets."

Japan's unique geography of volcanic islands leaves the future balancing on engineering skills boastfully weighed against the titanic uncertainties of nature's power. Earthquakes crack and destroy the earth's surface, as well as creating islands. While this case study was being conducted thirty years ago, Japan experienced a series of dangerous earthquakes. The May 1983 earthquakes were not the first warnings. (and by 2014 there were 20 more earthquakes) On March 21, 1982 the southern tip of Hokkaido Island was hit by an earthquake with the intensity of six on a Japanese scale of seven, injuring over a hundred people and ripping apart highways. Strangely enough, a year later the government of Japan decided to build the first nuclear power plant in this very area. One day after the government's announcements, Southern Hokkaido was again hit by two earthquakes, not severe, but eerily untimely. Government spokesmen, speaking with the same conviction as nuclear engineers, claimed that the nuclear reactors could survive any future earthquake. Japanese citizens who once flocked to their shores protesting nuclear armed American ships in Japanese waters now looked inward at their own nuclear time-bombs, especially since all 48 reactors are located on the beaches of Japan's coasts, vulnerable to a tsunami such as the one that hit in 2011.

Japan appears to be at the most critical crossroad in its history since 1945. The antiwar provisions built into the Japanese constitution, the nation's unique victimization in the only nuclear war, and Japan's signature on the NPT (non-proliferation treaty), no longer seem to dominate Japan's perception of the world. The vulnerability felt from threatening nuclear testing by a North Korea who have fired rockets over Japan, a new Chinese navy capable of projecting China's ambitions over disputed islands, not to mention China's nuclear capabilities.

.   American politics, despite its mercurial pendulum of an Asian policy, has penetrated Japanese policy-making to a degree that has no counterpart in the economic sector. If American businessmen could penetrate the "Keiretsu" (a Japanese business group with the same exclusivity as exemplified by America's Federal Reserve Bank and American banks) with the ease exercised in political influence, American business interests would not be complaining of unfair Japanese competition in the market, second only to the complaints against China.

The 48 nuclear reactors on Japanese islands would turn the nation into a nuclear nightmare in time of war. The ghosts of Nagasaki and Hiroshima appear to have been relegated to past symbols and Japan appears to have completely shut down dissent about nuclear power until 2011.

I personally felt the brunt of the Japanese government's sensitivity to criticism of its nuclear industry. I once gave a lecture in New Zealand on China's ambitions in the Pacific, and in the midst of complementing them on their being the first nation in the world to declare a nuclear free zone I contrasted their decision with Japan's, when I said that "despite the experience of Nagasaki and Hiroshima, the country now derives more than a quarter of its power from nuclear energy...building nuclear reactors on volcanic islands, Japan reneged on its responsibility to its people."

My comments were published in an Auckland newspaper and two days later my speaking tour in Japan was cancelled; citing visa problems.

FUKUSHIMA, 2011

In the 1980s there was a very brave and beautiful young German woman who has been largely forgotten. Petra Kelly was a strong advocate for the elimination of nuclear weapons and power plants and pushed this agenda as a member of Germany's Green Party. I had the honor of meeting her in Germany and believe to this day that her death by gunshot wounds from her lover and former Army commander had more to do with those opposed to her advocacy than has even been investigated or proven. She would cheer from her grave at the current Chancellor of Germany, Angela Merkel, who since Fukushima has announced that she wishes to phase out nuclear power plants from German soil.

The earthquake and tsunami that destroyed Japan's reactors in Fukushima in 2011 were a vindication of the above case study, as well as remarks the author made about Japan's government reneging in its responsibilities to its own people who had suffered so directly from the American atomic bombs in WW II, during the speech in New Zealand

Japan became of interest to me, for having studied and taught Japanese history and culture, having taken a university course in geology that included the professor taking us on field trips to various mountain ranges in Pennsylvania, West Virginia., and Virginia to teach us how to touch, feel, and smell stones or soil in understanding faults and earthquakes, and having walked the majestic mountains and lands of Japan with my curiosity out there; it was dumfounding for me to comprehend why nuclear plants on the volcanic islands known as Japan.

The 2011 Fukushima disaster was not an accident, it was negligence on the part of the government, the result of a time bomb, and it will happen again. The company made a mess in failing to clean up the mess but in warning the people closest to the disaster. The earthquake and tsunami knocked out Fukushima's complex cooling systems in March 2011 that caused meltdown in three reactors. The release of deadly radiation was as great as the 1986 disaster at Chernobyl, rated at a " Level 7," the highest on the scale, a fact that regulators hid from the public.

Tokyo Electric Power, or Tepco, played down the deadly releases of cesium and strontium hundreds of times higher than legal safety limits and denied they were leaking into the sea. To cope, Tepco stored the leaking fluids into about 1,000 tanks but 500 yards from the Pacific Ocean. They not only made a mess of the cleanup but lied leaving thousands of vulnerable families in radioactive areas.

Geologists had warned that four of the five reactors in Fukushima were built on active faults, but as pointed out earlier with regard to the building of the first nuclear reactor in Hokkaido in 1982, such warning were ignored. Also ignored are reports that streams coming down from the mountains and running through Fukushima cannot be stopped and will be washing this radiation into the Pacific Ocean for a long period of time.

It was not until August 2013, when 300 tons of highly contaminated water leaked from one of the storage tanks into the

Pacific Ocean that Japanese regulators finally admitted any release into the sea. Can you image, this was the first time an admission of an environmental calamity. The concern, is that this one leak reveals that the other storage tanks could eventually leak...500 yards from the sea. The latest desperate solution is to surround the plant was a huge underground ice wall. Yes, an ICE WALL.

Japan's denial is rooted into a culture no Westerner can really comprehend. The individual will lived at the point of a blade, if that is what he or she is " supposed to do." I knew this when I originally wrote the case study, and this has only been a confirmation. If the Japanese government does not shut down all of its nuclear power plants this will happen again.

10/22/2013   " After Storm, Toxic Water Overflows In Japan,"

Reporter Martin Fackler reported that a storm had dropped so much rain that the barriers built to contain the toxic reactor waters from spilling into the Pacific Ocean were breached by overflows of this toxic waste now flowing into the sea. These concrete walls were not high enough; the barrier was breached in 11 places.

At some of these breaches the radiation levels were 71 times beyond the limit our bodies can take, and most disturbing of all, contained one of the deadliest forms of radiation, Strontium-90, that killed thousands upon thousands of young children during the heavy testing of nuclear weapons in the atmosphere before John Kennedy's Nuclear Test Ban Treaty of 1963 ended the testing. I find it so irresponsible that here we are in 2013 and this Strontium-90, that should have been banned from the earth, is going to eventually take the lives of children not yet ten, in the land of The Rising Sun. Strange to me, this is where it all began for me, the anti nuclear crusade. As I have written elsewhere, after my five year old son's death in 1968 I did more research, on why? And discovered it was strontium-90 from nuclear fallout being absorbed into the grasses and earth, cows eating the grass, we giving our children milk. Bingo. There are, as I have written, researchers who have examined teeth of children who died of cancer during certain periods and found high levels of strontium-90 in the teeth of those children.

Where did this strontium –90 come from? Just like nuclear war itself or testing bombs by blowing them up in the atmosphere; it came from the original explosion of the plant and the meltdown of three nuclear reactors. It was a hydrogen explosion that blew the roof off of the building of Reactor N. 4. What many do not realized is that it left 1,500 radioactive fuel assemblies exposed in 2011, and it was not until November 3013 that an attempt was made to remove this fireball from hell from the pool in which it sits. The trick is that when the rods are lifted out with cranes they must be kept submerged in water, the only way to block gamma radiation from being released, killing not only the construction crew but immeasurable damage as the now enflamed dry rods spew radiation into the atmosphere carried by winds and water into many communities far from the plant. The trick becomes more problematic for the rods have to be lifted at least one hundred feet into the air.

Reading reports from Japan brings me back nearly forty years to reading and listening to specialists, scientists, professors at Florida International University who read a few books on the subject for the first time speaking at academic conferences, right wing Republicans, and others so sure of themselves on these issues of nuclear dangers, and considered banning of nuclear power plants a position for poets and dreamers, not men and women of learning. It is incomprehensible to me that the Japanese government has allowed the company who caused all this, Tepco, to be responsible for fixing it. Not only should this be a Japanese government project; but I believe nuclear catastrophes of this severity should be addressed by the global community through the United Nations, for these are not just threats to any one nation, but many others, particularly those in the neighborhood.

Estimates suggest it may take 5 years to extricate the rods. What happens if this 90 ton package is lifted 100 feet up and an earthquake hits? Is this alarmist? Considering that a month before, in October 2013, an earthquake with a magnitude of 7.1 hit off the coast of Fukushima, followed by a small tsunami. By the time this book is published this will be a moot question, but not a moot point. We will not know just how global these nuclear threats are until future generations have the evidence before them. Reading a 2013 report from Costa Rica about large dead sea turtles washing up on their beaches, I was struck by the suggestion that gave concern to a question: could the turtles have been poisoned from the radiation being washed into the Pacific Ocean in Japan?

The arrogance upon civilization of those who put human health and life in such jeopardy by creating these monsters called nuclear power plants. China now selling nuclear power plants to Pakistan (whose Qadeer Khan had sold nuclear weapon components to Libya). There was a time when Pakistan stopped buying powered milk from China because contaminated milk in China killed a lot of children. Now they are buying nuclear power plants. At the end of what I call my anti-nuclear novel set in New Zealand I have a quote from the author of "Small Is Beautiful" that has more in it than anything I have written or could write. E.F. Schumacher wrote:

No degree of prosperity could justify the accumulation of large amounts of highly toxic substances which nobody knows how to make 'safe' and which remains an incalculable danger to the whole creation for historical or even geological Ages. To do such a thing is a transgression against life itself, A transgression infinitely more serious than any crime ever perpetrated by man. The idea that a civilization could sustain itself on the basis of such a transgression is an ethical, spiritual, and metaphysical monstrosity. It means conducting the economic affairs of man as if people really did not matter at all.

I believe this quotation should be carved into the walls of every government and judicial building in the world, and recited by school children everywhere. To me, this case study on Japan I began writing at a time when Japanese nuclear development was not even on the horizon is now at a crossroads in 2014; is this what we want for the remained of the 21st century. When I gave that talk in New Zealand in 1986 I accused Japan as abrogating its responsibilities to it own people who had suffered the effects of American nuclear bombing during WW II.

Now, in 2014, I am horrified with the reality that strontium-90 and other radioactive deadly poisons are being washed into the Pacific Ocean as a result of a stubborn Japanese psychology unwilling to recognize the mistake they made in developing nuclear reactors for electricity, now going beyond my original accusations to include such an irresponsible contamination of an Ocean Japan shares with many other peoples. Will Japan help with the medical support when thousands of children in other Asian countries develop cancer from radioactive elements in waters of the Pacific Ocean

In first edition of this book I theorized and subsequently predicted two very important events: the downfall of the USSR and Japan's current nuclear nightmares. I have another theory that I have been discussing in classroom for the last twenty years. As I have written in this chapter about the health affects of radiation, it attacks the weakest in the life chain, such as the fetus in the mother's belly before the mother herself. Think of radiation as a coward. What parent, if they had the option, would not take the hit of radiation themselves to save their children.

Think: what are the two most important parts of the female and male bodies for the reproduction of the human race? Hint: the male animal spreading his sperm and the female animal nurturing the young: the male prostrate and the female breasts.

I believe that the huge increases of breast and prostate cancer will someday be traced to radioactive poisons that remain in our environment that are difficult to trace. True, most of these cancers occur in men and women after their most reproductive years, but that may not necessarily hold true in the future if wars release this cowardly devil.

Today, you can be sure that terrorists are desperately trying to acquire nuclear weapons, and when they do, they will use them. Or imagine conflict in Asia over the competing claims to the islands and rocky outcroppings in the East and South China seas. Conventional weapons unleashed in conflict would be able to destroy many of the nuclear power reactors in all the country's involved, be it China, Taiwan, Japan, etc. Or a war between North and South Korea that destroyed all of South Korea's nuclear power plants. Or a war between India and Pakistan. Nuclear weapons need not be used; conventional weapons destroying a countries nuclear power reactors would not be as violent as a bomb doing its mission in a few minutes, but the release of radiation from the electrical nuclear power plants would make the regions not only uninhabitable, but affect the reproductive cycle of peoples in the most horrible and unimaginable ways.

This time span may seem like science fiction, but the concerns previously discussed in the above pages may have seemed to have gone away from history and the consciousness of most people in today's world, but as the fearful theme running through all the above problems with things nuclear; they never go away. At one time I was trying to find a part of the world that might possibly survive the WW III that the USSR and USA seemed destined to bring about, and settled on New Zealand, the purest nature preserve in all the world, a pristine environment David Henry Thoreau would have wished to live in were he alive today. As one who has explored the world since I was 18, as a military man, a merchant seaman, and for the United Nations; I knew I had found a special place. I decided to not go back to America and stayed to live a simple Thoreau life. I was taken in by a Maori tiribe, the Nahi tahoe, and lived with them to learn and write. The Nahi Tahoe were the only Maori tribe that did not surrender to the

British in 1840 and refused to sign the peace treaty of Waitangi giving sovereignty to the British. They finally did sign the peace treaty with the British on August 1, 2008. What I particularly learned from the Maori was a fuller appreciation of our relationship to nature, one I had known about intellectually, but now I felt it in my very being, and in my soul. In my minds eye; there is a nuclear bomb, a nuclear power plant, and across from them stands a sacred mountain containing the hard green jade stone that is a gift from time, and a reminder of nature's beauty and hope. There is a feeling that cannot be transcribed to paper or put into words when nature allows you to touch its secrets. The closest I ever came to this again was among the ancient Maya ruins in Tikal, Guatemala in 2008.

As a child I was fortunate to experience the transcendence of nature up close spending summers in New England woods, lakes, and seaside beaches camping under the stars far from my family home in Philadelphia; my father had been born and raised in Connecticut. I learned early of the strong independent New England spirit and as I wrap this up I am somewhat lost for words with the anti-democratic, ant-federalist, anti republican stance taken this summer of 2013 by the U.S. Federal Courts in claiming that Vermont's government does not have the right to shut down its Vermont Yankee nuclear power plant, despite a decision by the state legislature to close it down. This plant that sits on the Connecticut River has the potential to not just cause catastrophic environmental damage to Vermont, but all the states through which it flows in reaching the sea.

In fact, this ruling by the United States Court of Appeals for the Second Circuit means that no state has the right to close any of its nuclear power plants; the states are "pre-empted" from regulating safety by the Atomic Energy Act of 1946 which gave the Federal government that responsibility and power.

Think, New York City and the Indian Point nuclear power plants situated on the Hudson River in West Chester County, 38 miles from NYC. I am sure there is today, a terrorist, or group of terrorists, who are dedicating their lives to blowing up these plants. We witnessed the panic after hurricane Sandy; just imagine the unthinkable outcome of such an attack. Governor Andrew Como has been trying to close these reactors owned by Entergy, the same company who owns the Vermont Yankee plant; and to think the people of New York and their governor do not have the power to close down this most dangerous of dangers.

New Zealand did not change history's course, but the Cold War did come to an end in 1989 and there was new hope that the nuclear proliferation could be managed. When the Wall came down in Berlin I stood there with great hope, for I had spent a great deal of time in Berlin during the Cold War, including some risky times on the eastern side of the Wall. At one time I felt like a Berliner, as John F. Kennedy proclaimed: "Ich bin ein Berliner." I say this for I was once engaged to the Berlin Opera's only Prima Ballerina 'Assoluta' (the 7th in only 12 since 1893) and would have lived with her in Berlin at a time when the escalation of short range nuclear missiles made Berlin potentially the deadliest place in entire history of the world. That day when The Wall came down I felt a hope that I had not experienced since being in New Zealand.

Where are we this year 2014? Four year ago in Prague President Obama issued a call for a nuclear free world and was also honored with the Nobel Peace Prize. But the reality is another thing. We are not just witnessing Iran working feverishly to develop nuclear weapons, if they have not already done so (which I am afraid is the case); but North Korea already has them.

In conclusion, two thoughts. The only country in the world to have been bombed with a hydrogen bomb, the Marshall Islands, and their suing 9 major nuclear nations; not for compensation, but for their failure to adhere to disarmament of nuclear weapons as proscribed by international law and treaties they have signed.

The other; the editorial board of the NYT times who argue that the US not only needs nuclear power in the future, but that it is now much safer. Where will these board members be if the Indian

Point nuclear plant, 38 miles up the Hudson River from New York City is ever destroyed from a missile or terrorist actions?

Chapter Eight

AMERICAN FOREIGN POLICY

CHEMICAL AND BIOLOGICAL THREATS (by Leo P. Brophy)

A SHORT HISTORY

Chemical-Biological Warfare

One important characteristic of chemical and biological weapons is that both are toxic. We have evidence from Greek mythology that even before the dawn of history poisons were used to exterminate one's enemies. The daughters of the Greek goddess Hecate were honored for their skill in concocting poisons and it was one of these concoctions that enabled Jason, the leader of the Aronauts, to acquire his kingdom.

Early recorded history mentions various instances of the use of toxics in war. For example, in 600 B.C. Solon, the renowned legislator of Athens, directed that roots of a poisonous plant be thrown into a stream which the enemy was using for drinking water. Thucydides, the great historian of ancient Greece, records that in the fifth century B.C. the Spartans saturated wood with pitch and sulfur and then set fire to it under the walls of certain cities in order to conquer them. In the second century B.C., Hannibal the famous Carthaginian General, in a naval attack on the city of Pergamum in Asia minor ordered that pots filled with poisonous snakes be thrown on the decks of enemy ships, a ploy that led to the defeat of the enemy. In the seventh century of the Christian Era, scientists in the Byzantine Empire invented an incendiary compound known as Greek fire, which was closely akin to the Napalm invented by the U.S. in World War II. This substance, whose formula was a closely guarded secret, could be hand-thrown by buckets or grenades, hurled by catapults, or shot from tubes, not unlike modern flame throwers. Greek fire was a terrifying weapon, and it is credited with having saved Constantinople from attacks by Moslems in the seventh and eighth centuries.

A well publicized instance of the use of biological warfare took place in the 18th century during the French and Indian war. In 1763 the Commander in Chief of all the British forces in North America, Sir Jeffrey Amherst, ordered that blankets contaminated with smallpox, a dreadful disease, be delivered to certain antagonistic Indian Chiefs. The Indians who had not developed immunity to smallpox soon became its victims.

Chemical war from the 1700s to World War I

One outcome of advances in the science of chemistry, dating from the late 1700's was the use of chemicals in war in a more sophisticated manner than ever before. By the middle of the 19th century it was a simple matter for men with a knowledge of chemistry to visualize the application of toxic chemicals to warfare, and to suggest specific methods of using them. It was World War I that saw the employment of poison gases on a massive scale for the first and only time in world history.

As mentioned above, Germany violated the spirit, if not the letter, of the Hague Declaration of 1899 when she released chlorine gas from charged cylinders near Ypres, Belgium, in 1915. Only Germany among the world's nations was in a position at that time to prepare for the use of chemical munitions, because she possessed the worlds largest and most varied chemical industry. Early in the war the German government appointed a renowned German chemist, Professor Fritz Haber, Director of the Kaiser Wilhelm Institute in Berlin to direct work on war gases. It was that research that led eventually to Germany's dubious distinction to be the first country to introduce chlorine gas, then phosgene gas, and still later mustard gas in World War I. In self defense against Germany, the allied powers built up their own arsenals of chemical munitions and employed them against the central powers. When the U.S. entered the war 'on the side of the allies in April, 1917, she too would employ gas warfare on a considerable scale.

When the Germans first released chlorine gas on the 22nd of April in 1915 near Ypres, Belgium, a cry of horror arose from all parts of the civilized world, and understandably so. For Germany had violated a sacred trust in its introduction in warfare of a truly barbaric and inhuman weapon which civilized men had been attempting for centuries to eradicate.

Post WW I

The government and people of the United States, like those of so many other areas of the world, raised a hue and a cry against gas warfare during and after World War I, and as has been pointed out, the highest ranking officers of the army and the navy in World War I were unsparing in their condemnation of poisonous gas. All the presidents whose administrations spanned the inter war years sought to eliminate gas as a military weapon. Herbert Hoover and Franklin D. Roosevelt, who saw eye to eye on this issue, were particularly outspoken. President Hoover steadily urged elimination before the disarmament deliberations which took place while he was in office. In 1937 when Congress passed a bill (Sl,284) to change the designation of the Chemical Warfare Service to chemical Corps. President Franklin Roosevelt vetoed the bill in a stinging message which expressed the White House's attitude and, ipso facto that of the U.S. government, said Roosevelt:

"It has been and is the policy of this government to do everything in its power to outlaw the use of chemicals in warfare. Such use is inhuman and contrary to what modern civilization should stand for. I am doing everything in my power to discourage the use of gases and other chemicals in any war between nations. While, unfortunately the defensive necessities of the United States call for study of the use of chemicals in warfare, I do not want the government of the United States to do anything to aggrandize or make permanent any special bureau of the army or the navy engaged in these studies. I hope the time will come when the Chemical Warfare Service can be entirely abolished."

To dignify this service by calling it the "Chemical Corps" is in my judgment contrary to sound public policy. It was not until after President Roosevelt's death that a bill was enacted and signed by President Truman on August 2, 1946 that changed the designation of Chemical Warfare Service to Chemical Corps.

In the face of so much opposition on the part of the government and the public, how did the Chemical Warfare Service manage to survive after World War I? It was mainly through the efforts of one man, Amos A. Fries, who was a lieutenant colonel in the Corps of Engineers, was selected as Chief of the Gas Service, American Expeditionary Forces (AEF) in France in August 1917. Fries succeeded in building up an effective organization whose duties included research and development, procurement and supply, and military activities. In June 1918 the Gas Service, AEF, was renamed the CWS, AEF, with Fries, who was promoted to the rank of Brigadier General, as its chief. Meanwhile a similar movement towards centralization of military chemical warfare activities had been underway in the United States, a movement that led to the creation of the CWS, national army, on June 28, 1918. Major General William L. Sibert was appointed chief of this organization, whose existence was limited by congress to one year.

Once the war in Europe came to an end there would obviously be no further need for a CWS there, and to judge by the attitudes of many American leaders there would be no such need at home either. While the fact that the CWS was headed by a major general added prestige to the organization, it did not necessarily guarantee its longevity. It was at this juncture that General Fries came to play such an important role. Less than two weeks after the close of hostilities on November 11, 1918 he had obtained General Pershing's approval for his return to the United States, where he would devote his energies to working for a permanent CWS. He was a personal friend of both the chairman of the Senate Committee on Military Affairs, Senator George E. Chamberlain of Oregon, and the Chairman of the House Committee on military affairs, Representative Julius Kahn of California. Fries lost no opportunity in conveying to those gentlemen his strong conviction of the need for a permanent chemical bureau in the army.

In his struggle Fries received the active assistance of the leading chemical scientists and industrialists, who had come to regard the existence of such a service as recognition of the growing importance of chemistry in the national economy. The first hurdle was to get an extension of the life of the CWS, National Army, into the year 1920, a suggestion to which Congress agreed. Then Fries and his backers devoted their energies towards amending the National Defense Act of 1916 to make the CWS a permanent part of the military establishment. This feat was accomplished despite the opposition of the Secretary of War, Newton D. Baker, the Chief of Staff, Peyton D. Marsh, and General Pershing. The CWS was made a permanent service of the army in June 1920, and was made responsible for the development, procurement and supply of "all smoke and incendiary materials, all toxic gases, and all gas defense appliances." These duties were further extended to include "the supervision and training of the army in chemical warfare, both offensive and defensive": the organization, training, and operation of special gas troops, and such other duties as the President may from time to time prescribe."

The lack of enthusiasm on the part of officials so influential as Baker, Pershing and Marsh did not argue well for the newly formed Chemical Warfare Service. To complicate matters still more came the Washington conference of 1921, which aimed at setting limits on armaments, including chemical warfare munitions. Indeed most of the two decades following World War I witnessed world wide disillusionment over the terrible destructiveness of modern war in terms of human lives and material resources. As a result, emphasis was placed on reduction of arms, rather than on their build-up.

Another factor that contributed to the curb on arms and the military was the economic recession in certain basic industries that characterized much of 1920's and reached a climax in the stock market crash on Wall Street in October 1929. National treasuries simply could not bear the burden of another arms race. Once World War II got under way in Europe in the late 1930's the situation would change dramatically and Congress would become amenable to making much longer appropriations for military preparedness.

Meanwhile in the U.S., the military was to feel the pressure of greatly reduced congressional appropriations after World War I. The newly founded CWS, unpopular as it was in the eyes of both the public and the military establishment was barely allowed to exist. In the 1920's and 1930's the War Department prohibited research on toxic gases, confining the CWS efforts to defensive measures only. The war department attitude had the general support of those within the army and navy combat forces, whose experience in World War I was that poison gas was not a decisive combat weapon, but rather more of a nuisance than anything else.

Chemical Warfare Service appropriations for the peace time years were among the very lowest for any element of the army, for example from 1927 to 1935 they averaged about one and a quarter million dollars a year. Manpower was a similar story. In 1927, CWS actual strength was 80 officers and 418 enlisted men. From 1920 until 1938 a dozen officers and a score of civilians constructed the entire personnel of the office of the chief, CWS, which was located in the munitions building in Washington, D.C.

The Washington disarmament conference of 1921-1922 was but a first step in a campaign aimed at international peace. The League of Nations during its existence worked towards that goal. In the early 1930's the United States, although it was not a member of the league, cooperated closely with England and other powers to bring about qualitative disarmament in 1932, at the suggestion of Lord Cecil of Great Britain. Representatives of 60 nations met in Geneva at what has been called the first world disarmament conference. Lord Cecil described the aim of the conference as follows: "to decrease the offensive power of armaments, while leaving defensive power untouched, for anything which diminishes the power of aggression proportionately to the power of defense necessarily increases the safety of the world."

In June 1932 President Hoover presented a comprehensive qualitative disarmament plan to the conference. The president stated that, "reduction should be carried out, not only in armaments, but by increasing the comparative power of the defense through decreases in the power of attack." He then went on to propose, "the abolition of all tanks, all chemical warfare, and all large mobile guns; the abolition of all bombing planes; the total prohibition of bombardment from the air; and the reduction by one third of battleships and submarines, and by one quarter of aircraft carriers, cruisers and destroyers."

After Franklin D. Roosevelt succeeded Hoover as president he wrote the following message to the conference in May 1933:

"If all nations will agree wholly to eliminate from possession and use weapons which make possible for a successful attack, defenses automatically will become impregnable, and the frontiers and independence of every nation will become secure. The ultimate objective of the Disarmament Conference must be the complete elimination of all offensive weapons."

Just a few months before Roosevelt wrote that message an event took place in Germany that few if any could foresee would eventually dash any hope for peace in Europe or in the world. That was the appointment of Adolph Hitler as chancellor by the senile president Paul Von Hindenburg on January 30, 1933. Hitler soon came to dominate the German government and by the following

October he was that nation's leading representative at the Geneva disarmament conference. One day, after delivering one of his flamboyant speaches on the evils of the Versailles Treaty, he announced that Germany would no longer obey the provisions of that document which forbade it to rearm. He then walked out of the conference for good.

That act led to the gradual disintegration of the disarmament conference and in the Summer of 1934 Great Britain announced that there was no reason for it to continue. On March 16, 1935 Hitler publicly repudiated all treaty limitations on her rearming and re-established universal military service. In March 1936, German troops took over the demilitarized zone of the Rhineland in violation of both the Versailles Treaty and the Locarno Pact of 1925.

Meanwhile in Italy another dictator, Benito Mussolini, had come to power in October 1922, after he and his ~fascist followers marched on Rome where they "convinced" King Victor Emmanuel III to put Mussolini in charge of the government. In October 1935 Mussolini violated Italy's international agreements when "Il duce", as Mussolini was called, directed an invasion of Ethiopia. In October of the following year Germany and Italy drew up a cooperative agreement known as the "Rome-Berlin axis". A month later, in November 1936 Germany joined Japan in an "Anti-Comintern Pact", aimed at Russia. The following July, Japan would start a war against China that would not end until Japan's defeat in World War II.

Thus by 1937 Germany, Italy and Japan had formed alliances, at the same time their opponents in Europe, Great Britain, France and Russia had joined in alliances. By 1937, then the world was formed into two armed camps and it was in this atmosphere that President Franklin D. Roosevelt appealed to the American people to modify its spirit of isolationism.

Deciding to make his sentiments known especially in the strongly isolationist Middle West, the president travelled to

Chicago, where on October 5, 1937, he gave a speech which has ever since been known as "Quarantine the Aggressors" speech. Roosevelt said that in the preceding few years the political situation in the world was "growing progressively worse", despite the 15 year effort of more than 60 nations to bring about an era of peace. Although he mentioned no nation by name, there could be no doubt that the president was referring to Germany, Italy and Japan.

Congressional appropriations for the CWS, which averaged about one and a quarter million dollars a year from 1927 to 1935, jumped to almost 3 million dollars in 1939. They would leap to 60 million in 1941 and in 1944 to over a billion. Manpower was a similar story. In 1935 the CWS had an actual strength of 83 officers and 450 enlisted members, in 1940 the members were 93 and 1,035, in 1941, 833 and 5059; and the peak in 1943, 8,013 and 61,688. Civilian employees ranged from 742 in 1931 to a peak of 29,000 in 1943.

As indicated above, the congress enacted special legislation in June 1938 under which the U.S. began to tool up for production of munitions. The objective of this legislation, which was known as Educational Order Legislation, was the training of selected industrial concerns in the manufacture of a half dozen army items.(13) One of the items selected was the gas mask, on which the CWS wrote its first contract in late 1939 and several more in 1940 and 1941. The educational order program was the first real step, so far as the CWS was concerned, in the direction of industrial mobilization in the emergency period. The lean years for the service had given way to the years of plenty.

In the two decades following World War I the primary mission of the CWS was to provide insurance for American military forces against the shock of a sudden gas attack. Hand in hand with this duty went responsibility for maintaining a state of readiness for quick retaliation. These two constituted explicit responsibilities. In a broader sense, another function of the service was to provide military support for a national policy that of dissuading others from resorting to gas warfare.

Unfortunately the chief of the CWS, from 1920 to 1929, the tough minded Amos Fries, balked at carrying out the latter responsibility which would require that the U.S. would become a signatory to the Geneva Gas Protocol. Fries felt that his highest mission in life was to insure that his country would be capable of winning any future war, which he was certain would be a chemical war. To achieve his objective he was willing to disregard the national policy of his government, of his commander in chief and of his more immediate superiors. General Fries could not have succeeded, of course, had he not continued to receive the active support of a few senators and representatives in key positions, as well ss the backing of the burgeoning chemical industry and of veterans organizations like the American Legion. This is an astounding example of how a small special interest group can frustrate the policy of an entire government. Fries, moreover, set a pattern that his successors, who in the years following World War II would emulate and carry his policy to a level that not even his vivid imagination could envision.

WORLD WAR II

On September 3, 1939, the day that Great Britain declared war on Germany, she sought assurances from the various belligerents that they would continue to observe the Geneva Gas Protocol of 1925, which prohibited the use of poison gases and bacteriological agents in war. Germany, Italy, Bulgaria, Rumania, Finland, and Japan replied that they would abide by the protocol. Thus was established the precedent for the non use of gas in World War II.

When Japan attacked the U.S. fleet at Pearl Harbor on December 7, 1941, it did not use gas. The U.S. declaration of war against Japan on the following day suddenly cast the U.S. in the role of a belligerent. Since our government was not a signatory to the protocol, what would be its policy on gas? An official answer did not come until six months later. Meanwhile a policy of silence was observed on the theory that it was preferable to keep the enemy guessing about U.S. interminably, while the war department conducted a crash program to activate, train and equip many more chemical units. When President Roosevelt finally made a public announcement on gas warfare on June 5, 1942, it was by way of a warning to Japan on its alleged use of gas against the Chinese, a charge that has never been definitely substantiated, said the President: "I desire to make it unmistakably clear that if Japan persists in this inhuman form of warfare against China or against any other of the United Nations, such action will be regarded by this government as though taken against the United States and retaliation in kind and in full measure will be meted out. Roosevelt was saying indirectly that the U.S. would not be one to introduce gas warfare, and that has remained the definite policy of the U.S., at least until recent years. U.S. policy at present seems to be uncertain.

Research and development, procurement and stockpiling of the poison gases used in world War I were accelerated in World War II. Research and development activities were conducted not only in government arsenals and laboratories, but also through contracts with universities and commercial laboratories. The CWS received guidance and supervision in research from several higher echelon agencies, the most important of which was the office of Scientific Research and Development established by President Roosevelt on June 28, 1941. Research was carried out on the poison gases developed in World War I; phosgene, hydrogen cyanide, cynogen chloride, mustard gas, lewisite. Further research was carried out on the World War I tear gases and vomiting gases. Neither the Americans nor their allies developed any new gases during World War II.

Much research was expended on protection against poison gases. In World War I reliance for detecting the presence of gas was through the sense of smell, except for blister agents on which the Americans and the British had devised a method based on color changes in a dye base. World War II saw great improvements in this area, not only for detection of blister gases but for other gases as well. Scientists and physicians made great strides in the treatment of the victims of gas, thanks to the discovery of the sulpha drugs and the development of better protective ointments.

After the German attack at Ypres in 1915, the various belligerents had labored feverishly to devise suitable gas masks. In World War II the CWS did much work on improving the World War I masks, not only for military personnel but for civilians and even for children. on the project of devising a mask for children, the chief of the CWS invited Walt Disney, the creator of Mickey Mouse, to assist in the development of a Mickey Mouse Mask. on still another item, protective clothing, the CWS worked on the development of a permeable suit for protection against both mustard vapor and fine mustard spray.

The CWS also had responsibility for other items that had been used on a limited scale in World War I. These included incendiary munitions, flame throwers, motors, shells, and smoke used to conceal the movements of troops and to designate target areas. All of these munitions were used on a much larger scale in World War II, and in the absence of gas warfare they loomed much larger in the responsibilities of the CWS. In carrying out its mission, the CWS had the assistance of a number of universities and industrialists.

Smoke Screening

In the case of smoke screening, for example, its use would grow as the result of the astounding development of air power, both military and civilian in the inter-war years. With all belligerents making use of airplanes, it became absolutely essential for the first time in history to conceal troop movements and targets over large areas of land and sea. Thus when German bombers flew over Mediterranean cities like Algiers and Naples intent on blowing allied shipping out of the harbors they almost always found an impenetrable haze covering the targets. On New Guinea and Luzon American paratroopers dropped safely to earth protected from bullets of Japanese riflemen by screens of white smoke. At beachheads, highways, and river crossings in Italy, France and Germany, troops and trucks went about their work under a shield of artificial fog. Never before had armies been able to protect their movements as successfully as the allied forces did in World War II.

Flame Throwers

After the Germans devised and employed flame throwers in World War I, the allied forces followed suit. The use of the weapons was very limited, however, and the Americans had such little respect for its effectiveness that the CWS dropped the flame thrower from its list after the war. Consequently when the corps of engineers requested the CWS for a supply of portable flame throwers in July 1940, research and development started all over again. By March 1942 acceptable weapons were coming off the production lines and by the end of that year some were arriving in the South Pacific area. On January 15, 1943 American portable flame throwers and their first successful appearance at Guadalcanal Island in the South Pacific. It was in the vast reaches of the Pacific area that the weapon would be chiefly used. Two circumstances were responsible for this:

(1) The nature of the terrain on which the Japanese constructed, camouflaged defenses and bunkers that were impervious to the effects of artillery and mortar fire.

(2) The personality of the Japanese soldier, who chose to flight until death rather than surrender.

It was from the Pacific area, also, that requests for mechanized flame throwers emanated. In World War I the CWS had designed its first mechanized flame thrower, but did not have time to carry the weapon beyond its experimental stage. In the late 1930's revival of interest in the mechanized flame thrower began in the United States as the result of reports in newspapers, magazines and newsreels that the Italian army had outfitted some of its armored units with this type of weapon. In the Summer of 1940 engineers in the U.S. constructed the first model by replacing the cannon, or main armament, of an M-2 medium tank with a flame gun. This model went through many modifications and delays, so that it was not until the Summer of 1944 that the first mechanized flame thrower reached the Pacific area. And it was not until the last battle of the war at Okinawa in the Spring of 1945 that the weapon was really effectively used.

The success of the flame thrower, portable as well as mechanized, was due in great measure to the development of a thickened fuel, know as napalm, to replace ordinary gasoline. Napalm was made by combining aluminum soap of napthenic and palmitec acids with gasoline to produce a jelly like substance about as thick a rubber. While it was originally intended to be used in incendiary bombs and was so used in World War II and later wars, it was also found to be equally effective for flame throwers, greatly increasing their range.

Incendiaries

Aerial incendiaries were used in World War I by the central powers and their opponents. Those incendiary bombs were at first very crude items, but as time went on they become more sophisticated. The first ones that German Zepplins and airplanes dropped on England consisted of a core of thermite wrapped with tarred cotton waste and tarred rope. Later the Germans devised a 2-pound bomb composed of a magnesium-thermite filler in a magnesium alloy casing. The English developed the Baby

Incendiary, which consisted of a special thermite mixture and weighed about two-fifths of a pound. The Americans developed heavier types of incendiaries, but due to the late entrance of the U.S. into the war they were never used.

In the years between the wars CWS interest in incendiaries did not entirely wane, especially after the Army Air Corps showed its interest in the potentialities of these munitions. In response to a request form the Chiefs of the Air Corps the Chemical Warfare Service and the Ordinance Department began work on an incendiary bomb in the mid 1930s. At that time these two bureaus of the army had joint responsibility for the munitions, the Ordinance Department for the design and the Chemical Warfare Service for the filling. By the end of 1936 an incendiary bomb had been standardized, the 100-pound M47. This was the only incendiary munitions in the U.S. arsenal when the U.S. entered World War II. In the interest of speed and efficiency the chief of the Chemical Warfare Service, Maj. Gen. William N. Porter, recommended to his superiors that the CWS be given sole responsibility for incendiaries and this was accomplished in the latter part of 1941.

During World War II the CWS, with the customary assistance of universities and industrial concerns, developed and supplied incendiary bombs of various types to the armed forces. They ranged in sized and shapes from the four-pound magnesium incendiary bomb to the five-hundred pound bomb. Incendiary grenades in the millions were also produced and distributed and incendiary rockets in lesser numbers.

Four pound magnesium bombs and other small incendiaries were not held together by devices called adapters. The device was made up of two end plates, two longitudinal bars, and four steel straps. One model held together thirty-four bombs, a larger model 128 bombs.

Elaborate and costly field tests had to be conducted to determine the effectiveness of different type bombs. Among the tests were bombing "raids" on a composite German-Japanese village at Dugway Proving Ground in Utah. After each "raid" the razed buildings were examined and then reconstructed. Among the points that had to be determined was the degree of penetration of the bombs, and the time temperature factor for igniting the typical Japanese target.

The type of construction of urban areas led to varying degrees of success in aerial incendiary attacks. For example, German construction was almost exclusively of brick or stone with a tile or slate roof, while Japanese was mostly of wood and paper. Consequently the damage inflicted in lives and property on Japanese cities was far greater than on German cities.

The most destructive raid of World War II took place over Tokyo on March 9, 1945, when more than 300 U.S. planes swarmed over the city, dropping about two thousand tons on incendiaries. Almost 16 square miles of the city was burned out and more than a quarter of a million buildings were destroyed.

It would be hard to improve on the following description of that raid:

Some people were able to escape through the wide fire lanes, but many other were encircled by the flames and died of suffocation and burns. Those who fled to the canals faced death in the scalding water or were crushed by the terrified mob which crowded on top of them. This raid alone caused the death of an estimated 83,793 people and almost 41,000 more received injuries. Over one million people lost their homes. The fire destroyed 15.8 square miles in the center of Tokyo. All buildings in the area were entirely destroyed or seriously damaged. Although some of the modern, fire-resistant structures were not totally destroyed, the majority of even this type was left as sagging skeletons. Glass, steel bars, and concrete melted in the intense heat; wooden buildings went up in flames before the fire front had reached them.

Such was the havoc wrought by the first of the "blitz" raids against the cities of Japan.

After pondering that description, written by two of his colleagues, this writer could not help recall how President Roosevelt in 1937 berated Germany, Italy and Japan for ruthlessly murdering from the air "civilians, including vast numbers of women and children". And I could not help but wonder whether the atrocities committed by the Axis Powers were any more reprehensible than some of the activities of the United Nations, including the United States, during the World War II.

BIOLOGICAL WARFARE

Biological warfare was not used in world War I and therefore in the years after the war little consideration was paid to it. By the early 1940's that attitude had changed because of simultaneous development of the science of bacteriology and of airpower. The threat of this type of warfare was causing concern not only to the armed forces, but also to certain nonmilitary governmental agencies and to scientific associations. The reason for this is quite obvious, if a biological warfare attack would possibly be conducted on such a scale that every known source would have to be employed to combat it.

To supervise all activities dealing with research the President appointed a National Defense Research Committee in June 1940. At about the same time a committee on medical Research was also established. Both of these committees a year later were put under the jurisdiction of the newly created office Research and Development (OSR). Cooperating with these supervisory committees were scientists and physicians from the National Academy of Sciences and the National Institute of Health, who took under advisement the offensive and defensive aspects of biological warfare. The attitude of these groups was not one of alarm. They believed that the relatively advanced state of public health in the United States put the population in a favorable position in the event of a biological attack, but at the same time they felt that the situation should be carefully watched.

All concerned elements of the military establishment from the Secretary of War down, welcomed the assistance and cooperation of nonmilitary agencies and groups. Especially pleased were the Surgeon General and Chief of the Chemical Warfare Service, to whom the chief of staff of the army, General George Marshall, had assigned responsibility for biological warfare activities. Representatives of all the various groups, military and nonmilitary, consulted among themselves and came to the conclusion that a civilian agency be delegated to supervise all aspects of this type of warfare. The Secretary of War, Henry L. Stimson, them sent this recommendation to President Roosevelt in June 1942, who gave it his approval. Thereupon the War Research Service headed by Mr. George W. Merck was set up in the Federal Security Agency in the summer of 1942. This service was a small coordinating organization which drew on the facilities, personnel, and experience of government and private institutions, including the medical services of the Army and Navy, the Chemical Warfare Service, the Department of Agriculture, G-2 of the army, the office of Naval Intelligence, the Office of Strategic Services, and the Federal Bureau of Investigation.

The War Research Service secured the services of outstanding scientists and administration for full-time duty with the armed forces. It was decided that exhaustive investigation of biological agents would require research and development of a scale not heretofore attempted and that the agency best suited to carry out these activities was the Chemical Warfare Service. A site outside Frederick, Maryland, was selected for a biological Warfare installation and construction of the future Camp Detrick was begun in the Spring of 1943. This was the first of four biological warfare installations built during World War II. The others were the testing grounds at Horn Island, Pascagoula, Mississippi; the Granite Park installation at Tooele, Utah; and a production plant at Terre Haute, Indiana.

In all research and development on chemical and biological items, the Americans worked closely with the Canadians and the British. After American forces arrived in the British Isles in 1942, CWS personnel could visit British installations and learn at first hand what the British were doing. The three powers established an advisory committee to eliminate duplication of effort, establish uniform test procedures, and establish cooperative work on various items.

CHEMICAL & BIOLOGICAL WAR POLICIES
OF THE ENEMY POWERS

Of the axis powers only Germany had real capability of using poison gas. German scientists had developed the first of the nerve gases, "Tabun", in 1936 and had also developed "Sarin" and "Soman". Yet Germany did not give serious consideration to the use of gas. The chief reason perhaps was that Hitler had been the victim of a gas attack in World War I and consequently abhorred its use. Another possible factor was that the Germans believed that the Americans had also developed nerve gases. The German high command, moreover, felt that the use of gas warfare in violation of international agreements would outrage international public opinion. Neither Italy nor Japan showed any intention of introducing gas warfare, despite the fact that the latter "had used it in isolated cases against the Chinese".

As to biological warfare, there is ample evidence that the Japanese experimented with this type warfare since 1931, that they conducted tests with deadly diseases that resulted in the killing of 1,500 to 2,000 human guinea pigs at an installation near Harbin in

Manchuria (then in Japanese territory), and that they made attacks with plaque on China that resulted in about 700 deaths between 1940 and 1944. This information was first brought to light in 1949 when the Soviets put twelve Japanese military prisoners on at Khabaroosk trial for use of biological warfare. One of the accused was the former commander-in-chief of the Kwantung Army. More evidence against the Japanese came in the 1950's in a report made by an international scientific commission which was set up to investigate Russian charges that the Americans were using biological warfare against the North Koreans and Chinese. The commission concluded that the Soviet charges were totally unfounded. In the course of its investigation, however, it discovered more evidence of Japan's biological warfare activities from the early 1930's until 1945.

Thanks largely to the efforts of the United States and Japan the science and art, so to speak, of biological warfare was revolutionized in World War II. How does one define this type of warfare as it exists in our time? In simple terms, biological warfare may be defined as the intentional cultivation or production of pathogenic bacteria, fungi, viruses, and their toxic products, as well as certain chemical compounds,. for the purpose of producing disease or death in men, animals, or crops. The definition also includes the development of defenses against these organisms and toxic substances. Potential agents might include the organisms producing the intestinal diseases of typhoid, cholera, and dysentery, through pollution of water supplies; the respiratory diseases of smallpox, diphtheria, epidemic meningitis, scarlet fever, and influenza, which are ordinarily dependent upon ideal epidemic conditions; the insect transmitted diseases of malaria, yellow fever, anthrax, gangrene, and the phylogenic diseases; agricultural diseases in the form of the boll weevil, corn borer, and Mediterranean fruit fly, as well as fungus diseases of crops and plants, and foot and mouth disease, Newcastle disease, fowl plague, and other diseases to which domestic animals and fowl are subject.

CHEMICAL/BIOLOGICAL WARFARE DEVELOPMENTS SINCE WW II

The chemical warfare service emerged from World War II with more prestige than it had after World War I. This was owing largely the change in its responsibility from offensive and defensive gas warfare to that of other chemical warfare munitions as smoke, flame throwers, and incendiaries. The change in the designation of the Chemical Warfare Service to Chemical Crops, under War Department General Orders 99, of August 1946, was a definite indication of the importance that the military establishment attached to these methods of warfare. Like all elements of the military establishment the chemical corps in the period of demobilization was reduced in size and members to conform to its peace mission. That mission was of course, to make preparations for any possible military emergency. The main installations and facilities that had come into existence before-procurement districts, arsenals, laboratories, proving grounds, training schools and during World War II were retained, through some in time were eliminated in a process of reorganization.

The most important duty of the Chemical Corps in the post World War II years was that of continuing research and development on chemical and biological agents. In closing months of the war the armies of the various United Nations had come into possession of the nerve gases that the Germans had been developing since 1936. Chief among the victorious powers to show interest in these agents were the U.S.S.R. and the United States, and those two countries have continued to this day to develop nerve gases until their toxicity is much greater than were the original specimens. The United States, incidentally, is alone among the great industrial nations of the West to concentrate on preparation for chemical and biological warfare; neither the United Kingdom or any of continental NATO countries emphasized such preparations, because they are intent on abiding by the terms of the Geneva Gas Protocol of 1925. Although the United States became a signatory to that protocol in 1975, there seems little evidence that the Reagan administration is taking its provisions seriously.

The military establishment lost no time after the close of World War II in emphasizing its interest and continued research and development in biological warfare on September 13, 1945, the secretary of war directed the chief of staff of the army to assume responsibility for the military aspect of chemical biological, and radiological warfare. As was the procedure during the war, the chief of the Chemical Warfare Service and the Surgeon General were to coordinate their activities in these areas.

The headquarters for chemical research was located at Edgewood, Maryland, the site of the chemical warfare arsenal that had been built in World War I. The arsenal continued as an important manufacturing installation throughout World War II, but at the end of the war it came to almost a complete halt. On lands adjacent to the arsenal, up-to-date laboratories and other facilities had been erected and during the war the installation was designated as the Chemical Warfare Center. In early August 1946 it was renamed the Army Chemical Center.

The headquarters for biological warfare activities continued to be located at the site outside Frederick, Maryland, known during the war as Camp Detrick. After the war it was renamed Fort Detrick. Interest in biological warfare seemed to become almost an obsession in pertinent circles of the military establishment and among certain elements of the scientific and pharmaceutical communities. For example, in 1949 Secretary of Defense James Forrestal issued a 1,400 world statement that announced that biological warfare was being conducted. At the same time Maj. Gen. Alden Waitt, Chief of the Chemical Corps, stated that he was confident "we are as far advance (in biological warfare) as any nation in the world... I think ahead". In 1952 a successor to Waitt, Maj. Gen Egbert F. Bullene, gave secret testimony in a congressional hearing that the pentagon had approved a shift from

239

research to the manufacturing stage in biological warfare and the Pine Bluff arsenal, Arkansas, had been chosen as the site for the 10-story biological manufacturing plant. The following year the Secretary of the Army, on October 22, 1953, established the position of assistant chief chemical officer for Biological Warfare to assure the accomplishment of the army biological warfare program.

To finance the entire chemical biological warfare program up to the late 1950's relatively modest funds were expended, from $50 million to $75 million a year. With the advent of the Kennedy administration in 1961 expenditures began to increase considerably, reaching at times a level of three times what they were in the 1950's. Several factors accounted for this development. One was the nation's greater involvement in Vietnam. Another was the change in strategic planning away from exclusive dependence on nuclear munitions, already discussed above. Still another was the appointment of Robert D. McNamara as Secretary of Defense. McNamara, who had been president of the Ford Motor Company, came to office with ideas of streamlining the Department of Defense in order to improve its efficiency. He directed a reorganization in 1962 which eliminated the Chemical Corps and assigned its functions to other elements of the army. For example, chemical and biological research and development as well as procurement and supply responsibilities were placed under a new organization, the Army Material Command, while training activities assigned to the Continental Army Command. To provide for high-level review of CBW programs and coordinate research among the Army, Navy and Air Force, the secretary established a joint Technical Coordinating Group.

With the abolition of the office of the Chief Chemical Officer in Washington, D.C. in 1962, the last Chief of the Chemical Corps, Maj. Gen. Marshall Stubbs, was transferred with a few of his staff to the office of the Army Deputy Chief for Operations in the Pentagon. This reorganization gave chemical biological activities greater prestige than they had ever experienced before.

Representation at the highest echelons led to greater coordination at the lower levels - a kind of military trickle down. As one writer described the situation in 1969:

"Every corps and higher military unit has a separate chemical, biological and radiological element (CBRE), whose mission is to plan and carry out CBW operations. These men work with the intelligence supply and chemical officers in smaller field units to coordinate attacks."

The sums allotted for CBW activities led to greater accomplishments not only in military installations, but also in those of private contractors and university laboratories. Thanks to the development of more sophisticated computers and other technological advances, startling improvements took place in making nerve gases more toxic and germ agents more deadly. Improvements were going on, meantime, in methods of disbursing all these various agents, whether it be by hand grenades, artillery shells, guided missiles, or whatever. All these research development, manufacture and distribution activities were carried out under a veil of strict secrecy.

Campaign-to Popularize CBW

While the work done on the development and manufacture of the poison agents was secret, propaganda on their alleged benefits were not. In the-latter 1950's the Chemical Corps and its sympathizers conducted a campaign, known as "Blue Skies", to win over public support for chemical biological weapons by stressing their "humanness" and their low production costs -much lower than nuclear weapons. In 1956 two events occurred that facilitated the campaign. One was a statement by Marchal Zhukov, the Soviet military leader to the effect that a future war would witness the use of atomic, thermonuclear, chemical and bacteriological weapons. The other was a report of high-level civilian advisory committee, headed by Otto N. Miller, vice president of the Standard Oil Company of California, to the Secretary of the Army Wilber M. Brucker. This report regretted that the public perceived of these weapons as "horrifying in character" and it recommended that an educational program be undertaken to convince the public that these weapons were no worse than other munitions, and that they should be included in military planning and training.

In carrying out "Operation Blue Skies", high ranking chemical officers addressed public gathering such as businessmen's clubs, conventions of scientists, and medical society meetings. Moreover, they targeted magazines, newspapers, and even medical journals to feature articles boosting the merits of chemical-biological weapons. At first the reception was quite favorable and such articles appeared in such staid publications as The Wall Street Journal, Washington Star, Harpers, and the Saturday Evening Post. Another means used to get the message to the public was to send a caravan throughout the country carrying exhibits of chemical defensive items like protective masks and clothing. Included in this display was a film featuring a cat that had been subjected to the psychochemical ZZ and a mouse that was in full possession of all its faculties. The cat cringing at the sight of the mouse. This experiment had actually been carried out. The purpose behind the film was to convince the public how easily battles would be won, if only enemy commanders could be treated in the same way that the cat was.

Closely associated with "Operation Blue Skies", was the campaign that the Chemical Corps leaders conducted in the late 1950's and early 1960's to woo the members of congress to their cause. In doing this they were of course following the example of General Fries in the 1920's and 1930's. Their efforts were directed at not only at obtaining more funds, at which as indicated they were eminently successful, but at convincing their fellow congressmen and others that chemical biological weapons were acceptable in modern warfare.

At the annual hearings of the House Appropriations Committee the Chief Chemical Officer or his representative would appear. The chairman of the committee, representative George H. Mahon of Connecticut, was booster of chemical biological warfare preparations, as were also the following committee members; Robert Sikes of Florida, Daniel J. Ford of Pennsylvania, Glenard P. Lipcomb of California. The efforts of these gentlemen were not confined to fiscal matters. They used their influence with the higher echelons and even with Secretary McNamara's office in stressing greater consideration for chemical-biological warfare.

An indication of how the efforts of the congressional backers of chemical-biological warfare paid off was the decision of the House Committee on science and astronautics, chaired by Representative Overton Brooks of Louisiana, to take the unusual step of holding special hearings on the subject in June 1959. The committee listened to the testimony of a former chief of the Chemical Corps, Maj. Gen. William M. Creasy, and were so impressed that the following month they sent a report, running to 17 pages of text plus 20 pages of indexes, to the House of Representatives for consideration. Included in the report were the following points:

There is an urgent need for a higher level support on a continuing long run basis in order to develop better detection and protection measures against possible employment of CBR weapons against this country.

It is also recognized that in the present world situation with other countries pursuing vigorous programs of CBR development, the best immediate guarantee the United States can possess to insure the CBR is not used anywhere against the free world is to have a strong capability in this field, too. This will only come with a stronger program of research.

At the present time CBR research is supported at a level equivalent to only one-thousandth of our total defense budget in the light of its potentialities, this committee recommends that serious consideration be given to the request of Defense Officials that this support be at least trebled. Only an increase of such size is likely to speed research to a level of attainment compatible with the efforts of Communist nations.

In CBR is to be considered a deterrent force in the U.S. arsenal of weapons, the program of research advocated here will have to be accompanied by an adequate program of manufacture and deployment of CBR munitions. (25)

The report, which its critics believed was a snow job, scored a definite triumph for the advocates of Chemical-Biological warfare. The report proved successful on two fronts. The House went along with increasing the CBR budget and the Army reprinted the report of the House Committee on Science and Astronautics as Army Pamphlet No. 3-2, dated March, 1960 and distributed it by the thousands. (26)

Popular reaction to the Chemical Biological publicity campaign did not prove so successful. The initial spate of booster articles began to slacken and by the fall of 1959 an adverse reaction was evident. For example, on October 1,

Reporter carried an article entitled, "The Campaign To Make Chemical Warfare Respectable", by Walter Schnier, which stated the attempt to portray Chemical and Biological Warfare as humane was a charade to get increased congressional appropriations. In February 1961 the Bulletin_ of Atomic Scientists featured a witty and caustic article, "Comments of Biological Warfare", by John Barden in which he describes a visit he made to the 137th national meeting of the American Chemical Society the previous April. The meeting featured a Symposium on Nonmilitary Defense-Chemical and Biological Defenses in Perspective. One speaker, Dr. Harold

C. Lueth of the American Medical Association, described the effects of nerve gas on the human body as follows:

Early symptoms include headache, blurring of the vision, tightness of the chest, and dizziness. Rapidly there will develop severe headache, profuse salivation, dimness of vision, early fatigue, drowsiness, cyanosis, collapse, convulsions and death.

The speaker pointed out that the symptoms ran their course in less than ten minutes, until death intervened. Barden came away less than enthusiastic over the humaneness of chemical warfare agents. Nor was he any more favorably impressed about biological warfare after listening to a report by Dr. LeRoy D. Fothergill, an adviser to the Chief Chemical Officer, which included the following statement, "an attractive feature of anti-crop warfare is that it does not destroy man's physical assets - his cities, his bridges, his railroads, et cetera". That was a theme that other speakers would harp on in addition to their stressing the fact the Chemical and Biological Warfare were inexpensive. Other types of agents that were discussed were the incapacitating drugs that caused temporary mental confusion, blindness, lack of balance, and the like. In commenting on those agents, General Stubbs remarked, "Incapacitating compounds might permit a force to gain its objective without killing or maiming personnel-military or civilian. That is, they get you so they have you to work for them."

Reactions to the campaign of the Chemical-Biological Warfare boosters would continue and lead to further divisions of opinion, not only in the scientific and medical communities, but also among the general public. As early as 1959 a group of Quakers and their sympathizers led a vigil outside of Fort Detrick to protest the use of these weapons, a vigil that would continue for months. In 1961 the Kennedy administration approved the use of plant killing defoliants and herbicides and nausea-producing gases in Vietnam. That decision would lead to protests by foreign powers (friendly and unfriendly) and to more publicity on their use in the U.S. press. Newsweek Magazine, for example, reported that by the end of 1961, American troops were training South Vietnam airmen how to spray rice and other plants with the poisonous agents.

As the Vietnam dragged on and public reaction to it intensified, criticism of the use of Chemical and Biological Warfare would likewise grow harsher. To understand the basis for this criticism, it is necessary to give more consideration to the actual employment of these weapons in Vietnam. But before dismissing the subject of "Operation Blue Skies", it is pertinent to make mention to an important book that epitomizes the views of all the boosters of Chemical and Biological Warfare.

In 1964 a retired Chemical Corps Officer, Brig. Gen. Jacques H. Rothschild had a book published by a house that specialized in text books for schools and colleges. This book was obviously meant to serve primarily as a text for advance students in military schools, because of its clear and explicit explanations of how Chemical-Biological agents could be used to advantage in certain strategic and tactical situations. But it was also intended for the instruction of the public, as the author indicates in the book. Rothschild states that over-classification of documents by the military has led to lack of public information on Chemical and Biological Warfare. How such a statement squares with "Operation Blue Skies" that began in late 1959 is somewhat puzzling. Perhaps he felt that propaganda campaign had not gone far enough and that a more forceful approach was necessary. Whatever his intentions were, he left no stone unturned to convince his readers of the virtues and advantages of Chemical and Biological Warfare. How effective his approach was among laymen is difficult to assess, but that his work made a great stir among scientists and historians with a special interest in the subject there is not the slightest doubt. This writer has not found any book published since the latter 1960's that fails to refer to Rothschild's work. Those who oppose the use of chemical and biological agents view the book with alarm, while those who look upon those agents with at least some degree of tolerance employ the very same arguments that Rothschild does in his book.

I want to dwell on only one aspect of Rothschild's book, namely its underlying philosophy. At the very beginning of the book under a section labeled "The Morality Of Toxic Warfare", he makes the following statements:

It appears illogical, then, to accept an agreement to ban any specific method of warfare and expect compliance therewith.

Are gas and germ warfare inhumane compared to other, seemingly acceptable, methods of warfare? This is the critical question insofar as morality is concerned. First, let us face the fact that no weapon of war may be thought of as humane.

In those few sentences the General disposes, at least to his own satisfaction and also to the satisfaction of many of his colleagues, the question of the morality of using chemical and biological agents. Never mind that from at least the time of the Greeks through the medieval and modern period of European history highly intelligent individuals have been giving thought to the morality of war and its methods. And their conclusions have been, as has been indicated above, that some types of warfare are more inhumane than others. Among those that have been considered totally unacceptable were the use of poisons of any kind. For centuries theologians have been making distinctions about wars that are just and those that are not. But that, of course, is a matter that military men are generally not in a position to consider.

General Rothschild writes from the point of view of a career professional soldier, a role which he fulfilled, incidentally, with great distinction. As a followers of the philosophy of Amos Fries, he does not feel that international agreements such as the Geneva Gas Protocol of 1925 are acceptable and he hold that the entire conduct of war should be left primarily to the military establishment. As one who disagrees with the General's point of view, I cannot help but recall the old age, "war is too important to be left to the generals".

To General Rothschild's credit, he does favor the establishment of a strong world organization having the power to prevent future wars and he does understand that it is possible to negotiate with the Russians:

While any step, small or large, is difficult to negotiate with the Russians, we have been working for years on small ones. A major agreement can be reached with the Soviet Union when they feel a real need for such an accord, that is when they have arrived at the decision that the risk of nuclear destruction is greater than the risk they would undergo by the acceptance of some new system. However, the groundwork for such an agreement would have had to be laid by negotiation.

Rothschild believes that the way to prevent war is through an organization established along the following lines.

The first step would be the preparation and acceptance of a charter which would describe the fundamental principles of the system (for preventing war), and which would include safeguards to protect all nations. The charter would establish the world organization required. The most logical organization would be the United Nations, although a separate organization, such as the International Disarmament Organization suggested by both the United States and the Soviet Union in 1962, might do. If this separate organization were used, its relationship with the United Nations would have to be carefully spelled out. It might be just as well to revise the charter and structure of the United Nations so as to permit it to perform the task for which it was originally designed--preventing war.

CHEMICALS IN COMBAT SINCE WW II

By the end of November 1961, according to Newsweek magazine, American servicemen were instructing Vietnamese airmen in the art of spraying crops with herbicides and defoliants. By the following year the U.S. was equipping the South Vietnamese Army with the standard riot control gases:

CS, CN, and DM. In the Spring of 1963 occasional notices appeared in the U.S. press about chemical-biological activities in Vietnam. On March 16, 1963 U.P.I. Correspondent Charles E. Smith wrote:

"Chemical defoliants and herbicides are used in certain places in the central highlands where the Vietcong terrorists grow crops. In such cases the aim is to eliminate sources of food."

On April 14 reporter Jack Wilson stated in the Minneapolis Tribune:

"Crop spraying has been limited to areas dominated by the Montagard tribesmen. Defense Department officials who receive regular reports on food spraying campaign feel that the Vietnam Government is conducting it with proper regard for its touchy aspects."

But is was not until 1965 that wide publicity was given to the use of those agents and it was only then that strong protests against their use was heard in this country. A question that would be asked persistently was whether the employment of gases and plant and forest killing agents was a violation of international law. It is true that the U.S. was not then a signatory of the Geneva Gas Protocol of 1925, but official and popular sentiment was against those methods of warfare. Had president Franklin Roosevelt's policy not to use these type of warfare in World War II undergone a change?

That the Pentagon itself was uneasy about using chemical biological weapons is evident from a request it made in 1964 to clarify the issue. The State Department after some hesitation, replied that the gases being used in Vietnam were riot gases and were therefore not among the toxic agents prohibited under international law. As to defoliants and herbicides, these had never before been used in war and therefore were not mentioned in any international agreements. Covered by international law or not, the use of these agents continued to be draw condemnation throughout the U.S. and other countries. After all no gases of any kind had been used at all since World War I, except for such rare occasions as the Italy's use of mustard gas against the Ethiopians in the 1930's and although the agents used in Vietnam were dubbed "riot gases", they did at times cause great discomfort and even death, as will be described below. The same thing can be said about the spraying of herbicides and defoliants.

OPERATION "RANCH HAND"

In December 1961 President Kennedy gave his approval to the use of herbicides and defoliants in Vietnam under a program known as "Operation Ranch Hand", whose official slogan was "Only we can prevent forests". Although the slogan sounds cynical, the original objective was to defoliate jungle areas from which Viet Cong snipers could attack the South Vietnamese and U.S. troops. For about a year U.S. special troops trained the South Vietnamese how to do the spraying, but without much success. Then the South Vietnamese became more efficient, so efficient in fact that they began spraying not only jungle areas, but also rice and other grain fields.) Later U.S. fliers also conducted spraying missions in jungle and crop areas.

The spraying was done by planes that were equipped with special tanks to hold the defoliants and high-pressure nozzles. The agents used were designated by a color code as follows:

Agent Orange, a 50:50 mixture of two commonly used defoliants, 2,4D and 2,4,5T. This mixture is used against heavy jungle and crops.

Agent Blue, a neutralized cocodylic acid sprayed over tall elephant grass and heavier crop concentration.

Agent White, also known as Tordon 101, a weaker mixture of unknown chemicals used in areas of sizable population. (34)

Agent Orange was the agent most commonly used. The Federation of American Scientists,, a non-political organization, lodged a complaint against the use of chemical and biological warfare in March 1965, in a statement that said:

The use of United States-produced chemical and biological weapons in Asia will be interpreted widely as field-testing of these weapons among foreign people and will hurt our efforts immeasurably in good will and moral respect all over the world.

We find it morally repugnant that the United States should find itself party to the use of weapons of indiscriminate effect, with principle effectiveness against civilian populations.

In recent weeks we have been treated to a succession of stories which have included the employment of napalm against villages, the use of crop destroying agents so-called defoliating chemicals, and now the use of gas against civilians.

Whether a chemical which induces extreme nausea and acts as a cathartic inflicts lasting effects on its victims of all ages and in varying states of health, we cannot possibly know.

251

The following January 29, scientists and physicians from Howard University, Massachusetts Institute of Technology, and several nearby institutions condemned the use of anti-crop agents and urged the President of the U.S. "to proclaim publicly that the use of such chemical weapons by our armed forces is forbidden and to oppose their use by the south Vietnamese or any of our allies".

In its statement the group made the following comments:

"Even if it can be shown that the chemicals are not toxic to man, such tactics are barbarous because they are indiscriminate; they represent an attack on the entire population of the region where the crops are destroyed, combatants and non-combatants alike. In the crisis of World War, in which the direct threat to our country was far greater than any arising in Vietnam today, our government firmly resisted any proposals to employ chemicals or biological warfare against our enemies. The fact that we are now resorting to such methods shows a shocking deterioration of our moral standards. These attacks are also abhorrent to the general standard of civilized mankind and their use will earn us hatred throughout Asia and elsewhere."

That the use of chemical or biological agents had a deleterious effect on the Vietnamese people, there is not the slightest doubt. Numerous examples have been recorded and verified. For example American agricultural attache' to the United States Operation Mission at Bien Hoa near Saigon sent a report to his superior in April 1965, wherein he complained bitterly that the reckless use of defoliants was poisoning area where water spinach was cultivated. Several pigs had eaten the stems of sprayed plants and died. Parents were complaining that their children's health had been adversely affected. Early the following month 500 complaints or requests for damages were forwarded from that area to the province chief. The U.S. and South Vietnam troops deliberately mutilated arable land which they suspected of being under Viet Cong control. Seymour M. Hersh states they destroyed thousands of tons of harvested rice they found in areas dominated by the Viet Cong, by throwing it into nearby rivers or burning it. He describes a device that the military used to clear bush and jungle it Viet Cong areas where food was grown. Known as a Roman plow, its main feature was a sharp bulldozer blade that weighed 2,500 pounds. In the U.S. this mechanism has been used commercially to clear rough land. Using this device, American troops "have stripped hundreds of thousand of acres of jungle and bush in an attempt to locate Viet Cong food storage areas and prevent ambushes. In some cases herbicides are applied to prevent future growth". According to the New York Times troops in North Central South Vietnam cleared 102,000 acres of plant life in the period between July 1 and December 3, 1967. The result of this and other instances of such destruction led to severe shortages of food in South Vietnam, which noted that even before spraying had begun the average daily diet of the Vietnamese was only about one fifth of the North American diet. Consequently anemia was widespread, as were such other diseases as beri-beri, diseases of the mouth, tooth decay, and endemic goiter. Certainly the destruction of food did nothing to improve conditions.

Especially outspoken about the deliberate destruction of food are physicians whose specialty is nutrition. One prominent nutritionist is Dr. Jean Mayer of the School of Public Health at Harvard University, who is an historian in the field of public health and whose experience includes witnessing its use on three continents, of which Asia was one. In the Spring of 1966 he wrote that history shows that neither the destruction of an enemy's food supply nor the use of food blockades are determining factors in war. He points to such incidents as the attempt to starve out the troops of the commune in Paris in 1871, the Allied food blockade of Germany and Austria in 1918, and the siege of Leningrad by the Germans in 1941-1942. In none of these cases did the starving tactic prove successful, because the besieged troops always managed to obtain sufficient nourishment. Those who were the chief casualties were small children and unborn children whose mothers had aborted. Next in number were the elderly. Mayer points out that similar results appear whenever there is severe shortage of food, whether it be from droughts, floods, earthquakes, or whatever. He refers to the U.S. objective to destroy the food supply of the enemy and he concludes with this plea:

"We obviously do not want to take war measures that are primarily if not exclusively, directed at children, the elderly and pregnant and lactating women. To state it in other words, my point is not that innocent bystanders will be hurt. Our primary aim - to disable the Viet Cong - will not be achieved and our prolonged secondary aim - to win over the civilian population is made a hollow mockery."

The starving out technique did not, of course, prove successful in Vietnam. Instead it remains "an indignity and blot to our honor and religion", to borrow from the English poet, John Milton. To quote briefly just one of many criticisms hurled at the U.S. for its use of chemical and biological methods, a contemporary English specialist on the subject wrote in 1968:

As I write this chapter, American forces are spraying the crops of the Vietnamese with weed killers. By the end of 1966 they had destroyed some 150,000 acres of rice paddy fields. This is an activity which as caused strong moral objections to be raised not so much because of technique used is a form of chemical warfare but for other reasons. Crop destruction, whether by flamethrower, incendiary bomb, need-killer, or biological warfare, is an invidious method in waging war.

The use of herbicides and defoliants on Southeast Asia have had lasting effects not only on the Vietnamese people and their land, but also on U.S. military personnel, who were exposed to the spraying. Among the chief culprits was Agent Orange, which produces a very deadly poison, known as dioxin. Among the diseases caused by dioxin are skin ailments, cancer, sterility and birth defects in children. It has been estimated that at least 300 pounds of this deadly substance were dumped on Vietnam.

Much publicity has been given to Agent Orange in the U.S. because of the suits that many veterans of Vietnam have been bringing against the U.S. government, and this is as it should be. Not so much attention however, has been paid to the harm that has been inflicted on the Vietnamese people and their land. They were the victims not only of Agent Orange but of all the various chemical and biological agents that were used the U.S. In 1969 experts were claiming that perhaps lasting ecological damage had been done to rubber trees, rice and other edible plants, buds and fish.

During the Johnson administration protests poured into Washington on the defoliation program from plant physiologists and other interested groups. These protests reached a climax at the end of 1966, when the American Association for the Advancement of Science, with a membership of over 100,000 scientists, passed a resolution to notify the President of the U.S. of the grave hazards associated with the spraying of defoliants and herbicides and to urge him to take immediate steps to discontinue this practice. By that time many scientists had become so disillusioned with the attitude of many government officials on the war that they began to question the ethics of certain large universities who were accepting grants for research projects on chemical and biological agents. This issue led to much discussion, but there is little evidence to indicate that the universities discontinued the research.

GASES USED IN VIETNAM

U.S. Forces in Vietnam used the so called riot gases, CS, CN, and DM, on a massive scale and the psychochemical ZZ on a more limited scale. One of the occasions on which B, was used was reported in the French paper, L'Express, by Pierre Darcourt in March 1966. He stated that the lst. Cavalry Airborne had sprayed this agent on a Viet Cong Battalion (350-500 men) and that only 100 of the guerillas had escaped from the attack. An American reporter, Sterling Seagrave, commenting on the effect the E, had on enemy troops, says that it was not at all like it was in the case of the cat and the mouse in the U.S. experiment. Instead, he reports that the men under attack "had a disturbing tendency to run amuck and perform astonishing stunts of violence and mayhem."

The so called "riot agents" were not used so much to control riots as they were to flush out caves and bunkers where Viet Cong guerillas along with children and elderly people had taken refuge. The agents were dispersed by such conventional weapons as grenades, artillery, or mortar rounds, but, more sophisticated methods were soon devised. One was dropping 80-gallon drums of the agent from aircraft as a means of flushing out caves and bunkers. Another was the conversion of an American made motor driven commercial fumigation machine into an instrument for distributing the agent. This device, which was dubbed the "Might Mite", weighed 25 pounds and could blow gas at a velocity of 185 miles an hour into the larger tunnels of Vietnam. As with the use of defoliants and herbicides, the chief victims were children and older people.

The most thorough coverage on the use of chemical and agents since World War I, so far as this writer has discovered, is John Cookson and Judith Nottingham, A Survey of Chemical and Biological Warfare, Monthly Review Press, New York and London, 1969. This 413 page volume list reports on specific gas attacks from countries both friendly and unfriendly to the U.S. In an effort to be objective as possible, I will confine my selections to reports by Americans or by observers from countries friendly to the U.S. The incidents listed below are a sampling.

The Swiss National Committee for aid to Vietnam stated that on September 5, 1965, a battalion of Marines, commanded by Lt. Col. Leon Utter, dropped 48 containers of toxics gas on civilians hiding in air raid protection trenches at Ving Quang (Bib Dinh Province). Thirty five were killed and 19 were wounded, 26 were women and 28 were children.

The New York Times reported on October, 1965, that General William C. Westmoreland, the U.S. military commander in Vietnam had again "received permission to use tear gas when it will save lives", and that "tear gas would be used almost as a matter of daily military routine."

On January 13, 1966 the Brisbane. Courier Mail carried a notice to the effect that an Australian corporal, Robert William Bowtell, 24, "died of asphyxiation" when he was trapped in a tunnel into which tear gas had been thrown. The corporal, incidentally was wearing a gas mask.

Science magazine stated in its January 20, 1967, issue that the use of chemical agents" was being left to local field commanders. When the magazine inquired at the Pentagon, on how many times and for what purposes the gas was being used, the reply was that nobody knew.

One of the most remarkable pieces of evidence of the deleterious effects of gases used in Vietnam is a letter, dated November 23, 1967, that Dr. Alje Vennema, Director of the Canadian Pfeiffer of the Department of Zoology at Montana University. This letter was later published, contrary to the wishes of Dr. Vennema. The doctor had been working for a period of three years at the Tuberculosis Hospital at Quang Ngai, where he had treated many patients, (men, women and children) who had been exposed to a war gas, the name of which he did not know. Most of the patients reported that they had been exposed to the gas while they were in hiding. There is no reason to mention the symptoms here, but it is interesting that the signs and symptoms were the same as those he had witnessed years before in veterans of World War I who were undergoing treatment at the Queen Mary Veterans Hospital in Montreal. The only difference, he noted, was that the

Vietnamese patients were more acutely ill. The doctor said that the mortality rate of adults was about 10%, compared to 90% for children.

PRESIDENT NIXON AND CBW

As has been indicated above, President Johnson's decision not to seek re-election in 1968 was prompted by the growing unpopularity of the war in Vietnam, not only among the populace but also among some key politicians of his own party. In his last months in office Johnson stepped up efforts to settle differences with the Russians by negotiation. Where Nixon succeeded to the presidency in 1969, he chose to continue U.S. participation in the war despite the ever growing protests by its opponents, but in time he turned to the negotiating technique, which his administration pursued with such marked success.

There was one aspect of the war in Vietnam, however, that was causing so much protest at home, in the United Nations, and abroad that Nixon felt he had to deal with quickly. That was the use of chemical and biological warfare. By 1970 he had ordered that all biological weapons in all government agencies be destroyed. Sterling Seagrave in his book Yellow Rain says that the President's directive was not carried out to the letter, because some official in the CIA circulated a letter within that agency to the effect that the stock of biotoxin at Fort Detrick was not to be destroyed but transferred to the Huntington Research Center, Becton-Dickinson Company, Baltimore, MD, for use by the CIA. The CIA Director Richard Helms, later claimed that he had never seen the memo and had in fact given an oral order that the poisons be destroyed. But that such a memo was circulated is made clear by the following remark that William Colby, Helm's successor made: "I think it was done by people who were so completely enmeshed in the subject and the difficulty of production that they simply couldn't bear to see the staff destroyed." According to

Seagrave, great amounts of poisons were stored at a special room at Langley, Virginia. The agency planned to use the material to dispatch enemy agents and to enable its own agents to take their own lives, should that prove expedient. There certainly was no shortage of toxics in that special storage room. Just one of the many substances would be "enough to kill tens of thousands of KGB (Soviet) agents and to permit tens of thousand of CIA agents to commit suicide."

CIA activities not withstanding, President Nixon, whose prestige was at such a peak in the period of detente, gave a positive new direction to the curbing of the future use of chemical and biological warfare. One indication of this was the announcement made at the Geneva Arms Talks on March 16, 1969, that the U.S.S.R. and the U.S. would work together to ban chemical and biological warfare. On November 25, 1969, Nixon ordered that the production of biological weapons be discontinued forthwith and he also pledged that the U.S. would not be the first nation to use chemical weapons, thus renewing the policy that President Roosevelt had established in World War II. Finally, in what he termed "an initiative for peace", he promised to submit the Geneva Gas Protocol of 1925 to the senate for ratification. But the president did not, at the same time, make any move to discontinue the use of defoliants and gases in Vietnam. On August 19, 1971, Nixon finally sent the Geneva Gas Protocol to the senate for ratification. Three years and four months later, the senate ratified the protocol, being the 104th country to do so.

President Nixon's 1969 initiative on discontinuing the production of biological weapons became an incentive for the 1972 Convention on the Prohibition of the Development, Production, and Stockpiling of Bacteriological (Biological) and Toxic weapons and on their Destruction. ~ At the 1974 summit meeting in Moscow, Nixon and Leonid I. Brezhnev agreed to open negotiations on this convention, and President Ford continued the process.

The Carter administration continued to negotiate with the Russians up till the Soviet invasion of Afghanistan in late 1979. During the Reagan administration such negotiations have all but ceased.

RUSSIA & CBW

On June 16, 1963, an article appeared in the London Sunday Times about a Telegram which stated that German chemists were working on a secret chemical-biological project in Egypt for the government of Abdel Nasser. Nasser, who at the time was the leading figure in the United Arab Republic, was on very friendly terms with the U.S.S.R. He was determined to extend his influence into Yemen, where, with Nasser's assistance, revolutionaries were attempting to overthrow the royal government. The article described how Egyptian planes were dropping toxic bombs on Yemen villages, which led the Saudi Arabian government and the Yemen loyalists to file reports on several recent cases with the International Red Cross and the United Nations. In 1963 somewhat similar reports appeared in the Washington Post. For the next three years occasional items on the subject appeared, but it was not until the end of 1966 that the items became numerous and more specific. By then more than 20 western correspondents had visited Yemen and filed their report.

Among the reporters was an American, Sterling Seagrave who at various times worked for the New York Times and the Washington Post. He became so fascinated with the subject that he travelled to such distant lands as Somalia, Afghanistan and Southeast Asia to verify incidents of the use of toxics. He lists his findings in his book Yellow Rain, A Journey Through The Terror Of Chemical Warfare, which has been referred to above.

It is not my purpose to discuss the evidence that has been uncovered by Segrave and others, but simply to observe that there seems little doubt that in the areas of the world where Soviet influence was dominant some very toxic agents were used. In no instances, however, were these agents a decisive factor in military operations. They were used against civilians mostly and, as might be expected, women and children were among the principal victims.

Where this writer disagrees with Sterling and some others who have studied the evidence is with regard to their proposed solution to the problem. They recommend the U.S. stocks be increased to a point where we are equal or superior to the U.S.S.R. What that amounts to is to agree that we intend to engage in uncivilized warfare just because our opponents do. It is my conviction that toxic agents and nuclear weapons should be eliminated, through negotiations from the arsenals of all nations. They are an abomination before humanity and God.

Post 9/11

By E. Ted Gladue

CHEMICAL & BIOLOGICAL

On September 11th 2001 and July 7th 2005 the national mindset of young America and old England were altered in the most fundamental ways, shattering an innocence of security held for over 200 years in the first instance, and deepening the psychology of vulnerability in the average Englishman as never felt in their long history of dealing with invaders and terrorists. But the horrible reality is: these experiences would pale with the helplessness, pain, agony, and despair that would result in the aftermath of a serious chemical or biological attack upon America or England. Not since the "black plague" of the Middle Ages would humanity face such an ordeal. Our human natures do not truly allow us to fully understand something vicariously. We have the visual, written, and recorded records and evidence of the chemical warfare used against the Kurds in Iraq or the victims of Syria; but how many deep down inside identify accurately with the true nature of such horrors. This defect in our human nature prevents us all from truly understanding anything we know, learn, or see unless we have somehow experienced that particular horror.

It is also true that this is manifested by its larger counterpart, one's generational experience is seldom translated with the same passion and depth that allowed those before them to "understand." After they experienced first hand, such as the generations who lived during the Great Depression in the 1930s. We don't know, and we don't want to know.

But many people would like to know where we are in relation to this shadow boxing with distance threats of chemical or biological attack upon our communities. The use of chemical warfare against the Kurds and Syrians, and the nerve gas terrorist attack in the Japanese subway system draws a smaller lesson for Americans than the anthrax attacks in America after 9/11 and the terrorists London bombings of July 5, 2005. We are more aware and at the same time want to know at what level of preparedness we happened to be at any one time.

A 2004 study by distinguished scholars and scientists at George Mason University looking at our current threats through their research and study in the fields of Molecular and Microbiology in regards to our "Bio-defense" needs paint a not very encouraging picture of our ability to protect ourselves. The authors find that it will take two or three decades for effective defensive programs against biological attacks to catch up to the deadly destructive power of advanced biological weapons and the ability to deliver these weapons.

At the heart of this problem is the alarming fact that although biological weapons can be developed very quickly, the vaccines take a long time of trial and error to prove there effectiveness against such weapons. It can take up to fifteen years to develop a vaccine and have it approved by the FDA (Food & Drug Administration).

Another problem is the uniqueness of any antibacterial or antiviral vaccines that could possibly be used to protect against infectious pathogens released by explosive devices or aerosol agents dispersed by air or other creative devices. It is not the same as treating diseases transmitted by ticks or mosquitoes. Any target population the bio-terrorist would attack, that population would have had been vaccinated weeks in advance of being attacked. How can that decision possibly be made? This problem does not exist with military personnel for they can be vaccinated long before being placed in such a combat situation.

To make matters even more complicated one vaccine will not protect again all pathogens. The CDC (Centers for Disease Control and Prevention) list six pathogens that may be used by bioterrorists that are listed as "Category A." Then there are classified pathogens that are listed under a "Category B" that few ever know about. The general population of any area or city in America would have to have been vaccinated against any or all of these pathogens listed under "A" or "B."

The George Mason authors of this study entitled *"Bioshield or Biogap?"* conclude that attempting to vaccinate civilian populations against Anthrax, Ebola, Botulinum (the most lethal toxin known), or Tularemia (named after Tulare County, California is useless at this time and resources should be put into new treatments so infected populations can be best treated after an attack. If one recalls, the anthrax attacks in 2001 did their deadly damage days following the actual contact or inhalation of anthrax. Simply put, systems today are ineffective in prevention, and that all resources should be put into dealing with the victims after an attack.

I very much miss my co-author Leo at times like this for we made it a habit to think outside the box. I learned so much from the James Madison University study but as always with me I try to first look at problem solving in simplistic terms. My first reaction: what do I personally do to give myself a defense against harmful elements in my own home? I sometimes tend to forget my basic principles for survival. First, I find a way to filter the air in my bedroom not just to filter out dust but also pathogens during those hours when I am asleep and unable to know if I am in any danger. Secondly, since I have set up more homes in more states and countries than anyone I have known (I am not talking about hotel rooms...but a primary residence that was usually intended to be my home for an indefinite period of time), I tried to make it environmentally healthy without the sophisticated knowledge others might have. How did I do that then, as I continue to the present?

When I moved into a place to live wherever it was the first thing I purchased once I was fairly settled were inexpensive plants, a fish tank and fish, and a birdcage for a canary if I could afford it, or, if not, an inexpensive parakeet. Then I would use the water from the tap to water the plants, for the fish tank, and to feed the bird. If my bird died, my fish died, and my plants died... I was out of there. These delicate and beautiful children of nature; plants, fish, and birds have always been my "environmental guideposts" that would alert me to poisons in the environment that would eventually harm me.

So my point is this: If it is true that there is no effective vaccines to prevent bio/chemical attacks from killing us, how can we create some kind of early warning system other than seeing in the news that dozens, or hundreds, or thousands of people are being admitted to hospitals alerting us that we are under siege by an enemy trying to kill us?

Perhaps every home, business, community begin thinking in terms of the canary in the coal mine that I once heard so much about years ago living in Western Pennsylvania coal regions to check killer methane gas. It is better to have birds, mice, and guinea pigs than our children to tell us we could be under attack from biological or chemical, anthrax being a little more complicated. More along this line of thinking will be discussed in with that of the anthrax threat.

How about Anthrax?

Unfortunately, we Americans have a case study of our own to weigh against the James Mason study conclusions. The mircrobial anthrax attack in post 9/11 that spread deadly spores in government offices and post offices around the country took us by surprise. People asked: "how could this happen"? And we watched images of closed-off buildings that had been tainted with anthrax spores, suggesting that every crevice was being examined. People died, and many were frightened, but we were told that various methods were being employed to kill anthrax spores, such as disinfectants.

One of the methods utilized was to fill entire buildings with chlorine dioxide that supposedly kills the bacteria from the outside in, perforate the protein shell of anthrax spores. That was the theory in the aftermath of 9/11, but it may have done little more than kill all the roaches. But chlorine dioxide gas does cause an oxidization that eats holes in the anthrax spores outer shell, throwing its metabolism in a tailspin, preventing it from transforming into a rod-shaped bacterium that allows it to then reproduce.

It appears better than using foams and other liquid agents for it can be sent through ventilation systems reaching every dead air pocket in any building. Of course bleach may be the most effective, but only "if" it can be applied directly to the spores themselves. Hidden spores would be saved from bleach applications.

As suggested above; are we going to wait until people beginning dropping dead from anthrax spores to warn us of an attack? Even when an environment is examined by checking table tops, swabbing nostrils, and looking in nooks and crannies for spores it often falls short since the age of the spores are difficult to determine. Using animals as sacrificial guard may hold the best key for prevention. Veterinarians have routinely checked cattle for natural anthrax, and while in New Zealand I learned of veterinarians using white rabbits to detect the form of anthrax that can be inhaled into the lungs. Besides the canary in the coal-mine mentioned above, birds have been used to check for West Nile fever, guinea pigs for tuberculosis, and chicken for viral encephalitis and flu virus.

Once scientists determine which animals are most susceptible to what diseases they can be placed not only in public places, but families would be able to purchase them at their local pet stores for their home defense. This may be the best defense again many strains of anthrax.

EPILOGUE

I call this conclusion an "epilogue" in respect to my co-author of this chapter (& our **"Gamble for Survival"**, Leo P. Brophy; for only Leo could write a true conclusion to his thoughts and wisdom, I am only the courier. His specialty being chemical and biological warfare left me with a responsibility to try and relate the wisdom I learned from thousands of hours of conversing with this amazing man.

Dr Brophy brought his study of history to problems of chemical and biological warfare as a medical doctor would bring his stethoscope and a mind filled with a knowledge of medical experience gleamed from textbooks, hands-on experience in emergency rooms, internships, residencies, lectures, and the smell and hopelessness of illness and death. My major political and intellectual concerns dealt with those apocalyptic nuclear bombs and their delivery systems; and Leo brought me down to earth in looking more closely of what history teaches us about the unmanageable horrors of biological disasters through war, nature, human folly, or accident. He insisted, that what makes it imperative we contain the threats is the ease with which assessable biotechnological knowledge can theoretically allow anyone to produce a biological agent capable of killing millions, and that was years before the internet.

I lack the expertise he brought to examining these threats and problems but I can recall his concerns in the mid 1980s that a terrorist would get their hands on the smallpox virus that had been eradicated from the globe, save for deposits held by both the U.S. and USSR. Today, in 2014, one would not have to tap into these two sources of natural virus, but could create their own smallpox virus. Today, the ingredients can be researched on the internet to make your own brand of a new insidious biological weapon.

We now know that during the Cold War the Russians had designed a deadly biological weapon by inserting a virus inside a bacteria; so when physicians treated the bacteria with antibiotics and killed it, the virus would be released. A "stealth" virus can infect a person and show no symptoms until it is activated by some food, beverage, or chemical.

A few years ago a deadly lethal virus was accidentally created in Australia by scientist attempting to develop a birth-control contraceptive by implanting an immune system gene into a mouse-pox virus.

E. coli contaminated Spinach and lettuce from California in 2006 sent a warning bow-shot across American consciousness; not too many sickened people, not too many deaths, this time. If you go back and review the TV news accounts it appears frightening, but this is "chicken-feed," if I many use a pun, compared to what could happen if bio-terrorists had discovered Dr. P.C. Stemmer's experiment that produced a strain of E. coli over 30,000 times more resistant to today's antibiotics. Modern technology has enabled molecular biologists to create an E. coli strain in a few months that normally takes millions of years. Fortunately, the scientific group that created this deadly strain destroyed it; but, how secure can we be, for no knowledge created on this earth disappears.

E coli was just a common bug near the end of the twentieth century, then U.S. scientists transferred a lethal gene from a relative of the plague bacterium to create a new virulent strain of E coli.

A 21st Century Dilemma

In our post 9/11 world a debate is being conducted beyond the radar of most citizens. This debate, primarily between scientists and government officials is how to prevent terrorists from acquiring deadly biological weapons without killing creative biological research. Therein lies the dilemma; not just to regulate, but how deep and widespread should the government regulate?

In the pre 9/11 world the Bush administration was even against the internationalization of banning biological weapons, to the dismay of our allies in the world. The 1972 treaty prohibiting the development, production, and possession of biological weapons was ratified by 143 nations; but the treaty had always lacked a means of verification. To rectify this diplomats have met in Geneva to work out a protocol to the treaty that would put some teeth into verification, which the Clinton administration originally supported. This draft agreement that would give backbone to the treaty banning germ weapons was rejected outright by the Bush administration, following their rejection of the attempts to counter global warming with the Kyoto accords, and the Bush rejection of the awkward but workable Cold War efforts at reducing nuclear escalation with the 1972 Anti-ballistic Missile Treaty.

The Bush administration pathetically ran counter to a long United States effort to ban germ warfare, albeit not without problems real and imagined. Long after President Nixon signed the treaty in 1972 it was discovered that the Russians had violated the treaty. In 1992 Russian President Boris Yeltson admitted that the former Soviet Union had violated the treaty by maintaining a decades old biological weapons program for years after the treaty went into force.

Yet, the U.S. is not without fault for its own interests that work against verification; for American pharmaceutical and biotech corporations, which are huge and have enormous lobbying power in Washington, do not want foreign inspectors walking around their city-like compounds in places like Philadelphia and Maryland, fearful to protect their latest and future biological research secrets.

One may have wondered during the Cold War of those secretive Soviet germ and biological weapons factories on the other side of the Ural mountains; but a one day car ride outside just one American city such as Philadelphia would take you into a world far less sinister looking than those clandestine germ warfare cities I once viewed in the USSR during the Cold War, when I was risking my life and limb, for what? Then, I might as well might have been looking at a pulp mill in Georgia, for I was unable to get anywhere near the facility. But outside Philadelphia I did have access to these facilities that covered many more acres than those old Soviet germ factories. I had access as courier, delivering strange packages I picked up at the Philadelphia International airport. I was warmed when meeting so many wonderful support personal from local communities, Philly boys and girls; but the serious work was done behind closed doors by scientists raised in countries far from Philadelphia whose research forced them to move often, between U.S. government bio-defense installations and American pharmaceutical corporations such as the many city-state installations outside Philadelphia. As I drove away from these secretive installations I wondered about what type of germ or aerosol agents these scientists were developing for the government that could be used as warfare weapons.

The efforts to strengthen the inspection powers of the treaty was quite practical, such as demanding that official parties be allowed to travel to a suspicious site within 108 hours after an approval for inspection. My question is: during the Cold War we would have been delighted if the USSR had accepted such inspections; but, would we ever accept such inspections in this new 21st Century environment of American Imperial power? But, why should we; we can be trusted, not like Saddam Hussein and Russian Communists who lied to everyone, including their own citizens who work in these lethal environments such as the one in

Sverdlovsk, Russia where anthrax spores from a biological weapons plant caused a local pandemic.

Hold on to your righteous seat. During this same Cold War the U.S. military conducted chemical and biological warfare test on American sailors without their knowledge. Janie Blankenship wrote in the December 2002 publication VFW that the sailors involved with these secret tests were used like "Lab Rats" by the government of the United States. Over 5,000 U.S. sailors and their ships were sprayed with deadly chemicals like VX and Sarin, followed by decontamination using the substance Beta-Propiolactone that tests indicate may cause cancer. These exercisers know as SHAD (Project Shipboard and Hazard Defense) were conducted nearly 50 times between 1962 and 1973 off the coast of Newfoundland and in the Pacific, but these deadly experiments with young American sailors were covered up for 40 years.

Blankenship now tells us stories of sailors on those ships who had no voice at the time. Such as a sailor aboard the USS Power who said they had no idea any exercise was goings to take place until they saw a Marine aircraft spraying their ship with a cloud of something or other, followed by another plane, a C-47, spraying another chemical over the entire ship. Now we know the first plane was spraying a spore-forming Bacillus bacterium,; while the second plane sprayed Zinc Cadmium Sulfide, a substance now know to cause cancer.

This SHAD project's mission was to test a ship's ability to fight in combat while under a chemical and biological attack. When the planes passed over the sailors were told the ship was being tested for "tightness." If they asked questions they were told to shut-up and do their jobs. What can a 19 year old sailor do in such a situation, except jump overboard? Many of these young guys never reached middle age, and many who did have chronic health problems.

272

The Pentagon has finally revealed that at this same period in the 1960s it conducted chemical and biological weapons testing on U. S. soil, on unsuspecting American citizens and military personnel in Florida, Alaska, Maryland, Utah, California, and Hawaii. In exotic Hawaii E. coli bacteria and bacillius globilus were released in populated areas, not in the wild. So as Leo Brophy has suggested earlier, it is difficult to trust government, any government, even your own.

Governments and scientists in post 9/11 find themselves grabbling with the complexities of trying to keep terrorists from acquiring knowledge of cutting edge germ warfare, or the germ itself, without stifling biotechnological scientific research, some of which may find antidotes to chemical and biological agents. Regulations? What type, how far, and who decides; and are we any safer after laws are passed that are to protect us? These are issues of security we never needed to deal with before; a new day, confusing, random, unpredictable, with loopholes any determined terrorist group can exploit.

Let me give you one example. There is a federal law that regulates the exchange of germs and toxins from one biotech research center to another. The law regulates the exchange of nearly 40 different toxins and germs from one facility to another by requiring these institutions to be registered with the government. Makes sense, sound secure; but any imaginative terrorist could figure out the weakness in the chain of delivery between two licensed agents. A courier picks it up, puts it in a car or truck, takes it to the airport where it is handled by baggage personnel before being placed on a plane, it is picked up by another courier who takes the package to the receiving facility. You do not see regulators overseeing these exchanges while they are in route. Recent legislation has focused on disallowing illegal immigrants, felons, or other undesirables from handling such potentially dangerous cargo; but who is going to do this low-paid work? It reminds me of the death toll lists from Iraq; one sort of intuitively knows that the names on the dead list are not going to be families in Washington, D.C., Manhattan, West Chester, Scarsdale, Santa Barbara, Ashton, Lower Merion…you got the point. Law and regulations, in my mind, are fine when we all play by the same rules. But a terrorist, intent on inflicting death and destruction, although playing on the same field, plays new games we are not familiar with, until it is too late. The dedicated civil servant, trained and educated to protect us, if often too fearful of irritating his superior to think outside the box, less he be passed over for promotion.

Then there are the scientists themselves who maybe placing us in great danger. Could scientists working on experimentally modified germs actually create a superbug that would unleash a new plague? Remember the story out of Australia as a case in point. Scientists attempting to design a virus that would make mice infertile accidentally created a virus that kills them. The new virus scrambled their immune systems so badly they all died. The scientists were so un-nerved by the surprise outcome of their experiment that they signed statements arguing for enhanced global treaties to ban germ warfare.

My concern is what happens when a scientist stumbles upon such a potential deadly pathogen and he or she is having a crisis in their personal lives, and this personal crisis get out hand. I am reminded of the rule during the Cold War that no husband and wife team ever be allowed to work in a launch control center during the same shift, in the event that a marital dispute between them end in a suicide pack whereby they both push the buttons (since both operators had to push the buttons at once), thereby releasing cruise missiles aimed at the USSR, starting WW III. A mad scientist may be a fictional character; but fiction does often mirror reality.

Such are the new realities of the 21st century. A reality that was lost on President Bush and his inner circle who were hell-bent on destroying global agreements and treaties that have keep us humans from our deep irrational animal selves.

AUGUST 2013 ... CHEMICAL ATTACK – SYRIA

Its appears that chemical agents were used to kill hundreds, perhaps thousands, of men, women, and children. President Assad's forces were known to have large amounts of Sarin, VX, and Mustard Gas; and Israeli intelligence suggested that rockets fired upon the civilians may have been a "cocktail" mix of these three deadly chemicals.

The rockets fired upon the civilians came at 2 a.m. in the morning while most were sleeping. But those who lived to tell about it heard the explosions that sounded like a water tank bursting or like the sound of a soda bottle being opened. The next came the strange smell, then the burning eyes and throats as if they had eaten onions or drank chlorine. Many died right there in their beds as they slept.

The rockets were fired into crowded neighborhoods on both sides of Damascus. Terrified families who sough protection in basements instead became trapped in death by suffocation as the gases found their way down into the lower reaches of buildings and settled there. News reported one physician who compared it to a horror film, with entire families, fathers, mothers, children being brought by vehicles to the hospital, all dead. Even in low doses Sarin can kill in one to ten minutes after direct inhalation; suffocation and lung muscle paralysis

The only antidotes to chemical weapons available was Atropine or Biperiden or Pralidoxime, whichever they had. These help to stop the attach on a person's nervous system, but even people who absorb a non-lethal dose can suffer permanent neurological damage. In Syria hundreds of victims poured into the local hospitals, the supply of antidotes ran out.

On the political side: President Obama had previously stated that the U.S. would act if Syria crossed a "red line" by using chemical weapons. A team of U.N. investigators sent to investigate where not permitted into the contested areas for five days. In an interview with a Russian journalist President Assad of Syria said that claims of his using chemical weapons were an "outrage against common sense," evidence later proving him a lier.

Some chemical weapons specialists have maintained that it is not always easy to detect their use for they can mimic other chemicals such as insecticides. As Brophy has pointed out the Germans in mid 1930s developed the very potent nerve gases tabun and sarin that were first used as insecticides, but later stockpiled for use in warfare.

But with Iran's accusations of Iraq's use of chemical weapons on several Iranian villages in 1988, Iraq's bombing Kurdish villages with sarin and mustard gas, and usage during a conflict between Azerbaijan and Armenia; the United Nations has developed sophisticated teams of scientists to investigate such claims of atrocities. An expert of biological and chemical weapons, Amy E. Smithson, claims that " They can pinpoint chemicals long after the fact;" and in the same reporting William J. Broad reveals in his **"Chemical Attack Evidence Last Years, Experts say"** two complex instruments lie at the heart of advanced chemical detections: the gas chromatograph and the mass spectrometer." The former breaks up chemicals into their components and the later identifies them " by comparing them to libraries of known substances."

Broad further quotes a former official at the United States Army Medical Research Institute of Chemical Defense at the Aberdeen Proving Ground in Aberdeen Maryland, David H. Moore: " If adequate samples are collected, there's a high probability that they will find 'conclusive' evidence of exposure to chemical warfare agents. (I added the quotation marks to the word "conclusive")

With regard to the latest accusations in Syria, William Broad points to the opinion of a former British military specialist and director of verification for the Organization for the Prohibition of Chemical Weapons, Ron G. Manley, who claimed that the " clock may be ticking not only on environments clues in Syria, but biological ones as well." His reasoning: the human body " eventually metabolizes traces of nerve agents, erasing the chemical evidence," even though " British scientists had managed to find unambiguous signs, ' in blood and urine samples for up to two weeks ' after a chemical attack."

At the heart of the recent, and past, uses of biological and chemical weapons is the 1993 United Nations treaty, the Chemical Weapons Convention that prohibits the development, stockpiling, and use of chemical arms. It is enforced by The Organization for the Prohibition of Chemical Weapons that is based in The Hague that utilizes a world-wide network of laboratories to analyze field samples. These dynastic test were brought to the investigation against the Syrian government.

Photos of young children and mothers who died in their beds have brought attention to many who heretofore thought of these issues in abstraction. Reading about the use of poison gases in WW I was an abstraction in my own mind, but I still remember some of the old veterans I had met when I was young, they long ago passed, like my next door neighbor during the time I was studying for a Master's degree in history. His name was John McNicole, an Irish immigrant to America who was sent to Europe with the U.S. Army not long after he came off the boat. He brought to life the fact of fighting during gas attacks in the battles I was reading about in Carlton J. Hayes classic history text. John himself had suffered from lung infections and lost many of his pals and comrades, many of whom he had worked with him on the farms of wealthy estates in suburban Philadelphia. I vividly recall his words as he related the horrible scenes to me, but most dramatic I remember the eyes of this old man watering up with tears as the names of his long dead pals rolled off his tongue. He would wipe his eyes with a big old hanky and reach for another shot of Irish whiskey. In the next moment of silence, his pain sort of floated into the air along with the smoke from his pipe.

I also remember my father's oldest sister Anna, the mother of my five cousins whose father was German and also fought in WW I, in the U.S. Army. As a young child I was confused as to why they had no father until I learned he had died after returning home from Europe. He was a big strapping man who was a boxing champion before the war, but died of lung disease from being gased in the " Great War." I was only a child, but I still remember Anna wiping tears from her eyes whenever mention was made of her husband, my uncle.

Just hours before this book went off to the press reports revealed that the Syrian military may have dropped chlorine bombs from airplanes and helicopters in an attack on insurgents in the village of Kafr Zita. It was chlorine gas that afflicted my uncle in the story above along with thousands of his fellow shoulders.

To many I suppose it makes no difference how you die in wartime; be it a rifle shot, an explosion, an atomic bomb, artillery, starvation, or hundred of other ways. Wars do kill people. But the international laws against chemical and biological weapons were not devised by machines, but by a global recognition that there be limits beyond which human beings and communities conduct warfare. For those of us who have taught International law we usually set the starting point for emergence of the " rules of war" written by Grotius who reflected on the horrors of the religious wars of Europe in the 17th century; or, with the thinkers at the University of Salamanca in Spain centuries before who reflected on the horrors inflicted upon the indigenous peoples of the Americas by the Spanish invaders.

Perhaps, thousands of photos of young babies and children who appear to be sleeping or in the arms of their dead mothers published on the internet may seal the acceptance of approval for zero tolerance for the use of chemical or biological weapons, anytime, for any cause, anyplace. I think Dr..Leo Brophy would approve.

\

APPENDIX

Game of Chinese mirrors

By E. TED GLADUE JR.   Monday, June 5, 2000   a Gannet newspaper
For the Courier-Post

Which reflection of China do you want to see? How does China, as a great state, see itself and its future? What do we really know beyond the debates and hype of trade and jobs? Can America really have a say in China's future direction? Will China become more like us politically as it becomes more capitalistic? Will China live by rule of law like we do?

From what angle do you view the Chinese mirror? Perhaps a reality check may be in order.

■ China's future as a rising great power in this century cannot and will not be affected by whatever trade policies the United States or European countries enact. Germany at the beginning of the last century, and the Soviet Union at mid-century, developed into formidable powers despite economic attempts to stifle such growth.

A realist deals with China as the United States once dealt with the Soviet Union; there were limits to the expansion of our interests.

■ At the center of China's psychology is the world's oldest surviving egotism. There is the Chinese way of doing things and then all the others. The people who invented gunpowder, paper and the compass also invented "nationalism," a very centrist way of seeing themselves as the center of the universe and all others as inferior.

■ Law and democracy. In the Chinese experience, it is best to rule by authority, not laws — stability and unity at any costs, for without them there is no order, without order there is chaos. Political power is rarely questioned if the leadership is able to maintain sufficient well-being for society. Even the father of the Chinese revolution, Sun Yat-sen, whose political philosophy included suffrage, recall, initiative and referendum, rejected political equality and argued for "wise leadership."

To tens of millions of Chinese, a home and material well-being are more important than freedoms of speech, press and assembly. The only time China was ruled by law was in 221 B.C. It lasted a mere 15 years.

In China, the law is something to avoid, for for the law punishes more than it protects. For 2,000 years, there were no law schools in China. Law is criminal law, and it's harsh; with children, immaturity is no excuse for murder, and punishments are the same as for adults.

To an American, a contract is backed by law, something that is to change now in China with the new globalism; but to Chinese businessmen, a contract is only as good as the understanding between the parties. If this understanding changes, so do the terms of the contract.

So, law and democracy must conform to the Chinese way of civility.

■ Capitalism. These are the tools China wants, not those of democracy. And capitalism is about profits and losses and eliminating competing. Corruption, at the heart of the economy, will be more difficult to eliminate than attaining democracy; the military has become the businessmen, and it is the military that controls most of the economy.

Chinese capitalism has arisen out of a totalitarian communist system, which the West hopes will change with more capitalism. Depends on which angle of the mirror one looks at.

The writer, a Gloucester City resident, is a novelist whose experimental fiction, *Chin Shi Huang Ti* & *The Birth of China*, set in the third century B.C., will be published this fall. He is the author of two previous books on China: *China's Perception of Global Politics* and *China's Diplomatic Behavior in the United Nations.*

At issue: The continuing War on Terrorism

How is war progressing?

YOUR VIEW

Infiltration will allow U.S. to defeat terrorism

By E. TED GLADUE
For the Courier-Post

Fighting global terrorism is one thing; defeating it is another. Can defeating it is another. Can defeating global terrorism be accomplished? Yes, but first we have to not only organize globally, but we have to fight in the most parochial way.

There is need to organize globally by sharing and integrating intelligence resources and information no less than we are discovering at home in creating a homeland security department. Larger seems better.

Recent attacks in Bali and Mombasa display the global reach of terrorists be they Al-Qaida, Al Ittihad al Islami, Herzbolla, Hamas or Islamic Jihad; and the use of hand-held surface-to-air missiles against civilian aircraft dis-

play the vulnerability of everyone, everywhere.

There is no place to escape the threat of terrorism, thus it demands global efforts in uncovering future plots and trying to understand what they may be thinking and planning.

Intelligence is key

I do not think we can read the mind of terrorists. Having studied the mind of the terrorist in the department of psychiatry at New York's Mt. Sinai Medical School and interviewed terrorists in Spain, Germany, England, Italy and the Middle East in preparation to revise a book I wrote earlier, *Gamble for Survival: Politics of Nuclear, Chemical & Biological Conflict*, I reached the conclusion of the futility of trying to read their minds years be-

fore terrorism became a global phenomena. So how can we detect in advance what terrorists will do?

The global coordination of intelligence technology cannot in itself defeat terrorism. What is needed is a global agency to train operatives from those shadowy areas of the world that breed terrorists.

Any group in the world has those individuals among them that can be co-opted to turn on that group. The best intelligence in the world is that gleaned from an infiltrator.

Sun Tzu, in his Chinese classic *The Art Of War* argued that you must "seek out enemy agents who have come to spy on you, bribe them and induce them to stay with you, so you can use them as reverse spies. By intelligence thus obtained, you can find local spies

and inside spies to employ."

In the simple world of the Cold War, the CIA sent young recruits to Yale to study Chinese and Harvard to study Russian. Today's imperative is to tap into Asian, African and Middle Eastern communities, as well as European and American immigrant groups, and train non-white-skinned men and women to infiltrate communities, tribes and terrorist organizations, no matter if these recruits are educated, impoverished or criminal elements.

Once in place, they can complement the global technological efforts to predict terrorists' attacks. It is only at this basic level that terrorism cannot just be fought, but defeated.

The writer is a novelist/essayist and maintains an office in Gloucester City.

Thursday, January 11, 2001   a Gannett newspaper

PERSPECTIV

Protecting our sailors' lives

By E. TED GLADUE JR.
For the Courier-Post

Who is to blame for the deaths of our sailors on Oct. 12? During congressional hearings on the USS Cole, Pentagon officers gave many explanations, but have not accepted any blame for poor judgment and bad planning.

I am reminded of Pogo who said, "We have met the enemy, and he is us." During the hearings, we heard the absurd contention that the sailors were like all other Americans — open and friendly, and thus not suspicious of the two terrorists with arms raised in friendship, fast approaching the port side of the USS Cole, the most expensive and sophisticated destroyer ever to sail. I nearly fell out of my chair when I heard this explanation from such a high-ranking Naval officer.

It is the responsibility of the U.S. Navy to ensure that our young men and women serving on ships in terrorist-infested areas be given operational procedures, instruction and orders that ensure their safety.

How could this have been prevented? Common sense dictates not to let terrorists get close enough to do damage. How to do this? The same procedure that is used to protect the environment when a tanker discharging oil or other hazardous chemicals springs a leak. The ship discharging the hazardous chemical is "boomed." The tanker is encircled with a floating plastic "boom" whose presence theoretically will limit the damage to the environment from the leak. The same principle should have been applied to the USS Cole and other naval ships.

A "boom" or other device set up around the vessel as a line of demarcation beyond which no supply ship, water or bunker barge, or any other boat may enter. Standard operating procedure commands no vessel to cross the line of the boom, until escorted by a support vessel from the ship itself.

Fundamentally, this is about communications. Everywhere today we see people with cell phones. With all the sophisticated electronic equipment on the USS Cole, nobody should have been allowed near the ship without first communicating, and then being escorted to the ship by armed sailors or Marines.

It is the responsibility of high-ranking naval officers in the Pentagon or the military headquarters for the Persian Gulf to plan security measures that leave no doubt in the sailors' minds. A ridiculous statement by the commandant of the Navy in the congressional hearing was that the sailors on guard with guns in their hands waved back. because as Americans. "We are friendly people." Their job should have been spelled out in an order: Shoot to kill anything not given permission to proceed toward the ship.

I have interviewed terrorists in Spain, England, Germany, Italy and the Middle East and have studied the "mind of the terrorist" as a student in the psychiatry department at Mt. Sinai Medical School, and I remain convinced that there is no way you can read the mind of terrorists. All you can do is try to protect yourself and prevent them from carrying out plans that always are different.

I worked with peace-keeping for years at the United Nations and was appalled when we sent U.S. Marines into Lebanon in the early 1980s and put them up in an unsecured hotel in Beirut. A simple decision such as secure concrete barriers could have prevented that attack. After these 247 Marines died because of dumb Pentagon planning, I had hoped we would change our thinking.

True, our presence in this part of the world always will be fraught with danger and unexpected attacks, each different. In May 1987, I was teaching anti-terrorism to U.S. naval officers in Rota, Spain, where 37 U.S. sailors were killed when an Iraqi missile "accidentally" hit the USS Stark; at that time, the United Sta even was leaning toward Iraq, wi

the Reagan administration having been selling arms to Iran in the hope of freeing American hostages.

A year later, in July 1988, a blip on the radar screen of the USS Vincennes warned of an approaching aircraft. With only a few seconds to decide and a fresh memory of the USS Stark, the captain of the Vincennes gave the order to fire, killing all 290 passengers of a civilian Iranian airliner.

In this dangerous area of the world, there are no guarantees, but we must have common-sense policies that enable our service men and women to carry out security measures that are planned for them. The killing of American troops on June 26, 1996, also could have been prevented. American commanders were repeatedly warned about possible terrorist attacks and failed to take basic security precautions before the bombing of the Khobar Towers barracks near Dhahran, Saudi Arabia.

This time, the catastrophe of the USS Cole could have been prevented. The best defense against terrorist attack is common sense.

TICO TIMES

Founded in 1956 by Elisabeth Dyer
Publisher 1972-1996 Richard Dyer

1981   IAPA - Pedro G. Beltrán Award for distinguished service to the community
1980   Special Citation Mora Morales Cárdenas Award
1990   National Conservation Prize
1995   IAPA Grand Prize for Press Freedom
1995   Salvadoran Army Others Award
        National Tourism Chamber Media Award

In memoriam - Linda Frazier (1945-1984)
Vol. LIX N. 2007

Publisher Dery Dyer
Associate Publishers Anita Daniels
Editor Dery Mack
Weekend Editor Meg Yamamoto
Online Editor Alex Leff

Staff & Contributors
Ana Jeanne Salgado Beeler-Mora, Ed the Kramr, Sasha Cordero, Franck Fitzgerald, Feliz Salazar, Vanessa Saurwein, David Boddiger, William Gilley, Ellen Zoe Golden, Marco Sibaja Gaby Peyton, Steven Lemon, Vicky Longland, Dorothy MacKinnon, Devon Mayer, Jack O'Brien, Morgan Vanschaick, Michael Saucie, Holly A. Timmerfeld, Mitzi Dean, Jeffrey Van Fleet

Photographers
Ronald Reyes, Kent Gilbert

Systems
Edwin Cisneros

Advertising
Marsha Kerr-Rios (Coordinator), Genoveva Kopp, Bad Hughes, Tatiana Renovir, Marcella Venegas, Cindy Morgan

Circulation
Diego Ramos (Manager), Alexis Rivera, Johnny Maidana, Linton Patience, Clara León, Mynor Murillo

Finance
Clinton Chacón, Ana Reynolds, Maylen León

Production
Mayra Solís (Manager), Ery Argandas, Yerry Quesada

Customer Service
Ana Lucía Espinoza, Maricely Brenes, Bernardita Madrigal, Luis Méndez, Flora Poveda

The Tico Times (ISSN 1017-1799) is published every Friday for $50 per year by The Tico Times S.A., Avenida 8, Calle 15, Apartado 4632-1000, San José, Costa Rica. Tel: (506) 2258-1558. Periódicals postage paid in Miami, FL. Postmaster - Send address changes to The Tico Times, c/o TTP, P.O. Box 025331, Miami FL 33102-5331.
Copyright Corporation - unauthorized reproduction in whole or in part is strictly prohibited.

Perspective

What Is China's End Game?

By E. Ted Gladue

The Tico Times Jan. 9 presented a wish list for 2009 entitled, *"Headlines We'd Like to See in 2009,"* and second on this list with the title: *"China Allows C.R. to be Friends with Taiwan and the Dalai Lama."* Having spent a good portion of my lifetime studying and experiencing the way China perceives other nations and the world, I wish to address this by questioning Costa Rica's recent moves to abandon its friendship with Taiwan and reserve its sympathy for the Dalai Lama in order to appease China?

With U.S. tourism revenues down in Costa Rica, resulting largely from an imploding U.S. economy, and China's uncertain future highly visible in train and bus stations in industrial areas, as an estimated 20 million suddenly out-of-work Chinese men and women scramble to return to their traditional villages, Costa Rica's decision is an important one. Walk into any large store in Costa Rica and many of the goods you see labeled "Made in China" are no longer being produced by the very workers that made that very item you are holding in your hands, because they got fired and the factory is closed. Translated: Costa Rica's old and new trading partners are both in deep economic trouble.

These are not the times for Costa Rica to abandon its foreign policy principles and perceptions of its place in the world over concern for its emerging economic relationship with the PRC (or Peoples Republic of China). Costa Rica's relationship with Taiwan and its sympathy for the Dalai Lama were natural outgrowths of the very core of Costa Rica's culture and history, and, like Taiwan, it has had to play the games of international politics in the midst of more powerful and sometimes hostile neighbors.

But Costa Rica has set a unique and courageous example to the world in this already dangerous, volatile and nuclear armed world: The abandonment of a standing army since 1948. It makes no difference that a close study of Tibetan history reveals quite different relationships with China than are often presented in the mass media, some historians claiming that Tibet has never been an independent country, and that Tibet has at times actually welcomed China's protection from foreign invasions and threats.

The Dalai Lama's message of compassion and non-violence is one that is consistent

The question is: What does China want from Costa Rica beyond a place to sell its products?

with Costa Rica's "no standing army" lesson to the world. I love impossible causes. Perhaps Costa Rica's example of no standing army is the only salvation for humanity, an example more universally ignored than the Dalai Lama's words echoing up against violent realities in the Middle East, Africa, and the most dangerous nation in the world today, Pakistan. You cannot put a price tag on this peaceful lesson Costa Rica has to teach, a rare quality in this new and violent 21st century, and which is in solidarity with the Dalai Lama's vision.

The question is: what does China want from Costa Rica beyond a place to sell its products? China has a strong presence in the Panama Canal Zone, but how does Costa Rica fit into China's Central American strategy? To test this future, one must know China's past. No nation in the world is more influenced by its history than China, and it makes no difference who is ruling or the type of political system. What is important to Costa Rica is how China deals with smaller nations, especially when these nations take positions at odds with issues China claims as vital to her national interests, such as Taiwan and the Dalai Lama. Even with the smaller nations of Southeast Asia, we see the same pattern stemming from the cultural belief that China is "superior" to all others, sometimes carried over into contemporary trade relations; not as obvious as it was in the 18th century, but there, and as deeply engrained as Confucian values of filial piety (respect for parents and ancestors), education and family. The negotiating styles of Chinese businessmen and diplomats are the no different in the 21st century than they were when China was first unified in 221 BC.

It is imperative that Costa Rica study China's recently developed trading relationships with African and Latin America countries, particularly those without rich natural resources, in order to obtain some clues as to what China might want from Costa Rica, as well as gaining a better understanding of China's negotiating style and tactics. Since China will become more important to Costa Rica as trading relationships grow, perhaps one university here in Costa Rica will create a China institute to study and explore how Costa Rica can benefit from this new relationship.∎

E. Ted Gladue lives and writes in San Isidro de El General. His most recent book, a novel, "A Great Tale: The Adventures of Sean Seminceaux," is about an intrepid traveler from Philadelphia. Gladue can be reached at harborlightspress@yahoo.com.

ABOUT THE AUTHOR

Written and transcribed by Bob Morgan of Harbor Lights Press, after the insistant urgings of editors and friends: an interview with E. Ted Gladue.

E. Ted Gladue was born in Philadelphia and came to maturity during high school on the tough streets of West Philadelphia. The only book he read in its entirety during high school was a yet unpublished manuscript by the boxer Rocky Graziano, "**Somebody Up There Likes Me.**"

After high school he turned down several university scholarships to play football and joined the U.S. Marines with his pal "to see the world", until that pal's mother pressured them to switch this decision to a four year enlistment in the USAF, so he and his pal could "learn something else besides fighting."

In the USAF he was sent to military intelligence schools where he learned: cryptography, coding and decoding, trained in parchuting into snow and jungles, and air sea rescue. His international education came quickly, learning things about the world that sent shivers through his soul during dangerous missions of the Cold War.

After four years of the military he ventured to Havana Cuba where he was hired as a diver by explorers looking for sunken 17th and 18th century Spanish ships that went down with gold and silver, encountering intense basic research with his employers who studied old maps obtained from the universities of Madrid and Salamanca. Watching the wealthy men who financed these searches, all of whom seemed unfulfilled, and after far too many encounters with sharks in Bahamian and Caribbean watrers he decided, to return to Philadelphia and attend college.

His college years failed to answer questions generated by his worldly experiences, so he ventured into a very demanding two year traditional Master of Arts degree in history at Villanova University, followed by years of teaching at universities from Pennsylvania to Florida. Now married with three children the professorship at the university did not bring in enough money so with a friend he began buying depressed houses in Miami, fixing them up for resale in the growing real estate market of the time. He then studied for his real estate licence, followed by financial success leading him to take the fifteen week course to become a Florida real estate broker. He was fortunate when several older and successful investors took him under their guidance, but when he and his family became secure, he still felt that there was more to life than financial success. He had seen the hollowness in the spirits and souls of the wealthy men who long ago had financed the diving explorations for gold and silver, and his reactions now where no different. At this time he remained a full time professor teaching Russian and Chinese history, American Foreign Policy, American Constitutional Law, and to quench his hunger for intellectual stimulation would seek out events at the University of Miami's international affairs center, and other colleges where he would teach.

A chance encounter at one of those events brought him to work at the United Nations headqurters in New York City for the Acting Director of Political & Security Affairs, for whom he traveled the world, ofen utilizing techniques he had learned in military intelligence. He maintained his own office for six years at the United Nations, and during this time and for three years after intensely studied the thinking and behavior of the Chinese representing the ROC, continuing after the Communists of the PRC took that seat at the United Nations, which he wrote up in a dissertation earning him a Ph.D.

The timing of the dissertation, **"China's Diplomatic Behavior in The United Nations,"** could not have been better, for it was in 1979 that the US switched recognition from the Republic of China, ROC, on Taiwan, to the Peoples Republic of China, the PRC and established diplomatic relations for the first time with the Communist government on the mainland. Job offers for advising international businesses on China came swiftly; the first from a global hotel chain, but dealing exclusively with Corporate types bored him; so he began working with importers and exporters bringing expensive Chinese wedding beds into San Fransico, along wih the Chinese carpenters needed to rebuild them. After an intense year of study he became involved with inporting rare Chinese porcelains that Chinese families were beginning to dig from the earth buried during decades of war and turmoil. But the pull of writing and travel was again greater that the lure of money and comforts.

His years in military intelligence and then with the UN convinced him that nuclear, chemical, and biological threats to life on earth demanded anyone with knowledge of these things to attempt to do something about it. He recruited his father-like friend and scholar Leo P. Brophy to write a book with him. Leo, a Ph.D from Fordam University, had been the Chief Historian for the US Army Department of Chemical & Biological Services, and the editor of definitive studies and books on the subject, his work internationally respected.

They divided the book up into chapters each would write. Brophy, now retired, was near completion of his chapters when the President of the publishing house became very supportive. Gladue had been writing his chapters with pen and ink; and the President, Mr. Brown, a very scholarly old school intellectual, not only gave a financial advance for Ted to complete his chapters, but had a secretary at the publishing house type them as he finished each, claiming that "Gladue's writing at times becomes so powerful, it may even change peoples minds."

When they completed the book they were invited to New Zealand, that had recently declared itself a NFZ (nuclear free zone) nation, that would require US naval ships to declare if thery were nuclear powered or carrying nuclear weapons before entering NZ ports, making it a controversial issue within New Zealnd as well as between two old allies. Brophy was too old and frail to take on this venture; so Gladue went and spoke in New Zealand, Australia, and other Pacific nations for a year and a half. The adventure highlight of these times was a trip spent in Antrartica, for he had spent a great deal of time near the Artic Circle in Greenland while serving in the Air Force and wanted to "feel" the difference. He got into Antrartica not as a tourist, but utilized his US Merchant Mariner's Document, know as Seaman's Papers, to work aboard merchant ship sailing from Lyttelton, New Zealand, at times behind an ice-breaker ship, then into McMurdo Bay with scientitsts concerned with everything from environmental issues to fears of the posibility of nations storing nuclear wastes or weapons in this last pristine land on earth.

In the years that followed he found that his Ph.D. from the most demanding and perhaps the top political science department in the entire world, CUNY (the professors were world class; Hans J. Morgenthau, Isaiah Berlin, Harold Lasswell, Donald Zagoria, Dankwart Rustow, Ivo Duchacek, John Stoessinger, Arnold Rogow to name a few), was not given its proper respect by universities in America; he again ventured and wrote books. He sailed the world briefly, until hired during the Cold War by the Defense Department to teach Masters level graduate courses to U.S. Naval, Marine, and Air Force combat officers during some of the most dangerous years of the Cold War. These were the men and women who flew the fighter planes, had their fingers on the buttons of nuclear weapons, manned the nuclear submarines, air craft carriers, and long range bombers with nuclear weapons. Every ten weeks he'd drive to a different European country to teach on military or naval bases, from Rota Spain, to Turkey, to Germany, then England, and back, often detouring to Paris to take in the mystries once breathed by great artists and writers. Sometimes in country with bases stretched from Saarbruchen to Berlin, or traveling from Plymouth England to Basque country in Santander Spain by ferry, then down through Portugal to Southern spain; but never boring.

When returning to the states, his knowledge of ships enabled him to get hired as a Ship Agent; a job he describes as the most demanding and most challenging of any he ever encountered. His experience with oil tankers, lumber, steel, fruit, and container ships with Transmarine Navigation Company landed him a job with one of, if not the, largest shipping agencies in the world, Inchape Shipping. While with Inchape he had an office on the pier in Wilmington Delaware where he handled fruit ships from New Zealand, Argentina, Chile, and Central America, the small fleet of ships from Dole Fresh Fruit, whose Grandfather company was the infamous "United Fruit Company" whose exploitation of native peoples were often backed-up by US Marines in Central America and the Columbian Army in Columbia. He wished that I emphasize that he was one of the rare college graduates in the business; but, he was always leaning on other Ship Agents for advice and knowledge that he did not possess. In his mind, many Ship Agents are more intelligent than many professors he has known. When teaching International Politics at Princeton Univerity he recommended to his students that instead of spending their time in the library trying to understand the direction of the economy they should go to east coast ports and observe the number of ships embarking and debarking, and interview the Ship Agents and port authorities.

Then there were his years of experience in Central America, first living in the most dangerous city in the world, San Pedro Sula, Honduras, and then in Nicaguara, Guatemala, and Costa Rica. There he could see and feel first hand the poverty that bred populist moments like those described in the fiction of Fererrico Garcia Marquez's famous novel, **"100 Years of Solitude,"** and that which led to the Sandinista in Nicaragua in the 1980s and populist movements in Honduras in 2008/09. He was not just a tourist; but worked a low paying job in Honduras before selling his home on the Delaware River in New Jersey and moving back to Costa Rica in 2008. He has written two novels set in Central America and some of his finest poetry

In preparing this "about the author" piece I was instructed to include certain details about his background that were important, for they are about the "real struggles" that writers, scholars, artists, poets, muscians, and other creative people encounter, not like a person from a wealthy family trying to learn about the world that their privledged upbringing sheldered them from. Ted demanded me to write about aspects of this life, the life of struggle he often encountered since boyhood.; that he has dug ditches and graves with a hand shovel, carried heavy building blocks, mixed cement, drove trucks, loaded trucks from a dock, a laborer on moving vans, moved beef as in the "Rocky" movies before Rocky fame in a South Philly meat warehouses, swung a heavy sledge-hammer all day long bureaking rocks, delivered pizza for more resurants than he wishes to remember, worked as a football and swimming coach, worked horrible phone sales jobs; everything from commodity options on Wall Street, truck and airplane cleaning materials to businesses in southern and western states from an office in Queens, NY, to sleezebag operations selling cigarette lighters with sex slogans no man would let their children read; worked as a bartender, drove a gypsy cab in NYC, drove delivery trucks, sales jobs of many stripes, all done, not for experience, but to eat, pay the rent, electricity, and trash pick-up. Many jobs where accompanied with what many artists go through and decline to speak of: humiliation at the hands of very insecure, nasty, and hatefilled employers.

E. Ted Gladue earned a Master of Arts degree in History from Villanova University, and a Ph.D. of Political Science in International Politics, Chinese Studies, and The Psychodyanamics of Human Behavior from City University of New York Graduate Center, and Mt Sinai Medical School of Clinical Psychiarity.

Many of his influences from these educational experiences are described in the text of this book.

Bob Morgan, April, 2014.

ACKNOWLEDGEMENTS

The first person I wish to thank is Patrick Novak, a man of the sea and an Admirality lawyer, and my pal. I have learned from his knowledge of the world and his keen observations gleamed from not just his intellect but his experiences in dealing with international economics at its most basic level, shipping and trade, without which there would be no global economy. I want to thank Scottie Erwin for his scanning chapters of this book when I felt in a wasteland. Here is an auto mechanic whose father had fought in WW II and considered these important writings. I loved him for this support when no one else seemed to care. I want to thank Nicholas Christonikos who not only helped with my research at the United Nations for years, but offered tremendous encouragement then and now. His professional editing and imput with his knowledge of language is more appreciated by me than he knows; for he brought his decades of experience with his United Nations job and his keen intellect to advise me on what he thought important. And then there is Dr. Joseph viteritti who under tremendous pressure in completeing his magnificent book, **"Summer in the City: John Lindsay, New York, and the American Dream,"** took the time and patience to encourage me to complete my book. And then there is John A. Conroy who caught up in the tension of completing his wonderful novel **"Flashes of Life,"** took time to encourage my writing. And then there is Jim

Akers, who did two tours of Iraq in the US Army carrying a heavy assult weapon, gave of his time to edit and advise on portions of this book. And I can never forget the encouragement I received from the late Jim Boyle and his wife Helene O'Donnel Boyle who read earlier drafts of these chapters; in their way they kept me believing that it was all worthwhile, and I had something to contribute. I have always been grageful for the continuing support of Professor Richared Raleigh of St. Thomas University. Steve Bunnell, who has again come to my aid with his knowledge and support to help with my floundering computer knowledge. Steve Andrews who not only designed the cover but again helped with organizing the text for manufacture and printing. I could not have done without Steve's help. Leo P. Brophy, my co-author of the Gamble book whose words grace these pages. Leo, who died long ago, was a great teacher, scholar, and a man I loved like a father. His ideas bless this book.

Those parts of this book that appear professionally presented I owe to Jack Schrems, a former Chairman of Political Science, and my boss, at Villanova University who not only brought his political theorist mind to my text, but his own brilliant writing and editing skills. It was Jack who kept me supplied with some of my first computers during years of working outside the academy on my fictional trilogy, and his current interest in my work is both humbling and deeply appreciated, for Jack Schrems is one of those traditional political scientist's who taught students how to think about politics with razor sharp insights.

I wish to thank a wonderful class of students I taught at Penn State University in 2010 for allowing me to dedicated so much time in our psychology class to examine the minds of suciide bombers and terrorists, for participation in these discussions was 100%, and I was proud of the seriousness and insights of their contributions. Working on this book also brought fond memories of a group of students I taught at Rowan University in the Fall of 2001. I was teaching a course called **"Violence, War, & Terrorism,"** which I thought would be the last politics course I would teach for several reasons. The first, being that my fictional trilogy I had worked on for for over ten years was to be published in about a month; and secondly, it seemed to me at the time that students did not seem to care much about international politics; On the night of September 10th I gave my first full lecture of the semester. I put my heart and soul into it, attempting to get my students to realize what dangerous times we were living in with terrorist threats looming no where and everywhere. I was not only surprised by their attentiveness, but by their questions. At one point a student asked a question, and about five others spoke out spontaneously in support of his question. It was: where do you think this threat will come from? I was sort of caught off guard, so I walked over toward the window as I thought out my answer. As I looked out the window at the sky in all its majesty and beauty with the darkened setting sun, the answer came to me, in surrealist images. Up there, I said. The sky, its coming from the sky. Next day, 9/11.

Then there are the women I have loved and lived with who suffered from my obsession to travel and explore enough to write this book; one, an English lady, Jennifer, once sent me a postcard suggesting it could be the cover for an earilier version of the book: it was a photo of a man, his wife, and their child in their kitchen with a bomb sitting on their kitchen table. The caption read: **"Living With The Bomb."**

Any language problems in this text is the result of my failure to correct the editorial suggestions of all involved, or the mechanical distortions of text that sometimes occurs when transferring data, or at times in the printing process. Please be patient, for they will be corrected in the next printing.

I would like to conclude this book by honoring those who influenced the roots of my very soul. They were the Christian

Brothers at West Philadelphia Catholic High School and the football coachs, Frank Cooney and Jack Shields. The brothers did not teach us much about theology; but a whole lot about ethics. How to treat other people whom we know little about? To give the other guy a hand, or a sucker a break; for you never know when you are going to be where he is. Why it is important to stand by each other and think of other's before one's self. To respect family and community and not to be afraid to stand up for what is right, and to reach out above what is considered the limits of our talents, to follow our dreams no matter how beyond our reach them appear, for our success is not just for ourselves, but the common good of the community. That our good fortune thrusts upon us an obligation to try and do good in this world for not just ourselves, but for all. My adventures and journeys have been mostly solitary, often lonely ones, but the values instilled in me by those Christian Brothers and the football coaches, have not only saved my life, but perhaps brought me to write this book. I would hope they would approve of my humble contribution to our country, humanity, and peace in our times.

ETG, April, 2014